Also by Richard M. Ketchum

AUTHOR

Decisive Day: The Battle for Bunker Hill
The Winter Soldiers: The Battles for Trenton and Princeton
Saratoga: Turning Point of America's Revolutionary War
Divided Loyalties: How the American Revolution Came to New York
The World of George Washington
The Borrowed Years, 1938–1941: America on the Way to War
The American Heritage Book of Great Historic Places
Faces from the Past
Second Cutting: Letters from the Country
The Secret Life of the Forest
Will Rogers: His Life and Times
What Is Communism?

EDITOR

The American Heritage Book of the Pioneer Spirit
The American Heritage Book of the Revolution
The American Heritage Picture History of the Civil War
American Testament: Fifty Great Documents of American History
The Horizon Book of the Renaissance
The Original Water Color Paintings by John James Audubon
for the Birds of America
What Is Democracy?
Four Days

VICTORY AT YORKTOWN

VICTORY
AT YORKTOWN

*The Campaign That
Won the Revolution*

RICHARD M. KETCHUM

A John Macrae Book

Henry Holt and Company ★ New York

Henry Holt and Company, LLC
Publishers since 1866
115 West 18th Street
New York, New York 10011

Henry Holt® is a registered trademark
of Henry Holt and Company, LLC.

Library of Congress Cataloging-in-Publication Data

Ketchum, Richard M., date.
  Victory at Yorktown : the campaign that won the Revolution /
Richard M. Ketchum.—1st ed.
    p.   cm.
  Includes bibliographical references and index.
  ISBN 0-8050-7396-5
  1. Yorktown (Va.)—History—Siege, 1781.   I. Title.

E241.Y6K48   2004
973.3'37—dc22   2004042496

Henry Holt books are available for special promotions
and premiums. For details contact: Director, Special Markets.

First Edition 2004

Designed by Victoria Hartman

Maps designed by Jeffrey L. Ward

Illustration on page xiv from The Pierpont Morgan Library /
Art Resource, New York

Printed in the United States of America
10 9 8 7 6 5 4 3 2 1

This book is dedicated to our grandchildren

Derek and Ethan Murrow
Dylan, Diana, Ben, Bray, and Fred Ketchum

with the hope that they may find
the story of America's past
as captivating as I have.

CONTENTS

MAPS

VICTORY AT YORKTOWN

George Washington's life mask by Jean-Antoine Houdon, 1785.
(Morgan Library, Dept. of Drawings and Prints. Accession no. AZ151)

PROLOGUE

He was *the American Revolution*, this man whose life mask reveals so much about his character.

When the fighting erupted at Lexington and Concord, it was not yet a war for independence—not even a war, for that matter, but a sure sign that the ugly dispute between the colonies and Great Britain had reached incendiary proportions.

Less than two months later, on June 15, 1775, the Congress of sixty-four delegates from twelve colonies (Georgia's representatives were not present) unanimously elected the quiet, reserved Virginia planter "to command all the Continental forces raised or to be raised for the defense of American liberty." As grand as that sounded, it meant merely that he was to take charge of a ragtag collection of farmers and tradesmen who made up a volunteer "army" surrounding the British troops in Boston. From that moment on, for more than eight years, George Washington was the commander in chief of the Continental Army, known as His Excellency, or more often as the General, the capital letter signifying that, while there might be other generals, he was someone special.

The Virginian, who was selected in part because he was not a New Englander and therefore might unite colonies whose history was one of rivalry and distrust, had been slow to conclude that armed resistance to Great Britain was necessary or in the best interest of the colonies. After he passed that milestone, Washington still had little faith that he was capable of the immense task that had been entrusted to him. He admitted to a conviction of his "own incapacity and want of experience in the conduct of so momentous a concern." Nor was he reluctant to reveal these doubts in public. In his acceptance speech to Congress he declared, "Lest some unlucky event should happen, unfavorable to my reputation, I beg it may be remembered, by every gentleman in the room, that I, this day, declare with the utmost sincerity, I do not think myself equal to the command I am honored with." He was a proud man, ever conscious of what his peers thought of him, so anxious that nothing mar his reputation that the possibility of failure in the top command haunted him.

After all, he had never commanded more than a relative handful of men, had little experience or background in the tactics of warfare, far less in designing strategy. Yet here he was, responsible for using the Continental Army in a manner that would do the most damage to one of the best fighting forces in the world. He never had an adequate number of troops, nor access to a navy that might contain or at least frustrate the enemy. And most of the time he lacked the money to pay his men, buy the food for their survival, or purchase the clothing, shoes, and blankets to keep them even marginally comfortable.

Congress did not vote to go to war with the mother country. The members simply elected George Washington to command the armed forces and then resolved to "maintain and assist him, and adhere to him . . . with their lives and fortunes. . . ." They left it to him to wage war if that was what it took for "the maintenance and preservation of American liberty." Washington knew, as did most of his colleagues, what all of them risked by waging war against their king and country and what the penalties for treason were, and he recalled later that soldiers and congressmen alike chose independence "with halters about their necks."

As a Virginia delegate to the Continental Congress, he socialized regularly with other representatives, was reserved but eminently companionable, laughing at jokes, proposing toasts, amusing his companions with comments on the foibles of mankind, enjoying with relish an evening of dancing. He practiced the advice he once gave to his nephew: "Be courteous to all but intimate with few; and let those few be well tried before you give them your confidence; true friendship is a plant of slow growth. . . ."

In meetings he generally said little but absorbed everything that was discussed and occasionally summed it up for his colleagues. Thomas Jefferson served with Washington in the Virginia House of Burgesses and with Benjamin Franklin in the Congress, and as he put it, "I never heard either of them speak ten minutes at a time, nor to any but the main point which was to decide the question. They laid their shoulders to the great points, knowing that the little ones would follow of themselves."

Later, a French officer observed that the General's face was frequently grave or serious, but never stern, and usually became "softened by the most gracious and amiable smile. He is affable and converses with his officers familiarly and gaily." As John Adams's wife, Abigail, described him so aptly, he "has a dignity which forbids familiarity, mixed with an easy affability which creates love and reverence."

Along with his other qualities, George Washington had the look of a leader. He stood a head taller than most of his contemporaries, and he was an imposing figure, whose large bones, hands, feet, and thighs gave the impression of great physical strength. The life mask of him made by Jean-Antoine Houdon in 1785 captured his features so faithfully that it was, according to the French sculptor, "the most perfect reproduction of Washington's own face." As the painter Gilbert Stuart put it, the "features in his face [were] totally different from what I had observed in any other human being. The sockets of his eyes, for instance, were larger than what I had ever met before, and the upper part of the nose broader." His face, which bore a trace of smallpox scars, was usually sunburned, his hair reddish brown, the eyes gray-blue. What everyone also noticed was the astonishing grace with which this big man walked, with a stride that was fluid and quiet, as he had learned to travel through the wilderness.

He was accused at times of indecisiveness, and there was something to the charge, but Washington was a farmer and surveyor, who had learned through years of experience that results do not come overnight and that patience and time are required for goals to be achieved. In fact, one of his noblest assets was self-discipline, which was responsible for his astounding patience and composure under the most trying circumstances imaginable.

Some of his darkest moments came during the retreat across the Jerseys after the disastrous loss of New York, but gradually he began to take hold, gaining confidence. Realizing how foolhardy it was to meet a superior enemy head-on, he improvised, remained flexible enough to parry blows and anticipate his foe's moves, learned to run, feint, and strike an isolated detachment of the British army. He understood that his greatest asset was mobility, to hit and run as he did in the startling victories at Trenton and Princeton.

He asked more of his men than most commanders would, or did, and those men were willing to suffer terrible hardships partly because they believed in the cause they were fighting for and partly because the man who led them did more than lead; he inspired. He took risks in battle that terrified his aides while making his men love him all the more. Through all the years of disappointment and suffering—when the army was plagued with desertions for lack of food and clothing and pay, when Congress proved incapable of providing the army with more men* or the essentials for survival—Washington never quit,

---

*The story is told that Napoleon once remarked to Lafayette that during the American Revolution the future of the world was decided by forces no larger than corporals' guards. One reason conscription was never tried by Congress was that nationalism was not sufficiently advanced to overcome the states' resistance to a draft.

never lost his dedication to freedom, never ceased to believe in the possibility of victory.

Mostly he presided over defeats, but thanks to a boundless reservoir of optimism he never despaired for long. He was a man of deep moral principles, with a profound belief that Providence was an active participant in what he and his army were engaged in doing. Happily for the confederacy of states, Washington never forgot that he served at the pleasure of the citizens who purported to run the country. To the end of the war he was an unreconstructed civilian serving somewhat reluctantly in uniform.

He could so easily have taken a different road, one that led to a military dictatorship, but he believed in the supremacy of civilian rule and deferred time and again to the oversight of Congress, even when that body did its best to shirk responsibility. The fact that the army was the only effective force in the struggle for the country's survival and its independence, and that Washington was at the very center of that fight, made him more than an important personage; he became the very soul of the Revolution.

Washington was not a great general in the usual sense of the phrase. As the Prince de Broglie, who came to America with the French army, realized, "to award him the title of a truly great soldier, it will, I believe, be necessary to see him at the head of a larger army, with more means at his command and on more equal terms with the enemy." Yet his situation was unlike that of an Alexander or a Napoleon; it was a war in which the American armies consistently lost most of their battles, a war that was more often than not guerrilla combat, with the rebels all too often fighting under unequal odds, fighting under conditions that demanded unorthodox solutions.

To the great good fortune of the American states and the future of their patchwork country, in George Washington they had found a leader of unsurpassed persistence, with a will to win that simply would not be turned aside, a man whose one goal remained the same for more than half a decade: victory.

From the time Washington took charge of the New Englanders

who encircled General Thomas Gage's army in Boston, until 1781, when many of those same Yankees, and others who had been with him at the very beginning, surrounded the redcoats at Yorktown, in Virginia, he took a leave from the army only once—from the evening of September 9 to dawn on the 12th—when he returned to his beloved Mount Vernon for the first time, and then it was to entertain the French generals Rochambeau and Chastellux and their staffs.

After six years of fighting and indescribable suffering, George Washington's Continental Army left the Northeast for the first time and headed south toward Yorktown, on a mission that would demand every ounce of that army's remaining stamina and resolve, plus a great dose of luck and timely assistance from the "Providence" so often mentioned by the commander in chief.

George Washington had never won a major battle, but on this occasion he had an unparalleled opportunity. In addition to his Continental veterans he commanded a superb French army sent here by King Louis XVI, and he hoped to receive the support of a French fleet. How he used these forces could determine whether the war would drag on or whether America would at long last achieve its independence.

1

SO MUCH IS AT STAKE

❧

Five years had passed since that momentous third Wednesday in April of 1775—a day of sudden violence that began in the gray half-light of dawn, with young William Diamond frantically beating his drum as church bells from every nearby town clanged madly, calling the Massachusetts militia to arms. Who fired first was never known, but when a couple of gunshots rang out, some two hundred tired, anxious British regulars opened up with a ragged volley at four- or fivescore equally nervous farmers assembled on Lexington green, and King George's regulars and his American colonists had been fighting ever since.

Now it was 1780, and the Revolution that had begun in 1775 was expiring for lack of support. George Washington, the harried commander in chief of what passed for the military forces of the United States, was pleading with Congress for a draft that would produce a Continental Army of 22,680, with 17,320 militiamen to supplement them, but the likelihood of anything like an additional 40,000 men joining up was preposterous, as the General knew, given the unwillingness of the states to come up with their quotas.

At most, the Continental Army garrisoned at West Point was

estimated to number 9,000 men, but the reality was that only 3,278 of them reported fit for duty—meaning that they had shoes and clothing and were reasonably healthy. Out of a population of 2.5 million people, fewer than 1 percent were willing to join the regular army fighting for their country's independence.

Except for those troops who were in the Highlands of the Hudson River and soldiers in the southern states, the main army had spent the past winter in Morristown, New Jersey, twenty-five miles west of New York City, on high ground protected by the Watchung Mountains, overlooking the roads between New York and Philadelphia. Here the army's season of greatest discontent had begun on January 3 with a blizzard—a storm so terrible that "no man could endure its violence many minutes without danger of his life," according to Surgeon James Thacher, who watched helplessly as four feet of snow piled up in as many days, covering the tents and burying the men like sheep. A contemporary recorded twenty-seven more snowfalls that awful winter, with weather so frigid in the succeeding months that the Hudson River froze solid from Manhattan to Paulus Hook and the snow remained on the ground until May, surpassing anything the oldest inhabitants could recall. When spring finally came, some of the General's infantry companies could muster only four or five men, with the average complement about fifteen. One of his generals reported that he had officers who were embarrassed to come out of their huts; they were almost naked. Worst of all was the number of men suffering from hunger. At one time Private Joseph Plumb Martin, a Connecticut Yankee, had nothing whatever to eat for four days and nights, except some black birch bark he gnawed off a stick of wood, and after seeing several men roast their old shoes and eat them he heard that some of the officers had killed a favorite little dog for a meal. Other officers put themselves on a diet of bread and water so their men could have what meat there was.

In May the situation had come to a head when troops of the 4th and 8th Regiments of the Connecticut regulars mutinied; they had not been paid for five months, they had had neither meat nor bread for ten days, they were angry, mortally weary of suffering, and they decided to quit and go home. Fortunately, the mutiny produced little violence beyond a few scuffles and an apparently accidental bayonet wound suffered by Colonel Return Jonathan Meigs, after which some quick-thinking officers ordered other Connecticut regiments to parade at once without their arms. After they turned out, guards took stations between them and their huts so they could not retrieve their muskets. At that, the men of the 4th and 8th didn't quite know what to do and, still fuming, stalked back to their camps, where their officers appealed to them to remain calm. As they did so, soldiers of a Pennsylvania brigade surrounded the Connecticut camps, but when officers huddled to decide what should be done next, they wisely determined to withdraw the Pennsylvania troops—the risk was too great that those men, too, might join the mutiny.

As Washington knew, the only money available to pay these men was virtually worthless Continental currency, but he figured that food was a more important need just now and appealed yet again to Commissary General Ephraim Blaine, who was doing his level best to find some meat. That gentleman had his own problems prying money out of the Congress: "I am loaded with debt," he told the General, "and have not had a shilling this two months." This meant that the troops would continue to plunder the surrounding neighborhood for food, but there was no helping it and Washington's officers were as disgusted as he was. Major General Nathanael Greene grumbled that "a country overflowing with plenty [is] now suffering an army employed for the defense of everything dear and valuable to perish for lack of food," and Colonel Samuel Webb cried out in frustration, "I damn my country for lack of gratitude!"

Ever since the rebel victory at Saratoga, in 1777, had convinced France to sign a treaty of alliance with the United States, George Washington had been waiting and praying for French intervention to come soon, but as the weeks and months passed with no sign that help was on the way, his hopes waned. The situation suited many a Francophobe in America, like the New York attorney and loyalist William

Smith, Jr., who wrote, "I dread France—She will be guided only by motives of Interest—No Promises will bind her—She will percieve it more advantageous to her Ambition to ferment animosities than hastily to plunge into a War—She will decieve both Parties that her ends may be achieved at our Expence."

Fortunately for the patriots, the young French aristocrat Marquis de Lafayette, a volunteer who had been serving in Washington's army, returned to Versailles in 1779 and came back to America a year later with the welcome news that seven French ships of the line, ten to twelve thousand veteran troops led by Comte de Rochambeau, and a war chest of 6 million livres were on the way and should arrive in Rhode Island in June. Even more encouraging to Washington, who believed that the key to victory in this war was to recapture New York from the British, the French had orders to join the American forces in an attack on that city. But what of the rebels who were to fight alongside the French? When Lafayette rejoined Washington in Morristown, he was appalled to find "An Army that is reduced to nothing, that wants provisions, that has not one of the necessary means to make war." However prepared for such squalor he may have been by his knowledge of past distress, "I confess I had no idea of such an extremity," he wrote.

Washington was mortified to think that when the French finally did arrive, they would immediately see the desperate condition of the Continental Army and the helplessness of America, and sail away. Were they to arrive today, he warned the governors of the states, and "find that we have but a handful of men in the field," they would surely doubt that "we had any serious intentions to prosecute measures with vigor." In February, New York was the only state that had met its quota, and the deficiency of men in the ranks was reckoned at 14,436. By July 4, the fourth anniversary of the signing of the Declaration of Independence, the General's best estimate of new recruits who had come into camp was, at most, thirty men. He had no alternative but to appeal repeatedly to the states: "The exigency is so pressing that we ought to multiply our efforts to give new activity and dispatch to our measures," he wrote, "levying and forwarding the men, providing the supplies of every sort required. . . . So much is at stake, so much to be hoped, so much to be lost, that we shall be unexcusable if we do not employ all our zeal and all our exertion."

The plight of the army was so bad that Lieutenant Colonel Ebenezer Huntington, who was clothed in rags and had not been paid for more than six months, wrote in a rage to his brother in Connecticut, hoping to shame his relatives into sending aid.

> The rascally stupidity which now prevails in the country at large is beyond all descriptions. . . . Why don't you reinforce your army, feed them, clothe and pay them? . . . [Do] not suffer yourselves to be duped into the thought that the French will relieve you and fight your battles . . . they will not serve week after week without meat, without clothing, and paid in filthy rags.
>
> I despise my countrymen. I wish I could say I was not born in America. I once gloried in it, but am now ashamed of it . . . and all this for my cowardly countrymen who flinch at the very time when their exertions are wanted and hold their purse strings as though they would damn the world rather than part with a dollar to their Army.

★ ★ ★

FIVE YEARS OF unbelievably harsh circumstances had taught George Washington he must be patient, must never stop trying, and the wonder of it all was his capacity for resilience—his ability to bounce back again and again from shattered hopes and bitter disappointment, too many defeats, too few victories. Several disgruntled officers and certain New England members of Congress saw in that record confirmation that the General lacked ability, and they made every effort to discredit him and have him replaced. Generals Horatio Gates and Charles Lee—both former British officers who had joined the rebels—were continually scheming to undercut the commander in chief and (so each one hoped) succeed him. On top of these ugly rivalries, the Congress seemed incapable of providing

Washington's men with even the barest necessities. As the General put it, ". . . the history of the war is a history of false hopes and temporary expedients."

Until recently Congress had borne the financial burden of the conflict, doing so by printing paper money that was not backed by hard currency. Finally, the reckoning had come, the Continental money was now utterly worthless,* and Congress decided to make the states responsible for raising funds, since they had the power to tax the citizens and Congress did not. The idea was that each state would pay its own line, as its regular forces were called, and provide soldiers with the necessities. Seeing at once where this would lead, Washington protested, in words that foreshadowed later arguments for a constitution of the United States.

Unless the states were willing to let their representatives in Congress speak and act for them, he said, and unless Congress was given absolute power to wage the war, "we are attempting an impossibility and very soon shall become (if it is not already the case) a many-headed monster, a heterogeneous mass, that never will or can steer to the same point."

At no time in the long history of the war, Washington warned, has dissatisfaction been "so general and so alarming." The only glue that held the army together was the soldiers' extraordinary patriotism, but now some officers were resigning while the men in the ranks—who had no such option—"murmur, brood over their discontent, and have lately shown a disposition to enter into seditious combinations." There were limits to men's endurance, he told Congress, and observed that if the Connecticut regiments had marched off, as they had in mind to do, there would have been no stopping the rest of the army from following.

---

*In the Washington County, North Carolina, courthouse, one Samuel Tate was indicted for his "evil mind and disposition" and for "maliciously intending to stir up and excite . . . Disorder, Insurrection, and sedition among the good and faithful subjects [by speaking] the following English words, to wit, 'God damn the money' (meaning the Continental Money) it has ruined me."

To these worries were added personal frustrations. His wife, Martha, had bravely joined him in camp recently, but their landlady continued to occupy two of the four downstairs rooms while the second floor was still unfinished for lack of boards. The Washingtons had no kitchen of their own, their servants were all suffering from bad colds, and, worst of all, the General's favorite horse was laid up, another was still gaunt from the previous winter, his mare was in foal, and his reaction to a substitute animal sent him by a Virginia neighbor was to accept it "as men take their wives, for better or worse, and if he should prove a jade and go limping on, I must do as they are obliged to do: submit to the bargain."

Further thwarting the General was the knowledge that if his own army were not so weak, the British commander in chief, General Sir Henry Clinton, would never have dared sail from New York with an expeditionary force consisting of most of the British fleet under Admiral Marriot Arbuthnot, plus as many as 8,000 troops, to besiege Charleston, South Carolina. Clinton had left behind some 11,000 soldiers, two-thirds of them Hessians and the others Tories, and while it was tempting to think they were vulnerable to attack, Washington knew he could accomplish nothing without a French fleet and many more soldiers to bolster his own feeble ranks in New Jersey and the Hudson Valley—2,800 of whose three-year enlistments would be up at the end of May.

★   ★   ★

ONCE FRANCE HAD decided to ally itself actively with the United States, the entire complexion of America's war began to change, and for no one was this more significant than George Washington. Until now, everyone fighting on the rebel side had been directly or indirectly under his command, and his only involvement with sea power was to wish that a European enemy of Britain would bring it to his aid.

The French alliance called for a fresh approach to strategy and tactics. The Continental Army would be fighting alongside troops who neither spoke their language nor were directly subject to Washington's orders. And who could say how the introduction of France's warships would affect the existing equation? While England's sea power was superior to that of France, the former country also had to reckon with Spain, whose navy when combined with that of the French could tip the scales.

Since protection of the homeland was of paramount importance to the English, they decided to keep their main fleet in European waters unless an enemy squadron was detached to the West Indies or America, but only after assuring themselves that the ships were definitely bound for North America could they dispatch a detachment in pursuit. That meant, of course, that the French, sailing first, were more likely to have the advantage and beat the English across the Atlantic. But there were inherent uncertainties, one being control of the waters of the West Indies, where French and British each had valuable properties. This was the real center of the Atlantic trade, where the naval forces of England, France, and other European powers were on the prowl and where the best-laid plans could be undone in the blink of an eye.

European diplomacy in the eighteenth century was a mirror image of Niccolò Machiavelli's theory of practical statecraft. The end justified the means, and the end, as often as not, was the aggrandizement of the various monarchs and nobles. Not surprisingly, Europe's capitals swarmed with spies, who were a continuing problem for the more naive American envoys. Beginning in 1763, the goal of France's foreign policy was revenge—revenge for the humiliation it had suffered at the hands of England during the Seven Years' War. Crushed militarily and stripped of its colonies by the Treaty of Paris in 1763, France lost its position as the first nation of Europe and was reduced to the unprecedented position of a second-rate power.

Since the French king Louis XV and his foreign policy had been largely in the hands of his mistress, Madame de Pompadour, from 1745 until her death in 1764, she deserved much of the blame for bringing on the Seven Years' War, so disastrous for France. One of her favorites was Duc Étienne François de Choiseul, who managed the foreign affairs portfolio through the Seven Years' War and obtained the best terms possible (meager as they were) at the peace table. It was Choiseul who perceived in Britain's disgruntled colonies a likely tool for humbling France's enemy across the Channel. In 1768 the monarch's amours again played a hand in the nation's diplomacy. That year the king took another mistress—one Marie Jeanne Bécu, who had until then performed the same services for Chevalier Jean du Barry while presiding over his gambling house. (It was a complicated life Madame du Barry led. She caught the eye of Louis XV and became his paramour while married to her former lover's brother, Comte Guillaume du Barry. In 1770 she dismissed Choiseul, and she retired from the court when the king died in 1774.)*

Fortunately for the American colonies, Choiseul's successor, Charles Gravier, Comte de Vergennes, saw their usefulness to France in precisely the same light as the duke. A clever, subtle statesman with experience in a number of the smaller European courts, Vergennes as early as the 1750s had observed presciently that if France lost Canada, "England will soon repent of having removed the only check that could keep her colonies in awe. They stand no longer in need of her protection. She will call on them to contribute towards supporting the burdens they have helped to bring on her, and they will answer by striking off all dependence." Vergennes was also a guileful man, who once wrote to the foreign office from his post in Turkey, ". . . we should hide from the Turks the real end toward which we are driving them. . . . let us appear to be occupied only with what concerns them, without reference to ourselves. . . ." All of which suggests how he viewed relations with the Americans. He was wise enough, however, to be content to humble England, while avoiding the impression that "we are seeking her destruction.

---

*Arrested by Robespierre in 1793, Madame du Barry was tried and condemned by the Revolutionary Tribunal and sent to the guillotine.

She is necessary to the balance of power in Europe, wherein she occupies a considerable place. . . . We shall be feared less if we content ourselves with cutting off our enemy's arms than if we insist on running him through the heart."

While Vergennes's foreign policy differed little from that of Choiseul, at first he failed to recognize the effect Britain's infamous Coercive Acts were having on the Americans in 1774, and this was brought to his attention by Pierre-Augustin Caron de Beaumarchais, who had risen from apprenticeship to his father, a watchmaker, to become a favorite at the French court. A man of many talents, he wrote the comedies *Le Barbier de Seville* and *Le Mariage de Figaro*, which later inspired operas by Rossini and Mozart. In 1775 Beaumarchais happened to be in England on a clandestine mission for Vergennes, and there he became acquainted with Arthur Lee, who represented Massachusetts as its agent in London. From Lee he heard how desperate the colonies' situation was, and the two discussed the possibility that France might assist the rebels with arms and other necessities of war.

On the heels of these talks Beaumarchais returned to Versailles, where he spoke with Vergennes and the slow-witted king, who was not yet twenty years old, urging them to consider covert shipments of weapons to the Americans. His notion, as expressed by Spain's cynical foreign minister, who had been approached by Vergennes to join France in providing secret assistance, was that the English and Americans should "exhaust themselves reciprocally," enabling France and Spain to pick up the pieces. A resulting memorandum read by Vergennes to the king and his council set forth the reasons for supplying the colonial rebels with arms disguised as legal trade goods. First, it would diminish the power of England and increase that of France. Second, it would cause irreparable loss to English trade, while stimulating French commerce. Third, it would probably lead to the recovery of some former French possessions, such as the fisheries off Newfoundland and the Gulf of St. Lawrence. "We do not speak of Canada," the memoir concluded, indicating that any continental conquest would be up to the Americans, while the French would take over the prized British islands in the West Indies.

Vergennes argued further that the colonies—once they declared their independence—would undoubtedly form a republican government, which, by its very nature, would be weak and incapable of threatening European possessions in North America. (No one seems to have raised a question about the ethics of sponsoring a revolution. More astonishing, Vergennes and his master, Louis XVI, appear to have made no connection between a successful revolution against George III of England and the possibility that restive folk in another country might be encouraged to foment a revolution against their own ruler—especially in a land like France, whose shaky financial condition already contained the seeds that made future upheaval all but inevitable.)

As early as May 12, 1776, it was agreed that France would pursue a policy of secret assistance to the Americans, whereupon Louis XVI directed that 1 million livres' worth of munitions be delivered to the rebels from the royal arsenals. This was to be handled by a fictitious trading enterprise created by Beaumarchais, called Hortalez et Cie. Eventually, Charles III of Spain contributed an equal amount of money, as did a group of French businessmen, and this company— managed by none other than Beaumarchais—was the channel through which shipments of arms from French arsenals were sent to such entrepôts as Haiti and Martinique, where they were received by American agents and reshipped to the colonies.

For its part, Congress named five of its members to the Secret Committee on Correspondence, and that group began corresponding with Arthur Lee in London and Charles Dumas, a friend of Benjamin Franklin's who lived in The Hague, in an effort to ascertain the potential support for America in Europe. After the signing of the Declaration of Independence the Continental Congress dispatched an official mission to France, composed of Benjamin Franklin, Arthur Lee, and Silas Deane. When these three commissioners arrived in

Paris, they notified Vergennes that they were "fully empowered by the Congress of the United States of America to propose and negotiate a treaty of commerce between France and the United States." But such an agreement was a long time coming.

★　★　★

WHEN FRANKLIN STEPPED onto the scene in Paris, he was by all odds the best-known American in the world and one of the most politically knowledgeable. He had served on the most important committees in Congress and had unrivaled diplomatic skills as a result of dealing with British statesmen, plus a shrewd knowledge of human nature. The Paris into which he came as a conspicuous newcomer was seething with intrigue. The British ambassador, Viscount Stormont, was alert to every move the French made and had a host of spies (including one who was Arthur Lee's secretary) working for him, reporting what Franklin was doing, who his correspondents in England were, and even stealing some of his letters.

A thoughtful, witty, homespun philosopher, Franklin was a wise old owl who sensed immediately what the French thought of him and was more than willing to play the part. He was, after all, no backwoods bumpkin but an urbane gentleman who had lived among and corresponded with some of the world's leading scientists and scholars, politicians, clergymen, and merchants. The French who sought the primitive virtues extolled by Rousseau believed they were personified in Franklin, and he did nothing to disappoint them. He had debarked in Brittany wearing a fur cap that had warmed him on the November crossing of the Atlantic, and he kept it on, even in Paris. Writing to a friend, he told him, "Figure me in your mind as jolly as formerly, and as strong and hearty, only a few years older; very plainly dressed, wearing my thin grey straight hair that peeps out under my only coiffure, a fine fur cap, which comes down to my forehead almost to my spectacles. Think how this must appear among the powdered heads of Paris." He wore an old brown coat, carried a stick instead of a sword, seemed to relish his outmoded clothes, and if this jibed with the image Parisians had of an American sage, leader of a natural state against a corrupt, sophisticated empire, so be it.

He was the toast of France, but since it was impossible for every French man or woman to see him, they must have his likeness, an engraving of him over the mantelpiece, his image in the lid of a snuff-box or set in a ring, plus busts, prints, copies—so many of them, he wrote his daughter, that they "have made your father's face as well known as that of the moon. . . ."

Inevitably, it was to Franklin that so many French and other European officers came, hoping to be recommended to the American army. By the first of March in 1777 he had moved to Passy, which he described as "a neat village on a high ground, half a mile from Paris, with a large garden to walk in," and here he was all but overwhelmed by visitors and correspondents—most of them men whose imaginations had been fired by the idealism behind the rebellion. As one nobleman wrote of America's rebels, "Their cause was our cause. We were proud of their victories, we wept for their defeats." And of course many of these young Europeans saw opportunities for glory and advancement in their chosen career as soldiers. Two men in particular who came to America with Franklin's blessing proved invaluable to George Washington. One was the nineteen-year-old Marquis de Lafayette, eager to win fame by fighting against England; the other was the man who called himself Baron Friedrich Wilhelm von Steuben. The latter had served on the Prussian general staff as an aide to Frederick the Great, but when he was introduced to Franklin he was an unemployed captain, and Franklin—to persuade Congress to accept another foreigner—raised his rank substantially, noting that he was "lately a lieutenant general in the king of Prussia's service. . . ." Captain or lieutenant general, the baron brought new life to Washington's army, making it over in a matter of weeks, drilling the men into soldiers, instilling real discipline in their ranks.

All that summer of 1777 Franklin and his fellow commissioners anxiously followed the progress of General John Burgoyne's army of British regulars, German mercenaries, and Indian allies, southward bound from Canada, heading for Albany, New York, and a rendezvous with General Sir William Howe's forces. News reached Passy that Burgoyne had captured Fort Ticonderoga and Mount Independence, that Fort Edward had been taken, but none of these reports seemed to dim Franklin's optimism or alter his refusal to concede defeat. Then came reports of a battle near Bennington and the loss of a sizeable number of Burgoyne's German troops, but still no signs from the French about an alliance. In November the group at Passy learned that Philadelphia, Franklin's hometown, where his daughter and her young children lived, plus all of Franklin's property, had fallen to Howe. Even so, the old man was more determined than ever that the Americans would persist and win, even without French aid; nor would he agree to warn Vergennes that without a French alliance the Americans must come to terms with Britain. Since that "might make them abandon us in despair or in anger," the commissioners would wait until the news was better, he announced, when they could argue for more favorable terms.

It was late in the morning of December 4 when a Boston merchant named Jonathan Loring Austin rode into Franklin's courtyard in the village. He had come ashore at Nantes with dispatches, and rumors had preceded him to Passy, where the commissioners waited anxiously, hopeful of news. Before he could dismount, Franklin asked, "*Is Philadelphia taken?*" To which Austin replied, "Yes, sir."

Then, as the old man clasped his hands as if he had heard of a death in the family and turned to go into the house, Austin said, "But sir, I have greater news than that. GENERAL BURGOYNE *and his whole army are prisoners of war!*" Recalling the moment later, Austin said the effect was "electrical," and throughout France the rejoicing over the rebel triumph at Saratoga was as enthusiastic as if it had been a victory by French troops. Beaumarchais, ever on the alert for an event that would enhance his stock market speculations, was in such a hurry to get to Paris that his reckless driving caused his carriage to overturn, injuring his arm.

During these past weeks the English had been on tenterhooks of their own, waiting for word about Burgoyne's army. They had been in the dark for more than three weeks, wrote the British man of letters Horace Walpole, who complained that "impatience is very high and uneasiness increases with every day." On December 2 official news from General Sir Guy Carleton in Quebec reached Whitehall, announcing "the total annihilation . . . of Burgoyne's army," prompting Walpole to say, "we are . . . very near' the end of the American war," adding that the king "fell into agonies on hearing this account. . . ."

On December 17, one day shy of two weeks after the news reached Passy, the American commissioners were notified that His Majesty Louis XVI was ready to acknowledge the independence of the United States and enter into a treaty of amity and commerce. On the evening of February 6, 1778, that treaty was signed, embodying most-favored-nation trading privileges and certain maritime principles along with recognizing independence. A second treaty—a "conditional and defensive alliance" that was to have a profound effect on the revolution in America—provided that in the event of war between France and Great Britain as a consequence of the first treaty, the United States and France would fight the war together and neither would make peace with the enemy without the formal consent of the other. Further, they would not lay down their arms until the independence of the United States was assured by a treaty ending the war.

France at once conveyed to the British government the treaty of amity and commerce (though not the alliance), not realizing that a spy had already given George III's agents a copy of both treaties. The spy was an American double agent, Dr. Edward Bancroft. Originally from Massachusetts, he had studied medicine in England and settled there to pursue scientific interests, through which he met Benjamin Franklin. When the latter went to France, Bancroft arranged to work as a spy for him, as he did, beginning in 1776, for Silas Deane as well. At the same time he was an agent of the British, who paid him a handsome £1,000 annually, with a promise of a pension of £500 a year. (It might be added that he was rewarded further through speculations in the market, based on the secret information he obtained.) As a final achievement, he arranged to be appointed secretary of the American Peace Commission negotiating the final settlement with Great Britain, and so effective was his cover that his career as a spy was not suspected until a century after he had died. As he put it after the war in a letter to Britain's foreign secretary, he went to France and "during the first year resided in the same house with Dr. Franklin, Mr. Deane, etc., and regularly informed this Government of every transaction of the American Commissioners. . . ."

If the stakes had not been so high, the frenzied activity of espionage agents milling around in the little house in Passy would have seemed a joke. In addition to British agents, Louis XVI's secret service spied continuously on the American commissioners, suspicious that they might be carrying on behind-the-scenes negotiations with England while working for a treaty with France.

At the center of British efforts to divine the relationship between France and the American colonies and prevent an alliance between the two was William Eden, an undersecretary of state and chief of the Secret Service in London. His man in charge of the Paris operation was Paul Wentworth, an American loyalist, Harvard graduate and classmate of John Adams, and until recently the London agent for New Hampshire. He was related to Benning Wentworth, who served as the first royal governor of New Hampshire, and his reason for becoming a secret agent was not the £500 a year he was paid, but the promise of a baronetcy, which meant a seat in Parliament and a position of some prestige in English society. Always prepared, he carried with him a cipher with recipes for several invisible inks, used as many as twenty assumed names, and devoted himself unstintingly to his work, with results that were of incalculable value to the British government. He prided himself on being a gentleman, yet he was capable of such outrageous acts as stealing a friend's visiting card and seal and going to any lengths to buy or pilfer documents. However, he was never to achieve the goal he most desired. Lord Suffolk believed that Lord North should reward his services; Lord North thought the king should do it; but George III did not like Wentworth (or other agents, for that matter), who kept reporting French actions to assist the Americans, which the king didn't want to hear.

The monarch discovered a way to rationalize his prejudice against Wentworth: when he discovered that he liked to gamble, he took to calling him a "stock-jobber" and a "dabbler in the alley," who was not to be trusted because such men were easily hoodwinked. Thanks to Wentworth and Bancroft, among others, the British government was far better informed about the secrets of its rebellious colonies than most Americans were, but the reason this knowledge had so little impact on the conduct of the war was the king's unreasonable animus against financial speculation and his conviction that his secret agents were involved in gambling—which they were. If he had paid attention to his agents, he would have realized that no more than a handful of American leaders were advocating independence in the early stages of the war.

For example, a letter to William Lee in London, written in October of 1775 and signed "J.A." (almost certainly John Adams), was intercepted by British postal authorities and known to the Secret Service, if not the king's ministers. It read:

> We cannot in this country conceive that there are men in England so infatuated as seriously to suspect the Congress or people here to erect ourselves into an independent state. If such an idea really obtains amongst those at the helm of affairs, one hour's residence in America would eradicate it. I never met one individual so inclined but it is universally disavowed.

To be sure, that was written late in 1775, but two years later Benjamin Franklin was still reluctant to push the French too hard by revealing his advocacy of independence. Not until he heard the news of Saratoga in December of 1777 did he feel sufficiently confident that the French would back the Americans with an alliance and, better yet, warships and troops, so that he could speak openly about independence.

In other words, by heeding Lord Stormont's reports from his spies, George III might have understood that an opportunity existed to settle affairs with the Americans short of independence, while keeping the colonies within the empire. Not until after the American victory at Saratoga was Wentworth instructed to propose terms secretly to Franklin—terms which North announced in Parliament two months later. But by then it was too late by far.

In a last-minute desperation move aimed at reconciliation with the former colonies, a peace commission headed by Frederick Howard, Lord Carlisle, the twenty-nine-year-old, extremely rich friend of the opposition politician Charles James Fox, was dispatched to America in 1778, bearing terms that would take relations back to where they had been in 1763—basically granting the Americans everything they wanted except independence. The hope was that this proposal would persuade the Congress not to ratify the treaty with France, and a British ship bearing the commission and a French vessel carrying the treaties raced each other across the Atlantic.*

The French won, though even had they not done so Congress would not have agreed to any proposal that did not include independence. On May 2 the treaties were presented to the legislators in York, Pennsylvania, where Congress was sitting, and were ratified

---

*The Howe brothers—General William and his brother, Richard, the admiral—who were already in America, were on the commission, and Carlisle brought with him William Eden, a member of the Board of Trade who advocated reconciliation; Eden's wife, who was four months pregnant; George Johnstone, an American partisan who had been governor of West Florida; Anthony Morris, known as "the best dancer and skater in London"; and Adam Ferguson, a professor of moral philosophy. Also on the boat, but by no means part of the mission, was Charles, Earl Cornwallis, who had sailed for England after the battles of Trenton and Princeton and was now on his way to becoming General Sir Henry Clinton's second in command.

two days later. Their significance was soon evident. On July 11, 1780, an express rode up to General William Heath's headquarters in Providence, Rhode Island, with news that the fleet of "our illustrious ally" had been sighted off Newport. After dispatching a messenger to George Washington, Heath hurried down to the dock, boarded a packet to Newport that arrived about midnight, and next morning called on the Comte de Rochambeau, who had come ashore the previous evening with his staff, and was understandably perplexed when no American officer greeted them and they found "no one in the streets; only a few sad and frightened faces in the windows."

That was the beginning of a long, enduring friendship between the two men, and the down-to-earth Heath also had an opportunity to meet and size up a number of Rochambeau's fellow officers, one of whom was the Chevalier de Chastellux, a distinguished philosopher-soldier, veteran of campaigns in Germany during the Seven Years' War, darling of the Paris salons, a famous author and friend of the great Voltaire, with a coveted membership in the forty-member French Academy. The group also included Admiral the Chevalier de Ternay, commander of the squadron of seven sail of the line and five smaller vessels that had escorted the transports carrying more than five thousand French soldiers. The fleet had sailed from Brest on May 2 and traveled by the southern route, where it was less likely to encounter British men-of-war, but even so, they had had several brief engagements.

An indication of how terrible these long ocean journeys were for the soldiers who were sandwiched like sardines in quarters that were inhuman, to say the best for them, is that as many as 2,600 soldiers and seamen were sick by the time they landed—two-thirds of them suffering with scurvy—and the first order of business on shore was to set up hospital facilities for them. On board one ship, with two servants and all his personal effects (which included "large stores of sugar, lemons, and syrups"), was Baron Ludwig von Closen, a Bavarian whose adopted country was France. On the crossing he had shared what he called a "large compartment" with nineteen others.

The space was fifteen feet long, twelve feet wide, and four and a half feet high; it was "not too comfortable," according to the baron, especially considering the noise, "exhalations and other bad odors produced by the passengers." If these were quarters for officers, those for the troops and ordinary seamen can only be imagined.

The Deux-Ponts regiment alone lost nine men during the seventy-two-day passage and counted 450 sick when they disembarked. Those who had suffered most on the voyage were big, robust men, and the Germans among them proved to be the worst sailors. (Led by Guillaume, Comte de Deux-Ponts, this regiment came from the ever-shifting borderland between France and Germany; as many as one-third of Rochambeau's army was made up of German and Swiss troops.)

Happily for posterity, Closen kept a diary of his experiences in America and later wrote a full account of the French expeditionary force from the spring of 1780 until its return to France in June 1783. Sprightly, candid, and humorous, the memoir and the drawings he made reveal a great deal about life in colonial America as well as Closen's keen interest in the land's flora and fauna, climate, people, customs, and food (especially the food), his own love of liberty and antipathy to slavery, and his fascination with the notable figures he met (Washington, Jefferson, and John Hancock, among others). Closen was a short man—just five feet four inches tall—blond, with blue eyes and a slightly turned-up nose. A good enough linguist that he often translated for Rochambeau, he became one of his aides-de-camp* and a trusted "Count's Courier," partly because he was a skilled draftsman, spoke good English, and was related to a former comrade-in-arms of Rochambeau, a Bavarian major general from whom Closen had inherited "military virtues and an unalterable attachment to France."

---

*Among the others were two of the general's nephews and Comte Axel Fersen, the favorite of Marie Antoinette, and Comte de Vauban, a great-grandnephew of Louis XIV's famous marshal.

In addition to Heath, who was there to provide Rochambeau with information about the countryside and its resources, Washington had sent Lafayette and a small contingent of militia to join the French in what the American general expected to be an attack on New York. When the British commander, General Sir Henry Clinton, returned to that city from his victorious expedition to Charleston, however, Admiral Thomas Graves arrived at Sandy Hook with six ships of the line, which, added to Admiral Arbuthnot's fleet, gave the British a thirteen-to-eight superiority over Ternay's force, immediately foiling Washington's plans.

But the failure of British naval forces to attack the French before they could establish themselves in Rhode Island was deplored at the time by General Clinton, who saw it as a turning point in the war and wrote years later: "our not being able to crush this reinforcement immediately upon its arrival gave additional animation to the spirit of rebellion, whose almost expiring embers began to blaze up afresh upon its appearance."

2

FRANCE WILL TURN THE TIDE

Despite the arrival of the French force, what confronted Washington was a bulging inventory of disaster. From Newport came word that the French ships that had been unloaded carried no arms, no gunpowder, no uniforms for his destitute, half-naked veterans. At the end of July Nathanael Greene had written to the congressional delegates resigning his post as quartermaster general, informing them that nothing would induce him to stay on in that frustrating job, which had almost driven him to distraction. Apparently, some of the congressmen found Greene's letter offensive and thought he should be cashiered. Washington, alarmed by the criticism of his favorite lieutenant, who had been wearing two hats—one as a field commander, the other as quartermaster general—wrote immediately to Congress hoping to prevent them from creating a real crisis. It was essential that Greene be persuaded to stay on until the man Congress had named to succeed him—Timothy Pickering—could learn the rudiments of the job. Otherwise, Washington would be forced to cease preparations for the next campaign and "be obliged to disperse, if not disband the Army for want of subsistence." Happily, Greene realized he had been overly inflexible, Congress made no more of the problem, and it disappeared.

In addition to their other wants, Washington's troops did not have enough horses and wagons to join the French in an operation anytime soon. Not a day passed without Washington hoping for news of that "second division" of France's ships and soldiers that Admiral Ternay had told him was on the way, but all he heard on that front was silence. His plan for the army was to put Greene in command of the right wing and give the left to Benedict Arnold, but Arnold was begging off, saying his left leg—badly wounded at Saratoga—was still too weak for so active a command. He asked instead for a more sedentary post—specifically, to take charge of the fort at West Point—even though Washington tried to shame him out of it by saying his garrison would consist of militia and invalids.

So lackadaisical were the states about providing food for the army that the commander in chief was obliged to authorize a program he detested. Here it was the harvest season, a time of abundance, yet appeals to the states had produced no results worth noting, forcing the General to resort once more to scavenging his own country. "Either the Army must disband," he wrote, "or what is, if possible, worse, subsist upon the plunder of the people." The result was that every few days he moved his camp, letting the men forage for anything within reach, and when the area was stripped clean, move on to another and repeat the process.

Week after week the officer corps deteriorated. Brigadier General Enoch Poor, who had served with Washington at Trenton and Princeton and fought at Monmouth, died in September of "putrid fever," as typhus was called. Another brigadier, John Nixon, left the army because of health problems. Alexander McDougall, "sick of the stone," considered "laying by for the winter"; John Sullivan and Israel Putnam were soon to retire because of ill health. Still other officers threatened to resign, some jealous of another who was given an appointment they cherished, others simply worn out, physically and mentally, tired of being hungry, unpaid, and away from their families. A large body of militia—some 4,500 men from Pennsylvania who were marching to join in the planned attack on New York, and who would have been welcomed with open arms at any other time—were ordered by the General to return home. He could not feed them.

Meantime a nasty situation arose with the Comte de Rochambeau, whose orders were to put himself under Washington's command. All very well, but from the latter's point of view the language barrier made communication extremely difficult: the Frenchman spoke no English, the American's French was elementary at best, and Washington was dealing with a man whose nuanced language and charm were well suited to the king's court but difficult for a Virginia planter to match. To deal with the dilemma, Washington informed Rochambeau and Ternay that he would communicate with them through the young Marquis de Lafayette, "a friend from whom I conceal nothing. . . . I entreat you to receive whatever he shall tell you as coming from me."

Nothing could have been more impolitic. Washington did not know this, but during his recent visit to France Lafayette had put himself forward at the French court for the very command now held by Rochambeau, and where the latter was a seasoned veteran, wounded several times and commended for his bravery and skill, who had been fighting for France long before Lafayette was born, the Marquis was now only twenty-three years old and, before volunteering for Washington's army and being given the rank of major general by Congress, had been merely a captain in the French reserve with next to no military experience. In fact, one reason none of the regular French officers in America wanted to serve with Lafayette's command was that everyone but Rochambeau was outranked by the young American major general. Understandably, the French commander had difficulty accepting this turn of events, and the friction was apparent to the men on his staff, who sensed the cooling of relations. As an old army hand, Rochambeau was not about to deal through Lafayette; nor was he willing to accept the latter's suggestions for strategy, which he rejected in honeyed words, saying, "it is always the old father Rochambeau who talks to his dear son whom he loves. . . ."

To his government, Rochambeau reported frankly that America was "in consternation." The real strength of Washington's army, he said, was a mere three thousand men, and the country's currency was worthless. "Send us troops, ships, and money," he went on, "but do not depend on these people nor upon their means: they have neither money nor credit; their means of resistance are only momentary and called forth when they are attacked in their own homes." Washington's plan for an attack on New York was foolhardy, he observed—preposterous in fact; and very likely the last gasp of a desperate commander. He couldn't avoid wondering if the General's insistence on this plan was not a result of Lafayette's mischief making. If only Washington had not "sent Lafayette to me with full powers from him!" Finally, exasperated by Lafayette's overzealous behavior, the count wrote to Washington, "I beg of your Excellency to continue to give me your orders by the same direct means that you have done until now."

That ended the awkward dispute, but it also pointed up the difference between the amateurs and professionals who took up arms on the side of America in this war. Marie Joseph Paul Yves Roch Gilbert du Motier, Marquis de Lafayette, was one of the former. Before he was two years old his father, a grenadier colonel, was killed at Minden. His mother died when he was thirteen, and when his grandfather followed her to the grave several weeks later the young man was a titled, wealthy orphan. That year he entered the royal army and at the age of sixteen married Adrienne, a daughter of the powerful Noailles family, whose brother, a viscount, came to America with Rochambeau.

In 1775 Lafayette was suddenly captivated by the idea of joining the American cause, motivated by a romantic notion of a revolution by people struggling for freedom and independence, plus a characteristically French desire for revenge against the British, and a hope for personal glory. Aware that the king would not approve his plan, he persuaded Prince de Broglie to introduce him to Johann Kalb, who obtained from Silas Deane written agreements that Lafayette and Kalb would be commissioned major generals upon arrival in America. Then, without even saying good-bye to his wife, Lafayette chartered a ship and sailed for America. (Their firstborn child died not long after his departure, and a second was born when he had been gone only a few months.) His reception by Congress was a frigid one, but when Lafayette volunteered to serve at his own expense Congress appointed him a major general without a command and sent him to Washington.

This was in 1777, at a time when the General had had a bellyful of foreigners who soon "become importunate for offices they have no right to look for," and he figured the youthful Frenchman, who had no military experience whatsoever, was another of them. Yet this one was different. For one thing, of course, he had what Washington called "illustrious and important connections" with the court of Louis XVI. Slightly built, he was anything but handsome, with a long pointed nose, narrow, egg-shaped head, and receding line of reddish hair. The American commander was impressed by his efforts to learn English (which few of the foreign officers seriously attempted) and his willingness to admit his lack of military experience, so he invited him to join his military family as an honorary aide. The two got off to a slow start, but as time passed their mutual admiration grew into a relationship that is best described as that of father and son. The childless Washington found that he loved Lafayette as he would have loved a child of his own, and soon discovered that the Frenchman possessed a talent he admired and practiced himself, which was to learn from experience. Many a professional soldier sneered at Washington because his methods were often unorthodox, not realizing that he liked to be flexible, letting the situation dictate his actions. Lafayette was not only intelligent but also a fast learner, and he soon became his mentor's most successful military pupil.

Lafayette described their relationship to his wife, Adrienne: "surrounded by flatterers or secret enemies . . . [Washington] finds in me a sincere friend, in whose bosom he may always confide his most secret thoughts, and who will always speak the truth."

★ ★ ★

FOR THE GENERAL, the matter at hand was New York, and the question of attacking the city was resolved to his keen regret when Ternay announced flatly that he would not put his ships at risk in New York's harbor, where a superior British fleet and ground troops could bottle them up and hammer them from land and sea. The alliance seemed to be going nowhere, with the lack of personal contact keeping plans in limbo. As yet, Washington had not met the French officers; Rochambeau begged him to visit them, saying, "In an hour of conversation, we shall be able to settle things far more definitely than in volumes of writing." And although the American commander felt the same way, his army was in such dire straits he simply could not take the time for a face-to-face meeting. As he put it, "my presence here is essential to keep our preparations in activity, or even going on at all."

The fact that the French troops, who had disembarked on July 11, 1780, were firmly established in Newport was a reminder of the incompetence of Admiral Arbuthnot and his stubborn unwillingness to cooperate with General Clinton. The latter's knowledge that Rochambeau's army was bound for Newport came from the American general Benedict Arnold, who had secretly been in touch with Clinton at intervals during the past year. Sir Henry, who had a large garrison in New York and wanted to occupy Newport before the French arrived, was frustrated in this by Arbuthnot, who would not believe the intelligence and wanted to wait for reinforcements that had been promised him.

Failing in his hope of reoccupying Newport, Clinton prepared to attack the French when they landed and were at their most vulnerable, but Arbuthnot, who rarely missed a chance to do nothing, advised against it and the rare opportunity vanished. Indeed, neither the British general nor the admiral knew when the French arrived; on

July 5 Arbuthnot's frigates had sighted Ternay's fleet off Virginia, but Ternay then disappeared. (Why the frigates did not follow the French is a mystery. As Clinton said to himself, the admiral had learned about the French on July 5, "why then did he lose sight of them afterwards?") Meantime, Clinton was doing his level best to ready a force of six thousand men to hit the French when they reached Newport, but for now all he could do was wait.

Admiral Thomas Graves's squadron was expected any day from England, and he showed up on July 13 with seven hundred of his seamen sick and far from ready for duty, but in theory, at least, he added to the British naval strength.

Again Clinton argued for an attack; Arbuthnot kept finding reasons for delay, finally warning that the combined American and French artillery in Newport, added to Ternay's firepower, would be too much for his ships. And by now Clinton's enthusiasm for the project was waning, as he focused more on the risks than on opportunities. When he convened a rare council of war, the members unanimously voted that the army should stand down and Sir Henry concurred. With that decision he effectively abandoned the initiative and lost what he had regarded as the greatest opportunity since the war began. Ternay, after all, was reported to have seven or eight ships of the line and was convoying some six thousand troops under Rochambeau, and what a coup it would have been to destroy or badly damage the Americans' French allies.

After Clinton made his decision a British naval officer remarked that the fleet "would never see Rhode Island because *the General hated the Admiral*." That was true enough, and from Sir Henry's standpoint quite legitimate, for Arbuthnot had from the beginning opposed Clinton's plan, ignored a suggested alternative, collected no useful intelligence, produced no plan of his own, and then criticized Clinton for his failure to act. The final straw came in August, when Arbuthnot suggested that he and Sir Henry should confer at Gardiner's Bay at the end of Long Island. Clinton made the three-day trip by carriage in insufferable heat, during which his coachman perished—probably of heat prostration—and arrived only to find that Arbuthnot had departed, leaving behind a note saying that the French fleet was reported to be putting to sea (it was not) and that he planned to intercept it. To put it mildly, Clinton was apoplectic.

For sixteen days "the old woman" Arbuthnot cruised off Newport, learning nothing about the French disposition or defenses except to say, "The enemy were not to be come at." At last he sailed to Gardiner's Bay to refit and grouse about Clinton.

The middle of September came and with it Admiral Sir George Rodney with ten sail of the line. Suddenly, the British navy held an overpowering advantage over the French, who "gave themselves up for lost on the arrival of Rodney," according to a Newport loyalist. Rodney was by far the most famous officer in the Royal Navy, an aggressive fighter and first-rate tactician, who tended to be prickly and quarrelsome. Though the opposite might have been expected, he and Clinton were friends, and since Rodney outranked Arbuthnot and was the senior officer present, Sir Henry was delighted and Arbuthnot infuriated.

Admiral Rodney's initial inclination was to launch a combined attack on Newport, which General Clinton opposed vigorously. The general could spare only three thousand soldiers, he said (not the six thousand he had mustered before), and they would be badly outnumbered by the Americans and French, who were said to have ten thousand men. Furthermore, he told Rodney, he would greatly prefer "the plan I laid before you yesterday."

This was a reference to a top-secret plan to seize West Point, the fort that was the key to the Hudson Valley and New York's Highlands—a project that had come to the general's attention through an offer purportedly from the American Benedict Arnold to betray the post he now commanded.

Why this should negate an attack on Newport is unclear, but the simplest answer is that Sir Henry now believed it impossible to dislodge the French, even with a vastly superior naval force. In any event, Rodney agreed to give him the assistance he needed for the

West Point operation, and Clinton's agent, a young officer named John André, was instructed to continue negotiations with the mysterious figure who was assumed to be Arnold. When that drama had played out, it was time for Rodney to depart from New York. He was responsible for the West Indies and sailed away in mid-October after writing a warm note to Sir Henry, concluding, "God bless you and send me from this cold country and from such men as Arbuthnot!"

At the same time Rodney wrote to the Earl of Sandwich, first lord of the Admiralty, in sharply different terms, condemning the inactivity and lassitude of the New York command, the grievous error of evacuating Newport in the first place, and the procrastination in establishing a post in the Chesapeake. Writing to Lord George Germain, secretary of state for the colonies, he carped about Clinton's "four different houses" in New York, where "without any settled plan [the general] idles his time and . . . suffers himself to be cooped up by Washington with an inferior army, without making any attempt to dislodge him." The army officers, instead of fighting, put on plays, he added scornfully. What Britain needs here is a general who "hates the Americans from principle." Rodney was not the only officer to complain, as he did to Sandwich, about the divisive squabbles at headquarters: "When commanders in chief differ," he wrote, "how much do nations suffer!" The tension around Clinton's office was palpable. As one officer wrote, "The Commanders in Chief . . . have both written home complaining of each other, and Sir George [Rodney] has taken Clinton's side and has wrote also against Arbuthnot. Commodore Drake, second in command, is hardly on speaking terms with any of the three; so you may guess how the service is carried on."

The failure of the British to attack, and possibly fatally wound, the French at Newport was calamitous in the long run. Because of the feud between General Clinton and Admiral Arbuthnot the French troops, who were, after all, some of the finest units of a veteran, first-class army, remained unharmed and within easy sailing distance of New York. Their presence in Rhode Island was a constant threat to the British, and, as George Washington discovered, even the pretense of an attack was likely to alter whatever plans Sir Henry might have made.

Nor was the French army the only beneficiary of the British headquarters infighting. Ternay's capital ships—seven of them—remained in Newport, a menace Arbuthnot had to deal with by maintaining a blockade, tying up vessels that could be more profitably employed elsewhere. And the blockade, as the French were to discover, was no guarantee that those seven ships of the line could not escape.

During that summer of 1780 Sir Henry Clinton lost the initiative and never regained it. For eight more months he and Admiral Marriot Arbuthnot would remain locked in a harness of mutual hatred that precluded any possibility of cooperation between the services they led.

★　★　★

WHILE THE BRITISH high command vacillated about attacking Newport, Washington was at his wit's end, hoping for congressional guidance on what he was supposed to do when his army and the French finally did join hands, and, on another topic, what the legislators suggested he might do now that the latest appeals to the states for troops had fallen far short of expectations.

Speaking of the French, he informed Congress of his need for "measures which have been judged essential to be adopted for cooperating with the armament expected from France." The allies had arrived, yet he had "no basis to act upon" and no instructions regarding "what we can or cannot undertake." Unless he was informed as to what support he could expect from the states, he foresaw an "awkward, embarrassing, and painful situation" and was "altogether at a loss what to do." Lest the congressmen suppose that his need was for troops only, he told them of the army's humiliating condition: "We have no shirts . . . to distribute to the troops," who are "absolutely destitute." The same was true of overalls—a situation that was bad enough at any time, but "peculiarly mortifying" for men and officers when they were about to act with their new allies.

As for the militia, their numbers "will fall as far short of the demand as the Continental troops." Provisions had not been received in anything like adequate amounts; forage and transportation were still worse—resulting in a practice he abhorred, of impressing horses and wagons, which was "violent . . . oppressive and . . . odious to the people."

The atmosphere at Washington's headquarters brightened when news from Rochambeau reached the General on August 25, saying he had received a dispatch reporting the arrival of the French frigate *Alliance*, bearing much-needed arms and powder. But as usual, bad news accompanied the good: the long-awaited "second division" of fleet and soldiers was blockaded in the harbor at Brest. At best, the ships might break out in time to arrive in America in October, but to Washington that meant no campaigning until the following year and a lot of mouths to feed if his army was to survive. To his brother Samuel he wrote that no one could possibly imagine "how an Army can be kept together under any circumstances as ours is in." Determined as ever, though, he sent the militia home, ordered the Continentals to the vicinity of Hackensack, and told Benedict Arnold to collect his scattered troops and concentrate them so as to resist a likely attack in the Hudson Highlands.

Then came news of yet another calamity. Horatio Gates, popularly (though incorrectly) known as the hero of Saratoga, had been defeated and his entire army destroyed at Camden, South Carolina, by Lord Cornwallis's troops, exposing North Carolina and Virginia to invasion from the south. The rout was so complete that no one knew how many Americans were lost. Gates believed he had seven thousand men before the battle—a highly exaggerated figure, but whatever the number, most of them were killed, captured, or missing. Gates, whom Congress had appointed to command in South Carolina,* was said to have fled from the battlefield ahead of his routed militiamen, leaving the outnumbered Continentals to fight Cornwallis's entire force. As Washington's aide Alexander Hamilton described Gates's escape in a scathing letter to his friend James Duane, "was there ever an instance of a General running away from his whole army and was there ever so precipitous a flight? One hundred and eighty miles in three days and a half. It does admirable credit to the activity of a man at his time of life. But it disgraces the General and the soldier." And to his fiancée, Elizabeth Schuyler, Hamilton said that Gates seemed "to know very little what has become of his army. . . . He has confirmed in this instance the opinion I always had of him." In the wake of Camden, Congress removed Gates from command and ordered an inquiry into his conduct at the battle.

General Washington and the French leaders were determined to meet and shape their plans for future operations and finally fixed on the date of September 20 for a meeting in Hartford, Connecticut. In preparation for this crucial encounter, Washington and Alexander Hamilton composed a working paper consisting of three proposals. Since everything depended on the relative strength of the British and French fleets, and no one could say when the ships blockaded in Brest might arrive on this side of the Atlantic, the General hoped for assistance from another quarter—Comte de Guichen, the French admiral in the West Indies. Guichen had been alerted by Ternay that the fate of America would depend on French naval superiority: the efforts of France, he had written, "will turn the scale." If Guichen were to arrive by early October with enough strength to seize New York harbor, Washington reasoned, then the allied land forces should move on that city, and his paper included an elaborate description of how this operation would be conducted. But if no fleet under Guichen

---

*In selecting Gates, Congress had bypassed Washington, isolating him from the southern theater of action. Gates was frequently insubordinate and had done his level best to replace the commander in chief as part of the so-called Conway Cabal, so Washington was no admirer of his. At the time Gates was appointed, Washington made no comment to Congress, "lest my sentiments, being known, should have an unfavorable interpretation. . . ."

materialized, the allies would send a combined force of about twelve thousand troops south to take Charleston and Savannah.

That was the initial proposal. The second was evidently suggested by Nathanael Greene, whose idea it was for the French fleet to sail to Boston, where it would be safe without the protection of land troops (a move approved by Ternay, who regarded the harbor at Newport as a suicidal choice of anchorage for a fleet outnumbered by the enemy). That done, Rochambeau's troops would march to the Hudson, link up with the Continental Army, and carry on enough activity in that area to prevent Clinton from releasing any troops to join Cornwallis in the South.

The third scheme called for a winter campaign against the British in Canada. This had been petitioned by some inhabitants of the New Hampshire Grants (in what would become Vermont), who offered men and supplies, and the General proposed sending a force of five thousand men—half of them Americans, half French, with Rochambeau to be in overall command and Greene leading the American troops. Washington himself would not accompany the task force since "the general situation of the Country . . . requires his presence and influence within the states; for in the present crisis there is no saying what may happen and Congress [may] stand in need of support."

★   ★   ★

LEAVING GREENE IN charge of the army while he rode east to meet the French in Hartford, Washington and his staff officers on September 17 crossed the Hudson River at King's Ferry, where he spent the night at the home of Joshua Hett Smith, about two and a half miles from the ferry, near Haverstraw. Smith was the youngest of fifteen children, of whom the eldest was his brother William, a prominent lawyer and historian who had advised many a governor of the colony of New York and became chief justice of the province in 1780 after refusing to take the oath of allegiance to the revolutionary state. Joshua was also a lawyer, and although his father and oldest brother were known to have loyalist sympathies, he was a member of the New York Provincial Congress, was active in the patriot militia, and had directed the secret service of Benedict Arnold, among other general officers.

By chance, Arnold was at Smith's dinner table when Washington and his party arrived, and brought the commander in chief up to date on his efforts to safeguard the area from British attack. Then he asked Washington for an opinion: should he consent to see the writer of a letter, one Beverley Robinson, in whose house Arnold had his head-quarters? Robinson, who had married the wealthy Susanna Philipse and was one of New York's richest landowners, was a former friend of Washington with strong loyalist views and had written Arnold from the British sloop of war *Vulture*, riding at anchor in the Hudson, enclosing a letter to General Israel Putnam, which he hoped Arnold would deliver. Robinson wanted to meet Putnam under a flag of truce on a matter that must be kept secret, and hoped Arnold would grant his request.

Should he do so? asked Arnold, to which the General's response was an immediate and emphatic no. If Robinson had any private business to transact, Washington advised, he should obtain permission to do so from the civil authorities in New York. Surely Arnold could understand that a meeting between him and Robinson would be viewed with suspicion. This whole business of flags of truce was proving a nuisance, in fact, and revealed how easy it was for unauthorized persons to slip through the lines. Recently, Colonel Elisha Sheldon had reported to Washington that one John Anderson of New York had attempted to enter the lines on a matter "of so private a nature that the public on neither side can be injured by it," and when Washington asked Sheldon how he came by the letter from Anderson, the colonel replied that it came under a flag of truce. Arnold, it seemed, had recently opened a new avenue of communication to New York, and Anderson was a secret agent he employed.

Washington and his retinue, with the guards who accompanied them, clattered off on forty horses early the following morning, were ferried across the Hudson, and then angled off north by east. Over the wooded hills separating New York from Connecticut they rode, crossed the Housatonic and Naugatuck rivers, trotting through one little community after another—not much more than clearings in the dense forest (including one called Washington, after their leader). Finally, after two days' hard riding, they reached Hartford on the broad Connecticut River, bounded by rich bottomland between low hills, where they passed an uninterrupted collection of farmhouses and barns set amid trees and meadows.

★ ★ ★

IT IS DOUBTFUL if any of the conferees were aware of—or, if they were, gave much thought to—a profound change that had altered the dynamics of warfare at this stage of the eighteenth century. It began with the premise that Britain could no longer assume that it had command of the seas. Beginning in the 1770s, France had been investing heavily in its own navy. An annual naval budget that was around 30 million livres* during the Seven Years' War was consistently being increased until it would reach the staggering total of 200 million livres a year by 1782. By 1780, France had sixty-six ships of the line,[†] and those numbers were supplemented by its allies Spain with fifty-eight and Holland with twenty. So although the Royal Navy had more warships than any single rival, its enemies, collectively, outnumbered them. What's more, the British fleet had to be broken up into a number of squadrons in order to guard the homeland, watch over Gibraltar, patrol the Baltic Sea, the Caribbean, and the Indian Ocean, plus escort convoys in the Atlantic.

Furthermore, even if it still had maritime supremacy, Great Britain would be obliged to cope with the realities of geography and distance if it was to suppress the rebellion of its former colonies. The

---

*A livre was originally worth a pound of silver.
†A ship of the line was a warship with sixty or more guns.

land war with the Americans had to be supplied and fought three thousand miles from home, demanding that every musket ball, every shoe or shirt or cap required by a British soldier, every one of the hundreds of items needed by an army must be transported across the vastness of the Atlantic Ocean. Another critical—and all but unsolvable—problem confronting the British was communications. Instructions from Whitehall to General Clinton's headquarters in Manhattan might take two or three months to arrive, and the reply— even if Clinton responded at once, which was unlikely—could require another month or six weeks. So there was almost no way officials in London could effectively direct the war, much as the king and his ministers might wish to do so.

Finally, to conquer the Americans, the British had to hold on to the territory they had won, but with a limited number of troops they couldn't possibly turn them into occupation forces and conduct a war at the same time. Yet the moment they withdrew, the rebels moved back in—a pattern that was prevalent in the South, where guerrillas seemed to move about at will.

★   ★   ★

AT LAST THE General and his aides greeted the allies from France they had been longing to see. The feeling was mutual, for these French officers were intensely curious to meet the famous leader of the Revolution. They found him to be a man they admired immediately. "Enchanted," Claude Blanchard summarized their reactions, noting his "easy and noble bearing, extensive and correct views and the art of making himself beloved. . . ." Comte Mathieu Dumas was impressed by the way "His dignified address, his simplicity of manners, and mild gravity surpassed our expectation and won every heart." Baron Ludwig von Closen said, "I could not find strong enough words to describe" Washington's remarks to the group. Another count, the Swede Axel Fersen, who was rumored by gossips at the French court to be a favorite of the queen and who had sailed to

America in March as an aide to Rochambeau, saw Washington in a slightly different light: "His face is handsome and majestic but at the same time kind and gentle, corresponding completely with his moral qualities. He looks like a hero; he is very cold and says little but he is frank and polite. There is a sadness in his countenance, which does not misbecome him and indeed renders his face more interesting." Louis-Alexandre Berthier, already marked by his superiors as a young man with a promising military future, said of the General, "The nobility of his bearing and his countenance, which bore the stamp of all his virtues, inspired everyone with the devotion and respect due his character, increasing, if possible, the high opinion we already held of his exceptional merit."

As for Rochambeau, he had no illusions about the American commander in chief. His orders specified that he was "in all cases to be under the orders of General Washington," but a secret instruction added that he was to keep the French troops together, serving under their own officers, and not disperse them. He would do his utmost to remain on good terms with the American leader and to regard him as his superior, and he would obey orders scrupulously and serve as a cooperative subordinate, but he had doubts about the General's judgment and very real concerns about the quality and quantity of Washington's army.

The man Washington met—Jean-Baptiste-Donatien de Vimeur, Comte de Rochambeau—was fifty-five years old and, after training initially for the church, had embarked on a military career when his older brothers died, leaving him the only son. By now he had spent thirty-seven years in the army, principally in central Europe, where he had served as inspector of cavalry and maréchal de camp. He was stocky, considerably shorter than Washington (who was between six feet and six feet three inches), and had a battle scar over the left temple of his ruddy face and a bad limp from another serious wound. As Washington was to discover, this was a no-nonsense, matter-of-fact soldier whose concerns and conversation dealt almost exclusively with military matters—troop movements and battle plans. Rochambeau's assignment in America was completely unexpected. Suffering from inflammatory rheumatism, he had made plans to retire and in fact the horses and carriage were at his house in Paris ready to carry the family to his château in Vendôme when a messenger from the king showed up unexpectedly, ordering him to Versailles. There he learned that he was to lead an expeditionary force to America.

Of Washington's three proposals for combined operations, Rochambeau favored only the first—the capture of New York—but made it clear ever so tactfully that his orders required him to keep the king's fleet and troops together. The Frenchman clearly considered campaigning at an end for the year and had already turned his attention to 1781. As for the American, he had approached this meeting with one all-important consideration in mind. In the words of a position paper drawn up strictly for his aides, ". . . it should appear that we are ready and in condition to act. . . . It will therefore be good policy to keep out of sight the disappointments we met with in the number of men &c. and to hold up the idea that we should have been prepared to cooperate. . . . It will be necessary however that we should profess our wants and weaknesses very fully. . . ."

Hewing to this line, Washington mentioned that he hoped to have fifteen thousand troops by the spring of 1781 and—since Rochambeau told him that Louis XVI had promised to send a "second division"—urged the French to "complete" their army to that number. At the end of the conference Rochambeau said he would send his son to Versailles, slipping him through the naval blockade so that he could request reinforcements and hard money, to stimulate the American economy.

As the meeting broke up, Washington was disappointed with the lack of concrete achievement. Socially it had been a success; strategically, no. Writing to James Duane in Congress, he characterized the conference aptly: "We could only combine possible plans on the supposition of possible events and engage mutually to do everything in our powers against the next campaign."

Riding back to the Hudson and his camp, he must have wondered whether that next campaign would bring new hope and purpose to the army. Surely his men—and the country—had endured all the misery and disappointment they could absorb. He was certain that more hunger and deprivation lay ahead, but if no major disaster came their way, the army might somehow hold together and survive.

3

SO HELLISH A PLOT

A story made the rounds about Washington and Brigadier General "Mad Anthony" Wayne. It seems the two were discussing how some of the British-held positions on the Hudson River might be taken, and Washington asked Wayne if he thought he could storm Stony Point, a precipitous, rocky bluff that juts into the Hudson. The reply came at once: "I'll storm hell, sir, if you'll make the plans!" Washington looked at him silently for a moment or two and then, with a little smile, said, "Better try Stony Point first, General."

In September of 1777, at Paoli, Pennsylvania, Wayne's division had been surprised in a skillful night attack by the British and suffered 150 casualties. The redcoats, led by Major General Charles Grey, were ordered not to load their weapons since gunfire would reveal their position, but to rely on the bayonet, with the result that their commander was known thereafter as "No-Flint" Grey. A court-martial acquitted Wayne of charges that he had failed to heed "timely notice" of the attack, and his opportunity for revenge came three years later at Stony Point, when he did indeed storm that position. On July 15 his light infantry brigade landed under cover of darkness and with fixed bayonets, but with no ammunition in their muskets, assaulted the position, and took over when the defenders threw down their arms and cried quarter. As a British officer wrote, "The rebels had made the attack with a bravery they never before exhibited. . . ." What he had seen was the fruit of lessons taught the Americans by the disciplinarian Baron Steuben, formerly of Frederick the Great's Prussian army—the proper use of the bayonet.

Several weeks after Wayne's victory, Washington was standing on a height overlooking Stony Point, watching the last detachment of his troops cross the Hudson at King's Ferry, when Benedict Arnold rode up and asked the General if he had "thought of anything for him." It was a propitious moment for the commander in chief, who had admired Arnold's courage and bold leadership for years and rather regretted having had to reprimand him in general orders. Washington badly needed officers like Arnold, who was probably his best fighting general, and he was pleased to tell him now that he was to have a "post of honor" with the main army.

Arnold's reaction astonished the General. "His countenance changed and he appeared to be quite fallen," Washington recalled, "and, instead of thanking me or expressing any pleasure at the appointment, never opened his mouth." A long, uncomfortable silence followed; then, according to the General, "[I told] him to go to my quarters and get something to refresh himself, and I would meet him there soon." It was a while before Washington returned, and when he arrived one of his aides, Tench Tilghman, took him aside and said that Arnold was walking with a pronounced limp, complaining that his leg, badly wounded at Saratoga, would not allow him to play an active part in a campaign. He said he even had trouble riding a horse.

When the commander in chief spoke with him later, "His behavior struck me as strange and unaccountable," almost as if the man had lost his nerve and was fearful of going into action. It was a curious business, since Arnold was the captor, with Ethan Allen, of Fort Ticonderoga in the earliest days of the war, leader of the heroic winter expedition against Quebec, commander of a fleet of makeshift vessels that had prevented the British from taking Fort Ticonderoga in 1776, and the officer many army men credited with the great victory at Saratoga. For this soldier, who was known for his naked ambition and courage and daring in battle, to admit that he couldn't handle an important command was impossible to understand. Yet what he wanted, Arnold told Tilghman, was the post at West Point. Evidently, Washington believed he would change his mind, for when he announced the order of battle on August 1, Major General Benedict Arnold was to command the left wing. (When the news reached Arnold's wife, Peggy, at a dinner party in Philadelphia she went into hysterics, which was put down to fear that her husband might be killed or wounded on active duty.) The matter had been resolved almost immediately, when Washington's spies informed him that General Clinton had no intention of waging an active campaign outside New York, after which the commander in chief gave Arnold command of the garrison at West Point.

More than a month later Washington sent a note to Arnold, informing him that he would be passing through Peekskill on Sunday evening, September 17, on his way to Hartford to meet the French, and wanted a guard of a captain and fifty men, plus forage for about forty horses. In closing, he said, "You will keep this to yourself, as I want to make my journey a secret."

The day that message was in his hands, Arnold encoded the secret information for the British, alerting them that the American commander in chief would cross the Hudson on a specific day and at a particular place, the idea being that armed vessels might capture him in midstream. At the same time he alerted the British, Arnold responded to the General, informing him that the guard and the forage would be supplied.

When Washington returned from the conference, he was accompanied by Lafayette, his chief of artillery, Henry Knox, and members of his staff. They rode through Fishkill and were heading toward West Point and a planned meeting with Arnold when they unexpectedly met the French minister to the United States, the Chevalier de

La Luzerne, who was en route to visit Rochambeau. The minister was so eager to talk that Washington went back with him to Fishkill, where they spent the evening.

Next morning, September 25, the General headed off at daybreak—a ritual intensely unpopular with his staff, since it consisted of riding ten or fifteen miles before breakfast. He was eager to push on to Arnold's headquarters and teased his retinue by saying they could look forward to a good meal and the opportunity of admiring Arnold's lovely young wife, the former Margaret "Peggy" Shippen of Philadelphia (who happened to be first cousin to Tench Tilghman). Then he dispatched Lafayette's aide, Major James McHenry, and Captain Samuel Shaw of Knox's staff to ride on ahead and tell Arnold they were coming and to prepare for a number of hungry guests. Along the way to West Point, Washington made a careful inspection of several defensive positions on the east bank of the Hudson and shortly after ten o'clock came in sight of Beverley Robinson's house, which Arnold had taken over as his headquarters. The rambling, two-story mansion was about two miles below West Point, and the General anticipated a warm welcome from Arnold and his beautiful Peggy.

About ten-thirty the group reined up before the house and saw, instead of Arnold and his wife, a single figure, Major David Franks, Arnold's aide, who greeted them nervously and said that the major general had received a message at the breakfast table that required him to go immediately to West Point. When Franks asked if they had eaten, Washington said no, they would appreciate having some breakfast. Franks added that Mrs. Arnold was indisposed and in her bedroom, and that Lieutenant Colonel Richard Varick, the major general's chief aide, was laid up with a severe stomach disorder. Adding to Varick's discomfort was that nothing had come of his efforts to obtain a transfer from Arnold's staff. Franks was equally unhappy in his current job: he had suffered such "repeated insults and ill treatment from Arnold" that he was determined "not to remain with him on any terms whatever." What's more, when Varick appeared, he and Franks observed that Mrs. Arnold had episodes of nervous tension "during which she would give utterance to anything and everything on her mind . . . so much so as to cause us to be scrupulous of what we told her or said within her hearing." Service on the staff of Benedict Arnold was not an enviable assignment. Washington told Varick to go back to bed and not to worry, and after he and his officers enjoyed a leisurely breakfast they left Alexander Hamilton behind to receive any messages and rode to the dock, where Arnold's barge—an elegant vessel with seats and awnings—and a crew of eight oarsmen waited to take them upriver to the fort.

What greeted them at West Point was quite a sight—one the Chevalier Chastellux was to call "the most magnificent picture" he had ever beheld. Around the fort itself, which clung to the rocks at river's edge, the mountain summits bristled with redoubts and batteries—a complex that was an engineering triumph, designed by such skilled foreign engineers as Thaddeus Kosciuszko and Louis Duportail, and built with several years of hard labor by Continental soldiers. Above the fort were six additional works in the form of an amphitheater, positioned so as to protect each other. The highest and most formidable was known as Fort Putnam, named for General Israel Putnam, who had the lion's share of its planning and construction, atop a precipitous plateau of rock that made it virtually inaccessible. Once here, one had a spectacular view of thirty miles in every direction. To the north of West Point, angling into the middle of the river, was Constitution Island, which seemed to be secured to the west bank by an enormous iron chain, made of iron bars two inches square, with links twelve inches wide and eighteen inches long, floating on sixteen-foot logs, to prevent vessels from sailing upstream. The main guns of the fort were trained on this barrier, which was located at the point where the river made a ninety-degree turn to the east, creating a kind of embrasure formed over the eons through the sheer rocks of immense mountains. Below it the Hudson widened and plunged southward again.

As the barge neared the dock, where Washington expected to find a welcoming party, no sign of activity was evident other than a few sentries making their appointed rounds. Most unusual—no Arnold, nor had anyone seen him that morning. Probably, the General thought, he was at one of the outlying works and would undoubtedly be found during their inspection tour of the defenses. Of all the posts in the United States, Washington considered West Point the most important. Three years earlier the Burgoyne expedition's goal was to seize control of the Hudson and cut off communications between the northeastern and southern states, but fortunately that army of British, Germans, and Indians had been stopped at Saratoga in the victory that convinced the French to join in the war on the side of the Americans. West Point, which commanded the Hudson, had been called the Gibraltar of America, but when the General saw the condition of the place he was appalled.

The east wall and other portions of Fort Putnam had collapsed; Fort Arnold, constructed entirely of wood, was a tinderbox, certain to be set afire by a shell; and all the other defenses were in a state of advanced decay. Yet instead of crews at work on all these posts, Washington saw almost no one, and those he did see could tell him nothing of their commander's whereabouts. The artillery colonel, John Lamb, who had fought at Arnold's side at Quebec, where he lost an eye and part of his face, was in charge here and said he had not seen the major general all morning.

Thoroughly irritated now by Arnold's unexplained absence, Washington nevertheless completed his inspection in about two hours (reporting later that he had found the post in "the most critical condition") and with vague feelings of uneasiness left West Point after three in the afternoon and was rowed across the river to Robinson's house, where his boat tied up at the landing about four. Mrs. Arnold was still in her room, Varick was in his, and Alexander Hamilton reported that he had heard nothing from the missing commander of the post. Completely mystified by then, the General went to the room designated for him, and as he waited to be called for dinner, Hamilton entered with a packet of papers sent to the commander in chief by Lieutenant Colonel John Jameson, commander of the cavalry outpost at North Castle, present-day Mount Kisco. Jameson's covering note read:

Sir

Inclosed you'll receive a parcel of Papers taken from a certain
John Anderson who has a pass signed by General Arnold as may
be seen The Papers were found under the feet of his Stockings
he offered the Men that took him one hundred Guineas and as
many goods as they wou'd Please to ask I have sent the Prisoner
to General Arnold he is very desirous of the Papers and every
thing being sent with him But as I think they are of a very
dangerous tendency [letter torn] . . . ght it more proper your
Excellency should see them. . . . From every account That I can
hear they mean an Attack on the Troops at this place. . . .

The name John Anderson was vaguely familiar: wasn't that the
man Arnold had indicated was a secret agent for him in New York
City? When Washington perused the papers found inside Anderson's
stockings, he was horrified. A pass for Anderson, dated September 22,
was signed by Arnold. Other documents included a detailed summary
of troop strength at West Point, an ordnance return, the placement of
artillery in case of attack, a paper with the notation "Remarks on
Works at Wt. Point, a copy to be transmitted to his Excell'y General
Washington," with detailed descriptions: "Redoubt No. 3, a slight
Wood Work 3 Feet thick, very Dry, no Bomb Proofs . . . easily set on
fire—no cannon," and so on. Finally—most curious—a copy of minutes of the council of war on September 6, which Washington had
sent to Arnold.

What was the meaning of this? How did this man Anderson come to
have these secret documents, several of them in Arnold's handwriting?

Hamilton had also received another letter for the General, brought
by express rider from Jameson. Washington had been stunned by the
other package he had received, but this one was even more remarkable. Written in elegant script, the letter was addressed to him and
came from the prisoner Jameson had taken. The language of this
extraordinary document, written the previous day (September 24), was
as full of flourishes as the handwriting but, simply put, it was from
Major John André, the British army's adjutant general, to General

George Washington. André wrote, he said, not out of fear for his safety but to explain why and how he had been apprehended. He had been "conducted" inside the American lines to meet a person who was to give him certain intelligence, but in a manner that was "Against my stipulation, my intention, and without my knowledge before hand."

He came up the Hudson in the *Vulture* sloop of war, he wrote, dressed in his regimentals, but instead of being returned to the vessel had been obliged to remove his uniform and was "betrayed . . . into the vile condition of an enemy in disguise within your posts." He had been "in the service" of his king and was "involuntarily an imposter." His request was for "decency of conduct" toward him and the privilege of sending an open letter to General Sir Henry Clinton, and another to a friend requesting some clothing.

It was now clear to Washington that this British officer, André, had met with Benedict Arnold, who had given him the highly confidential information in the packet of papers, after which Arnold had fled—God only knew where. While he was digesting this bombshell in the presence of Hamilton and Colonel Robert Harrison, one of them reported what they had heard from James McHenry and Samuel Shaw, who had been sent ahead of Washington's party and had eaten breakfast with Arnold this morning. During that meal a courier had handed Arnold a letter from Jameson, which was evidently the same one that had been turned over to Washington just now. Without revealing anything about its contents to his guests, Arnold excused himself, saying he had to cross the river to West Point at once, and McHenry and Shaw could see from the expression on his face that he was deeply disturbed by what he had read. The message, McHenry said, had thrown him "into some degree of agitation."

Arnold immediately ran upstairs to inform Peggy about what had happened, told her he must leave at once in order to save his life, and on his way out of the house directed an aide to say he would return from West Point in an hour. Running from the house, he leaped on a horse and as he was rounding the stable saw several of Washington's party, who told him the commander in chief was coming up the road.

Arnold put spurs to his horse, galloped down a steep hill to the dock, where his barge awaited, and, after throwing his saddle and pistols into the boat, ordered the boatmen to row as fast as possible to Stony Point. He was anxious to get there in a hurry, he told them, so as to get back in time for a visit with the General.

When the barge was off Stony Point, Arnold told the boatmen his business required him to go aboard the *Vulture* and promised them two gallons of rum for rowing on as fast as possible. In a final contemptuous act, when they reached the sloop and went aboard, Benedict Arnold turned his crew over to the British as prisoners. These men, whom Washington described later as "very clever fellows and some of the better sort of soldiery," were dumbfounded to be declared prisoners, since they assumed they were under the protection of a flag of truce. Fortunately, Washington added, when they reached New York "General Clinton, ashamed of so low and mean an action, set them all at liberty."

★   ★   ★

GRADUALLY, AT THE Robinson house, the story of what had occurred began to emerge. Washington's note to Arnold, informing him he would be passing through Peekskill on the evening of September 17, en route to Hartford, had set in motion an elaborate plan on the part of Arnold to capture the American commander in chief and seize the post at West Point. Arnold immediately wrote to the British, stating that Washington would be at King's Ferry the following Sunday and planned to lodge at Peekskill that night. Providentially for the Americans, Arnold's letter was delayed and did not reach the enemy in time for them to catch Washington, but the plan to take West Point was still in effect. All that remained was for Arnold and Major André to work out the details, and to that end Arnold arranged for Joshua Hett Smith—brother of William Smith, royal chief justice of New York—to go on board the *Vulture* on September 22 and bring ashore André (or John Anderson, which was the name by which Smith knew him). Smith lived nearby, in a country home owned by his brother. He was known to be an active Whig and had hospitably offered to put up Arnold's wife if she should visit her husband.

The two plotters, Arnold and André, talked at Smith's house all through that night and were still conversing at dawn when American cannon opened fire on the sloop, inflicting some damage and forcing her to drop downstream, out of range. Smith's boatmen, who had rowed André to the meeting, realized the risks involved in taking him back to the *Vulture* and refused to do so. Arnold, disconcerted by this turn of events, told André he must change his uniform for a disguise, return to New York by a different route, and deliver the papers to Clinton. The Briton protested heatedly, but he was finally persuaded to put on some of Joshua Smith's clothes and let Smith escort him to the British lines. At nightfall André and his companion were warned by American militiamen that travel after dark below the Croton River was extremely hazardous, so they put up for the night at a farmer's residence.

Next morning the two set out together on the east side of the river, heading for White Plains, but Smith left André when they reached a place called Pine's Bridge, telling him he would have an easy time reaching the British lines from there, and the major went off alone, carrying a pass in his pocket from Arnold that would supposedly get him past any rebel patrols.

André was riding through what was purportedly neutral ground, which was in fact a no-man's-land—a savagely contested area where no one was safe, where loyalist partisans who called themselves "Cowboys" were on one side, fighting the "Skinners," who supposedly supported the rebels, with both gangs preying on hapless travelers of all persuasions for whatever they could steal from them. Between nine and ten André was suddenly stopped by three American militiamen, who rushed out of the woods where they had been playing cards and grabbed his horse. Confused and alarmed, the British officer did not produce his pass from Arnold, which might have saved him, but instead told the men he hoped they belonged to "the lower party" (the popular term for the king's supporters, who held territory at the lower end of the river).

"We do," said one of them.

"So do I," replied André, adding that he was a British officer on urgent business and must not be detained. Then he showed them Arnold's pass, adding, "I am in his service."

"Damn Arnold's pass!" one of the men said. "You said you was a British officer. Where is your money?"

André said he had none with him, at which they ordered him to dismount and strip. Finding no money in his clothing, they had him remove his boots and finally his stockings, and there they discovered the papers given him by Arnold—revealing the troop strength and defenses of West Point. André, realizing that they wanted money more than anything, offered them a substantial sum, but since he had none with him, they decided they were asking for trouble by keeping him and took him to the nearest outpost, which was at North Castle.

There, the temporary commander, Lieutenant Colonel John Jameson of the Second Continental Dragoons, looked at the papers and tried to decide what to do. He and other officers at advanced posts had been ordered by Arnold to keep an eye out for a John Anderson and if they encountered him to send him at once to head-quarters at West Point. Jameson had Anderson, all right, but those papers were something altogether different. They appeared to be "of a very dangerous tendency," and he decided to send them to General Washington, who was known to be returning from Hart-ford, at the same time he dispatched the prisoner to Arnold at West Point.

Shortly after André departed under guard, Major Benjamin Tall-madge, who was in Washington's secret service, returned from a scouting mission, heard about John Anderson, and suspected that there was a lot more to this than met the eye. He spoke with Jameson,* persuaded him to recall the prisoner, and John Anderson and his guards came back to Lower Salem on Sunday morning, September 24, to be held pending instructions from Washington. Here he was put in the care of Lieutenant Joshua King, who was to deliver him to Washington, and the lieutenant was not overly impressed by what he saw. "He looked somewhat like a reduced gentleman," said King. Over his undress military clothes, he wore a "coat, purple, with gold lace, worn, somewhat threadbare, with a small-brimmed, tarnished beaver on his head." A barber came in to fix King's hair, and when the lieutenant had him do the same for the prisoner, the ribbon André was wearing fell from his head. "I observed it full of powder," said King, knowing that powdered hair indicated a man of some elegance. "This circumstance, with others that occurred, induced me to believe I had no ordinary person in charge." Walking outside with the lieutenant, the prisoner confessed he needed someone to talk to, told King who he was, and requested pen and ink so he could write directly to the American commander in chief in an effort to convince him he was not a spy.

★   ★   ★

JOHN ANDRÉ WAS young—just twenty-nine years old—charming, handsome, with long black hair that hung down his back, tied fashionably with a black ribbon. Born in London, he was the son of a Swiss merchant who moved to England, and he had spent some of his early years in a London countinghouse, not regarded as suitable preparation for a military career. He was ambitious and industrious, and after being commissioned in the army and sent to America, he needed a patron in order to rise through the ranks. He found one in a protégé and kinsman of the powerful Duke of Newcastle—General

---

*Jameson was in command that day because his superior, Colonel Elisha Sheldon, had been arrested on unjust accusations against him made by a surgeon. Had Sheldon, an able intelligence officer, been in charge, the whole matter might have been handled a lot more aggressively than it was under Jameson's somewhat muddled direction.

Sir Henry Clinton—who eventually made him an aide-de-camp and adjutant general in America. André was something of a poet, had a talent for sketching, and participated enthusiastically in the amateur theatricals British officers engaged in to while away the long winters in New York and Philadelphia. In the latter city he was the guiding spirit behind an extravaganza called "Mischianza," staged in 1778 to honor the departure of General Sir William Howe from America.

Clinton had great confidence in André and was extremely fond of him, as were his fellow officers. In fact, Clinton had turned over one of the country estates he had confiscated to the young officer while the latter was recuperating from an illness. This was Mount Pleasant, James Beekman's estate,* where André spent his last night on York Island, as Manhattan above the New York City limits was known. By some extraordinary irony, this was also the house that had served as a headquarters for General Sir William Howe, and where a twenty-one-year-old former schoolteacher named Nathan Hale—a captain in Knowlton's Rangers—was brought after being captured on September 21, 1776, on suspicion of spying against the British. Since incriminating documents were found on his person and he was not in uniform, Howe ordered Hale hanged. He was executed the next day, after making a statement that closed with the words, "I only regret that I have but one life to lose for my country."

★   ★   ★

ON THE AFTERNOON of September 25, when Washington went to his room to clean up before dinner, Lieutenant Colonel Richard Varick appeared at the door, flushed with fever and unsteady on his feet. Varick reported that Mrs. Arnold had screamed at him from her room that morning, and when he ran to see what the trouble was, he found her running through the hall, almost naked; after he persuaded her to go back to bed, she asked if General Washington would come to see

---

*At the corner of what was to become First Avenue and 51st Street.

her. She said there was a hot iron on her head and that only the General could take it off. Would His Excellency go to the distraught lady? Varick asked.

The General climbed the stairs and found her room in a state of chaos and the lady herself in total disarray, her nightclothes half off, but exhibiting, as Alexander Hamilton wrote his fiancée, Elizabeth Schuyler, "All the sweetness of beauty, all the loveliness of innocence, all the tenderness of a wife and all the fondness of a mother. . . ." What Betsy Schuyler was to make of this is not known, but Hamilton's description may have caused her to wonder what was going on in the highest echelons of the army. "She received us in bed," he went on, "with every circumstance that could interest our sympathy. Her sufferings were so eloquent that I wished myself her brother, to have a right to become her defender." Poor Washington. He could face an enemy in battle without flinching, but this was something else. ". . . one moment she raved, another she melted into tears. Sometimes she pressed her infant to her bosom." When Varick said that her visitor was General Washington, she cried, "No! That is the man who was agoing to assist Colonel Varick in killing my child." The General did his best to disabuse her of this notion, but she persisted, saying, "General Arnold will never return. He is gone. He is gone forever . . . the spirits have carried him up there," she said, pointing at the ceiling.

Finally realizing he could do nothing to calm her, Washington went away, filled with pity for the unfortunate, half-crazed young woman. The predicament of the consummate Virginia gentleman, reserved, undemonstrative, always in charge of the situation, was excruciating, but it might have been entirely different had he and his associates known that the performance by the beauteous maiden in distress was a very clever act, from her feigned madness to her professions of innocence, her insistence that she had known nothing of her husband's plans.

Downstairs in the Robinson house at the dinner table that evening, Washington was as usual completely composed, but an uncomfortable meal it must have been, with neither the General nor anyone else mentioning Arnold's baffling disappearance. "Dull appetites surrounded a plentiful table," Varick wrote. When they finished eating, Washington asked Varick to join him for a walk and as they strolled around the grounds told the colonel that neither he nor Major Franks was under suspicion, but that they should regard themselves as being under temporary arrest. Varick understood, and told the General all he knew about Arnold's recent activities, citing in particular his own and Major Franks's suspicions of Joshua Hett Smith and how he might fit into the puzzle.

The next morning Washington sent Peggy Arnold home to Philadelphia with an admiring Major Franks as her escort. The commander had more important matters on his mind than Mrs. Arnold just then—above all, the security of West Point. Benedict Arnold had systematically weakened the post's defenses by refusing to invest time or money on maintenance or improvements, by neglecting the deficiency in munitions, and by sending large work parties—several hundred men at a time—out beyond the defensive works to cut firewood. The vigilant Colonel Lamb, horrified by what was happening, had written to a fellow officer: "What will become of this garrison? Exclusive of the guards, we have between four and five hundred men, daily on fatigue. This is murder to a garrison whose troops ought to have some little discipline." Sick at heart, he never suspected that the commandant was determined that when the time came for the British to attack West Point, the fort would be captured quickly and effectively.

★　★　★

THE ORIGINS OF the plot went back several years—to 1778, in fact, when Benedict Arnold, who had finally been promoted to major general after suffering the agony of a leg shattered leading the charge against an enemy redoubt at Saratoga, and surviving a long hospitalization, received some of the recognition he craved and was appointed commandant in Philadelphia, after the British pulled out. The son of an alcoholic father and a pious, domineering mother, Arnold and his sister, Hannah, were the only ones of seven siblings to survive childhood. He became an apothecary's apprentice, bookseller, successful merchant, horse trader, smuggler, married man, and father of three sons before turning out for the Lexington alarm and then talking the authorities into allowing him to try the daring, seemingly foolhardy plan to capture Fort Ticonderoga.

By the time he reached Philadelphia, his active military career appeared to be at an end and his black hair was beginning to gray. Yet anyone seeing him for the first time couldn't help being impressed by a man five feet nine inches tall who looked to be enormously energetic, restless, and strong, with penetrating, ice-gray eyes above a beak of a nose and heavy, jutting jaw. He had not been in Pennsylvania long before he began concocting schemes to garner quick illicit commercial profits by questionable trading (abetted by his aide-de-camp, David Franks). He moved into the elegant Penn mansion, entered into the high life of a city that probably had more loyalists than any other, and reveled in what he saw as a prominent role in high society. Soon he met and fell in love with eighteen-year-old Peggy Shippen. As a sample of Arnold's sense of honor, in September of 1777, when he was wooing her, he sent Peggy several letters that were almost word for word duplicates of love letters written to another young lady five months earlier. He had made copies of those at the time and preserved them for future use after his advances were rejected. Peggy was the youngest of three charming daughters, whose father, Judge Edward Shippen, was no loyalist but was too conservative to be a rebel. He insisted on a generous prenuptial settlement, which Arnold proposed to meet with a large tract of land offered him by General Philip Schuyler (for his role at Saratoga). But in the meantime he ran afoul of the Whigs in town, whose opinion of him as a Tory was confirmed by his association with a moneyed family. Arnold was more than twice Peggy's age, and his lusty, rather coarse, swarthy features were in marked contrast with her striking, feminine looks; but early in 1779 they became engaged, and in April, five days after Congress ordered Arnold court-martialed on four charges, they were married. By the end of the honeymoon, Arnold was ready to betray his country and Peggy was a partner in his plans.

Badly in need of money to maintain his newly acquired lifestyle and under attack for his dubious financial dealings, in early May he took the fateful step of offering his services to the British in New York. The go-between was Joseph Stansbury, a Philadelphia dealer in fine china with strong loyalist ties and useful connections to British intelligence, and the contact man in New York was then Captain John André, a dear friend of Peggy's from the British occupation days. Both men were probably suggested for their roles by Arnold's bride.

Unbeknownst to Arnold, he was under close scrutiny by the British. In June of 1780 Major André wrote in cipher to Joseph Chew, a loyalist and former colonel in the British army during the French and Indian War, requesting that he hire men to watch Arnold's movements when he traveled from West Point to Connecticut. Any information he gathered would give André "an idea of schemes in that quarter."

Arnold's decision to betray his country required no inward struggle of conscience, no long, agonizing assessment of the pros and cons. It all came down to money and the position he desired in society—two objectives that had driven him for most of his adult life. Unlike Arnold, most officers in the Continental Army or the militia were motivated by a deep commitment to their country's independence. Most of them possessed a strong sense of personal honor. Benedict Arnold had neither. Completely amoral, he had no hesitation whatever in betraying his country or the men around him like John Lamb and Elisha Sheldon, who served with him and considered him their friend. What Benedict Arnold wanted came before country or friend.

After a protracted period of uncertainty and no response by André or General Clinton to Arnold's traitorous offer, he and Peggy decided that whatever communication he had with British headquarters should be sent to Philadelphia and be forwarded to Manhattan by his wife—a circuitous route, to be sure, but essential until Arnold was able to establish a reliable system of couriers between what were to be his new headquarters at West Point and Clinton's in New York.

Finally, having heard nothing concrete about the rewards he could expect for betraying his country, he angrily demanded £10,000 sterling, "to be paid to me or my heirs in case of loss"; £500 a year to make up for the pay and other "emoluments" he would be giving up; and a bonus of £20,000 for delivering West Point and its garrison. As usual, Arnold was taking a risk, especially since he had not then been given the command on which the bargain depended; but this fell into his hands at last on August 3, when General Washington put him in charge of West Point.

And there matters had stood when Arnold learned that the commander in chief would soon be passing through Peekskill on his way to Hartford.

★　★　★

ON THE MORNING of September 26, Major General Nathanael Greene's general orders broke the news of Benedict Arnold's treason to a dismayed army.

> *Treason* of the blackest dye was yesterday discovered! General Arnold, who commanded at West Point, lost to every sentiment of honor, of public and private obligation, was about to deliver up that important post into the hands of the enemy. . . . Happily, the treason has been timely discovered to prevent the fatal misfortune. . . . Great honor is due to the American army that this is the first instance of treason of the kind when many were to be expected from the nature of the dispute. . . . His Excellency, the Commander-in-Chief, has arrived at West Point . . . and is no doubt taking the proper measures to unravel fully so hellish a plot!

Washington had indeed taken action, putting West Point in the hands of Alexander McDougall, an experienced, reliable man who was in poor health but could readily cope with the situation until General Arthur St. Clair arrived to relieve him. But Washington was still as much in the dark as Colonel Alexander Scammell, who wrote to a friend: "Treason! treason! treason! Black as h-ll. . . . Heaven and earth! we were all astonishment, each peeping at his neighbor to see if any treason was hanging about him. Nay, we even descended to a critical examination of ourselves." Not knowing if further treachery was afoot or if others were involved in the plot, Washington understandably turned to his most reliable veterans to man the fort, ordering men of Anthony Wayne's Pennsylvania line to join him posthaste. It was night when two of his brigades were ordered to march immediately, and one young officer recalled "the dark moment . . . in which the defection of Arnold was announced in whispers. It was midnight, horses were saddling, officers going from tent to tent ordering their men, in suppressed voices, to turn out. . . ." As Wayne proudly described his response to a friend, ". . . his Excellency (in imitation of Caesar and his Tenth Legion) called for his *veterans*; the summons arrived at one o'clock in the morning, and we took up our line of march at 2 and by sunrise arrived at [Stony Point], distant from our former camp 16 miles, the whole performed in four hours in a dark night, without a single halt or a man left behind." When Washington got word of Wayne's forced march and timely arrival, he quite rightly called the feat "fabulous."

Riding to Tappan, where the main army was encamped, the General ordered Major Tallmadge to bring André there for trial, triggering a remarkable change of emotions on the major's part, and of just about every American who came in contact with the British officer. Seated beside André in the barge that took them downriver to Tappan, Tallmadge listened to his prisoner's questions, the most important of which was how his actions would be viewed by General Washington and a military tribunal, which was certain to hear the case.

Tallmadge did his best to avoid replying but finally told André that he had had a much-loved classmate at Yale named Nathan Hale, and asked if André knew what happened to Hale after he was caught by the British while collecting information on the strength and probable movements of General Howe's army in New York.

"Yes," said André. "He was hanged as a spy, but you surely do not consider his case and mine alike."

Tallmadge replied, "Precisely similar, and similar will be your fate."

The American major didn't care much for André at first, but after his trial by a court consisting of Nathanael Greene as president, plus five other major generals and eight brigadiers, during which the defendant confessed to espionage and answered every question openly and honestly, Tallmadge wrote, "I can remember no instance where my affections were so fully absorbed in any man." That statement summed up the views of most of Washington's officers.

On October 1, having considered the board's report carefully, Washington announced that Major André "ought to be considered as a spy . . . to suffer death," and directed that the sentence be executed at noon the next day.

The American commander summoned Captain Aaron Ogden of the light infantry and handed him a packet of letters to take under a flag of truce to the British lines, saying he should report to Lafayette for further instructions. The young Frenchman suggested (as Washington could not do) that Ogden inform the commander of the British post that if General Clinton would turn over Benedict Arnold to the Americans, André would be released immediately. The British officer to whom this was confided galloped off and was back in two hours, stating gloomily that "A deserter was never given up."

★　★　★

BY THEN IT was clear to André that he faced death, but he wanted to die before a firing squad, not on the gibbet. General Clinton, who had done his best to have André released, wrote to Washington, arguing that he, Clinton, "permitted Major André to go to Major General Arnold at the particular request of that general officer" and that "a flag of truce was sent to receive Major André and passports granted for his return." But the American commander in chief would have none of that. André had come ashore from the *Vulture* and spoken with Arnold "in a private and secret manner." He had changed his clothes and disguised himself, when captured had at first refused to produce the pass Arnold gave him, and had asked the militiamen who caught him which party they belonged to before admitting he was a British officer. And when he was searched, the important papers Arnold had given him were found concealed in the foot of his stocking—"papers which contained intelligence for the Enemy." What was this if not the activity of a spy? Indeed, under questioning, André had confessed "it was impossible for him to suppose he came on shore under the sanction of a Flag."

Arnold, behaving in character, had the nerve to threaten Washington, saying that if the death sentence was executed, he would "retaliate on such unhappy persons of your army as may fall within my power." In fact, he continued, if General Washington suffered the unjust sentence to fall on André, "I call heaven and earth to witness that your Excellency will be justly answerable for the torrent of blood that may be spilt in consequence."

Until the last moment, André was left to wonder about the manner of his death, while his superior, Clinton, could not bring himself to accept the harsh penalty imposed on a young man who was his favorite aide. André's final letter to Clinton was to absolve the general of any blame and to thank him for his "profuse kindness." At the appointed hour, André walked the half-mile from the stone house in which he had been confined, arm in arm with two men of his escort, to the mournful sound of a "dead march" played by fife and drum. He betrayed no sign of weakness but bowed politely to several people he recognized in the enormous crowd.

As he came in sight of the gallows, the prisoner involuntarily stepped backward in revulsion. One of the American officers accompanying him asked, unfeelingly, "Why this emotion, sir?" At that, André recovered his composure and replied, "I am reconciled to my death, but I detest the mode," and resumed walking. John Hart, an army surgeon, said he appeared to be "the most Agreeable, pleasing young fellow I ever see, the most agreeable smile on his countenance that can be conceived of. . . ."

All eyes were upon André as he approached the gallows and stood there for a moment, placing his foot on a small stone and turning it over, unconsciously perhaps, in a last touch with earth. Then, in the words of an artificer in Benjamin Baldwin's regiment, he "stepped into the hind end of the wagon, then on his coffin, took off his hat and laid it down, then placed his hands upon his hips and walked very uprightly back and forth as far as the length of his coffin would permit, at the same time casting his eyes upon . . . the whole scenery by which he was surrounded." The surgeon James Thacher heard André say, in a small voice to himself, "It will be but a momentary pang." To which John Hart added, "there was not the least tremour or appearance of fear. Such Fortitude I never was witness of . . . to see a man go out of time without fear, but all the time smiling is a matter I could not conceive of."

The hangman, a fellow named Strickland, hideously disguised with black grease on his face, stepped into the wagon with a halter in his hand, but André pushed him away, unpinned his shirt collar, took the rope from the executioner's hand, and, placing the knot under his right ear, drew the noose snug around his neck. Colonel Alexander Scammell informed André that he had a right to speak, and he responded, "I pray you to hear the witness that I died like a brave man."

Then the Briton took a handkerchief from a pocket and tied it around his eyes. That done, the provost officer commanded that his arms must be tied, so André pulled out another handkerchief and handed it to the executioner, who fastened his arms behind his back. The rope around his neck was then made fast to the pole overhead and suddenly the wagon was drawn from under the gallows—so suddenly that it swung the victim violently back and forth until the lifeless body finally hung absolutely still. As the man in Baldwin's regiment said, "He remained hanging, I should think, for twenty to thirty minutes, and during that time the chambers of death were never stiller than the multitude by which he was surrounded."

"Thus died, in the bloom of life, the accomplished Major André, the pride of the Royal Army, and the valued friend of Sir Henry Clinton," wrote James Thacher, who, like so many of those present, was deeply affected by what was perceived as the final scene in a tragedy.

America's military men recognized that the gentlemanly, courtly André was the antithesis of Arnold, but even so, they asked themselves, why had Arnold done what he did? How could someone who had fought so hard for the independence in which he believed turn against his country and his fellow soldiers? They may not have liked him, but there was no denying the man's courage in battle, his utter determination to win at all costs, his disregard for his own safety, and his ability to inspire men to fight.

At the time no one imagined that Peggy Arnold was intimately involved in the plot; not for a century and a half would it be known that she was her husband's accomplice in the squalid affair.* With Benedict Arnold, who gave his name to traitors in America, the motivation is easier to understand. He was greedy—greedy for money, for position, for recognition—all denied him or given him only grudgingly despite his heroic actions in battle. He had been passed over for promotion several times by Congress and understandably resented that other men, less qualified and with far less experience in battle, were appointed to a higher rank than his own. Unfortunately for his career, Arnold was plainly disliked by a number of his contemporaries, who were rankled by his raw ambition and his naturally pushy nature. Although the world might see what he did as a despicable, venal act, to Arnold it was a commercial transaction, no different from the sale of the share he had claimed in the British sloop *Active*, captured by a Pennsylvania privateer while he was the commandant in Philadelphia. Instead of wooden timbers and armaments and rigging, the merchandise was his country. What's more, Arnold knew how desperate the condition of the American army was, and wanted to ensure that he would end up on the winning side.

---

*It was in the 1930s, when the British Headquarters papers, purchased by William L. Clements, were found to contain a detailed record of the negotiations and the participants in treachery, that Peggy Arnold's role as an accomplice was discovered.

Greed is a goad that has turned many a man to the devil's work. In Benedict Arnold's case, the man obsessed by greed had no hesitation in resorting to evil to satisfy his craving.

As Washington put it, "He wants feeling!" and went on to say that "he seems to have been so hackneyed in villainy, and so lost to all sense of honor and shame that while his faculties will enable him to continue his sordid pursuits, there will be no time for remorse."

Peggy Arnold was something else again. She had grown up with money, never having to worry about it. Money was always there, and what she wanted she was always given. Spoiled by her family, sought after by young men, the cynosure of all eyes in her charmed circle, she took it for granted that she was admired, adored, and would always be invited to dance when the waltz began. Then this dark, mysterious, powerful figure, with a limp that reminded everyone of his heroism in battle, appeared on the scene, and she was drawn to him, an outsider, as he was to her, the ultimate insider. Filled with desire for him, she wanted whatever it was that he wanted, and what he wanted must have seemed eminently appealing to an attractive, impressionable young woman who longed for excitement and adventure.

On September 25, aboard the *Vulture*, Arnold had written a letter to George Washington—which could, under the circumstances, fairly be described as an obscenity—in which he claimed that love for his country actuated his present conduct, "however it may appear inconsistent to the world, who very seldom judge right of any man's actions." Having blamed the world for misinterpreting his actions, he then asked the General to protect his wife from any insult or injury, for "she is as good and as innocent as an angel, and is incapable of doing wrong." And that assessment of her character was the one the public seems generally to have accepted for a century and a half.

Arnold enclosed a letter for his Peggy with the one to Washington, asking that it be delivered to her, and carefully included a sentence he intended Washington to read, so as to divert suspicion from his wife: "Thou loveliest and best of women, Words are wanting to express my feelings and distress on your account, who are incapable of doing wrong yet are exposed to suffer wrong."

In the wake of the treasonable act, authorities in Philadelphia seized Arnold's papers, and at once other repugnant activities came to light: his wrongdoing in office, his own and his wife's secret purchases in New York, his influence peddling, his apparent theft and sale of goods intended for the garrison at West Point. Accused in the *Pennsylvania Packet* of "baseness and prostitution of office and character," Arnold soon became a figure of derision across the United States, his effigy hanged or burned in village after village, his once-heroic image shattered for good.

When he reached New York, the traitor's reception was a far cry from the hero's welcome Arnold had foreseen before his plot was discovered. General Clinton did give him the rank of brigadier general of provincials, but that was a step down from his rank in the Continental Army, with a somewhat demeaning limitation of his command, which Arnold was obliged to accept. His reputation with Clinton's officers was suggested in a London newspaper: "General Arnold is a very unpopular character in the British army, nor can all the patronage he meets with from the commander-in-chief procure him respectability. . . . The subaltern officers have conceived such an aversion to him that they unanimously refused to serve under his command. . . ."

Arnold, brash as ever, wrote to Clinton, quoting André as saying that while he was authorized to offer Arnold only £6,000 for his services, he was certain that General Clinton would give him the £10,000 Arnold proposed (even though "No sum of money would have been an inducement to have gone through the danger and anxiety I have experienced," the traitor added). Clinton's response was immediate and spoke eloquently: he sent Arnold a draft for £6,000. When one of Arnold's former comrades-in-arms learned of the transaction, he wrote to John Lamb, saying that the hero of Quebec and Saratoga had shown himself "as base a prostitute as this or any other country" had produced. It would have been far better for Arnold and his friends, he continued, "had the ball which pierced his leg at Saratoga been directed through his heart; he then would have finished his career in glory."

Before long an announcement appeared in New York's *Royal Gazette*, a loyalist newspaper, addressed to officers and soldiers of the Continental Army "who have the real interest of their country at heart, and who are determined to be no longer the tools and dupes of Congress and of France." Brigadier General Benedict Arnold offered to lead the volunteers in what was to be called an American legion and to share with them "the glory of rescuing our native country from the grasping hand of France. . . ." For the next six weeks the announcement appeared semiweekly and in that time produced volunteers of only eight officers, three sergeants, twenty-eight common soldiers, and one drummer for Arnold's American legion.

In mid-November of 1780 a haggard, exhausted Peggy Arnold arrived in New York with her baby, Edward. She had been banished from the state of Pennsylvania by the Supreme Executive Council on grounds that her presence there was "dangerous to the public safety," and, fearing for her life, she had been escorted to the west bank of the Hudson River by her father. There they bade each other a tearful farewell, and she was soon united with her husband. Interestingly, while in Philadelphia she had agreed, if permitted to remain there with her family, to cease all correspondence with her husband for the duration of the war, but the authorities would have none of that. They wanted no part of Benedict Arnold.

Whether the relationship between Arnold and Peggy had changed during her exposure to what must have been a shattering experience in her hometown, where old friends turned their backs on her and she learned firsthand the meaning of treason, is impossible to say, but the two had a powerful physical attraction for each other and within several weeks of her arrival in New York Peggy was pregnant. Soon they became part of loyalist society in the city to which thousands of Tories had flocked during the war, consorting with the chief justice, William Smith, and his wife, with Sir Henry Clinton and others at dinner parties, dances, and the theater. Yet as much as Benedict Arnold may have enjoyed the limelight, he was not a man to adjust easily to the sedentary life. He wanted action, and suddenly Clinton gave him a shot at it. He was to lead a detachment of some seventeen hundred men to Portsmouth, Virginia, at the mouth of Chesapeake Bay.

★   ★   ★

AT THE END of what Washington called an "inactive campaign," he positioned his troops in such a way as to protect West Point while camping near sources of provisions he hoped would carry them through the coming winter. He was sure that Clinton would detach some of his troops from New York and send them to the South "to extend his conquests," but if that should happen, the Americans were in no position to do much about it. After Gates's horrific loss at Camden, no one wanted that general in charge of anything, and Washington's immediate thought was to replace him with Nathanael Greene, his most able, resourceful general. Greene was then at West Point and accepted the southern command reluctantly, knowing he could expect little help from the commander in chief, who was burdened with so many problems. Writing to his beloved wife, Kitty, Greene said, "My dear Angel, What I have been dreading has come to pass. His Excellency General Washington by order of Congress has appointed me to the command of the Southern army."

Happily for Greene, Washington gave him the best possible support in the form of two officers: Baron Steuben and Henry Lee. Steuben was incomparable as a trainer of troops and could also serve Greene well as an experienced adviser, while "Light-Horse Harry" Lee was a superb horseman with a small but well-trained cavalry force.

After graduating from Princeton at the age of seventeen, Lee was about to leave for England and study law when the war broke out. Patrick Henry nominated him for a captaincy in a Virginia cavalry regiment, and it was not long before his military proficiency and exploits attracted the attention of the commander in chief. For his conduct during the campaign of 1778 he won a promotion to major commandant and was authorized to increase the size of his cavalry command, which would serve as an independent corps. A victory at Paulus Hook in 1779 earned him one of the eight medals voted by Congress during the war, and he was promoted to lieutenant colonel when he was only twenty-three.

Before Lee headed south to join Greene, Washington had a conversation with him about a subject of utmost importance. The General wanted desperately to get his hands on Benedict Arnold—not to have someone kill him but to give him a trial, sentence him, and make an example of him before the army and the world. The only possible way to accomplish this was to kidnap him from the British army, and to do this Washington asked his young friend Henry Lee to suggest a man from his command. Lee believed he had just the man for the job.

On the night of October 9 Lee summoned a sergeant major named John Champe to his headquarters, locked the door behind him, and disclosed an audacious plan. The idea was for Champe to desert from Lee's cavalry brigade, flee to the British in New York, insinuate himself into the corps Benedict Arnold was raising—his American legion—and somehow work his way into the good graces of the traitor. On top of this, he was to meet every second day with an American agent who would make himself known as Mr. Baldwin. When the circumstances seemed auspicious, they should take advantage of a dark night, seize Arnold, gag him, and, pretending he was a drunken soldier, carry him to a boat provided by Baldwin, cross the Hudson, and head for Bergen Woods, where a rebel patrol would meet them and take them to headquarters.

Champe was a tall, strong fellow in his early twenties who had been chosen by Lee as "a very promising youth of uncommon taciturnity and inflexible perseverance"—two qualities that were essential in this bizarre assignment. Lee knew Champe's family in Virginia and was confident that he would be faithful to his duty, but at first Champe was reluctant, not because he was afraid of the hazardous mission but because he hated the idea of even pretending to be a deserter. Obviously, he would have to run the risk any real deserter would face, but Lee promised to delay any pursuit of him as long as possible. Beyond that, Lee assured him that he would receive a promotion, and that if the plan miscarried and he was caught, his name would be cleared.

Lee wrote to Washington, saying he had arranged for two men to carry out the General's wishes. Champe was to be rewarded with a promotion; Mr. Baldwin was to receive "one hundred guineas, five hundred acres of land, and three Negroes." Washington approved promptly, but only "with this express stipulation and pointed injunction": "that he A———d, is brought to me alive. No circumstance whatever shall obtain my consent to his being put to death. The idea which would accompany such an event would be that ruffians had been hired to assassinate him. My aim is to make a public example of him."

On the night of October 20, Champe and Lee met for the last time, the sergeant packed his gear in a knapsack, saddled his horse, and rode out of camp on his extraordinary mission. Thanks to Lee's efforts to delay pursuit, he had a head start of about an hour and a quarter and managed to reach the vicinity of a popular tavern, the Three Pigeons, on the ridge above salt marshes on the west bank of the Hudson. But there his luck ran out. As he was emerging from the woods about daylight on Saturday, October 21, he heard hoofbeats and saw dragoons near the tavern galloping after him. Riding hard for Bergen, about four miles distant, he managed to elude his pursuers, but they came in sight again just as he leaped from his horse, strapped his knapsack on his shoulders, and plunged into the Hudson.

Providentially, he had been spotted by a British officer on a frigate in the river, who realized at once that an American deserter was making an escape, and had a boat lowered to row toward him and pick him up while the ship's guns covered Champe. Hauled aboard ship, Champe identified himself and said he was seeking British protection in New York City.

On October 23 the escapee was interviewed by Assistant Adjutant

General George Beckwith at British headquarters at 1 Broadway, the beautiful home built by Captain Archibald Kennedy of the Royal Navy. The deserter's story of unrest and terrible conditions rang true to British officers, who had heard similar tales from malcontents of the Continental Army, and Champe was invited to enlist in the British army. He was ready for this: to accept would heighten the risk of his being caught and hanged by the rebels, he argued, so he was allowed to look for a job in Manhattan.

Fortunately, Arnold's quarters were next door to Clinton's headquarters, and almost immediately Champe arranged to run into the traitor, who spotted the deserter's Light Horse uniform and was impressed by Champe's story that he had been led to desert by General Arnold's example. At the end of their conversation, Champe accepted a rank in the American legion that was equivalent to that which he had held in Lee's corps.

Within a matter of days the "deserter" discovered that Arnold had a regular habit of walking in his garden around midnight, just before retiring, and decided that this was the time and place to catch him. He then worked loose a number of palings in the picket fence so that he and his accomplice Baldwin could pass through quietly, jump on Arnold, stuff a gag in his mouth, and drag him into the alley behind the house and to a waiting boat at the pier behind headquarters. These precautions took time, and Champe was such a careful, meticulous planner that it was early December before he was ready to make his move. He set the date for the 11th of the month.

That winter afternoon as he waited for darkness to fall, General Arnold suddenly appeared and handed him an order. Champe was to leave immediately with the American legion, which was embarking for Virginia with orders to take the town of Portsmouth on Chesapeake Bay. Champe's efforts had been to no avail; now he had to join the loyalists struggling up the gangplanks with their gear and wait on board until the fleet sailed on December 20, leaving him with no chance to seize Arnold or notify Mr. Baldwin or call off the Continental soldiers who would be waiting in the Bergen Woods for the three men to appear.

As the transports bearing Arnold and his seventeen hundred men, including John Champe, set sail and slipped out of New York harbor on the evening tide, no one could have known it, but the Revolutionary War in the North was over.

4

BEWARE THE BACK WATER MEN

In Newport, Rochambeau's French officers settled in for a comfortable season of sociability, having taken over a number of elegant houses after repairing the damage the British had done to them. But early in October they got their first taste of severe American weather when the howling tail of the hurricane that had devastated Martinique and Barbados blew into Rhode Island, driving ships aground, dismasting others, and blowing over all the tents in camp.

That same month came news of the "shocking treason" of Benedict Arnold as part of a plan to deliver West Point to the enemy. Washington had written to Rochambeau about it on September 26, saying, "By a lucky accident a conspiracy of the most dangerous kind . . . has been defeated. General Arnold, who has sullied his former glory, by the blackest treason, has escaped to the enemy." In an attempt to allay any fears the Frenchman might have, he noted philosophically, "in a revolution of the present nature it is more to be wondered at" that there had been so few traitors. Rochambeau responded in words calculated to console the American general, but which proved to foreshadow a host of events in the campaign on which they were to embark: "I know not whether I should pity you, or congratulate you upon the discovery of Arnold's frightful plot; be this as it may, it proves to us that Providence is for us and for our cause, and of this I have had several examples since the beginning of this campaign." Under present circumstances, it appeared that only the hand of Providence could save the rebel cause.

The tactful response was characteristic of Rochambeau, about whom Axel Fersen wrote, "Everyone was contented to be commanded by Rochambeau. He was the only man who was capable of commanding us here in America, and of maintaining that perfect harmony which existed between two nations so different in manners and language. His wise, prudent, and simple bearing did more to conciliate the Americans than four successful battles could have done."

At the end of the month, after Vicomte Rochambeau, the general's son, left for Versailles, preparations began for settling the French army in winter quarters. Winter came early and the brutal cold obliged the officers to make huge fires in open fireplaces in their rooms, but they soon discovered how expensive this was going to be. Unavailable locally, firewood had to be hauled great distances since the English—who had occupied the town from 1776 to 1779—had stripped the island of its luxuriant forests and its renowned orchards.

Some of the men, including the Chevalier de Chastellux, were eager to explore the interior of America and left town in early November,* while those who remained behind gradually learned something of the mores of their hosts. They were struck by how unlike their own customs were those of well-to-do Americans—very easy and free, so that what would be regarded as bad breeding in France was, in this country, regarded as suitable behavior and generally accepted. At the table Americans leaned on their dinner companions, rested on their elbows, and used no napkin (a diner wiped his or

*François-Jean de Beauvoir, Chevalier de Chastellux, wrote a book based on his journeys, *Travels in North America in the Years 1780, 1781, and 1782.*

her mouth on the tablecloth). Breakfast, the visitors learned, generally included coffee, chocolate, and slices of buttered toast, and the amount of sugar used marked the difference between poverty and affluence. Dinner consisted of boiled or roast meat with vegetables cooked in water. "They make their own sauce on their plates, which they usually load with everything on the table, enough to frighten a man, and pour gravy over it. . . . After dinner those in comfortable circumstances have the tablecloth removed, whereupon the ladies retire. Madeira wine is brought, and the men drink and smoke for quite a while."

At dinner parties given by the well-to-do, so many healths were drunk that "one rarely leaves the table without being a little tipsy. . . ." In the evening a rather light supper was eaten about ten o'clock, and in every household they visited they found that grog,* cider, or beer was served to the thirsty. No glasses were offered; the liquid was in a bowl. The master of the house drank to the guests' health, took a drink himself, handed the bowl to the guest next to him, and it was then passed around the table.

Claude Blanchard, the commissary, dined frequently with Americans and was struck by their consumption of coffee and tea. In the case of country people, breakfast consisted of quantities of both coffee and tea, which they drank with roasted meats, butter, pies, and ham. Then they had supper, and in the afternoon, tea. It seemed to him that Americans were "almost always at the table" in the winter, and since they had little to occupy them besides spending days "along side of their fires and their wives, without reading and without doing anything, going so often to table" was "a relief and a preventive of *ennui*."

Baron Closen was struck by the way an American's outward appearance often suggested carelessness or even thoughtlessness, yet despite this apparent indifference to the opinion of others, "these

---

*Grog was a drink made of rum and water. If sugar was added, it was called toddy; with the addition of lemon, it was called punch.

same people fight with so much bravery, can support a war, and have such trained and disciplined troops. Who would believe that an American, who scarcely dares to go out of his house on a rainy day, the moment he has a musket on his shoulder, braves every danger and the most difficult weather?"

One of his colleagues, the Comte de Clermont-Crèvecoeur, described the Americans as tall and well built, but thin, which made "most of them look as though they had grown while convalescing from an illness." They do not live long, he concluded: "one notices that they live to be sixty or seventy, and the latter are rare." Even so, he had seen a few octogenarians and one ninety-year-old man who was still riding horseback with ease.

As for the Rhode Island women, Closen found them unusual in their modesty and sweetness of demeanor, noting that they had very fine features, white and clear complexions, small hands and feet, but "their teeth are not very wonderful"—a fault he attributed to drinking great quantities of tea. The clothes and coiffeurs of most women were in the English style, but he hoped that "the visit of the French army will increase their taste for dress." Fortunately, "they all like dancing, and they engage in it unpretentiously, as is their manner in general."

The women struck Clermont-Crèvecoeur as very beautiful but also quite pale and rather frail. A girl of twenty would pass for thirty in France, he said, and while they have very little color, "nothing can compare with the whiteness and texture of their skin. They have charming figures, and in general one can say they are all pretty, even beautiful, in the regularity of their features. . . ." By the time he had been in this country for six months or so, he had given a great deal more thought to American women and reached a rather startling conclusion, which he phrased as a question: "In a country so new where vice should not be deeply rooted, why should there be such a large number of prostitutes?"

The answer, he decided, lay in the strange custom of bundling—an activity granted by parents that permitted a young man who declared himself to be in love with a girl to shut himself up in a room with her, lavishing tender caresses upon her in bed, but "stopping short of those reserved for marriage alone; otherwise he would transgress the established laws of bundling." A truly virtuous girl would resist and conform to the letter of the law, while "those more amply endowed by nature in this respect succumb to this tender sport." Bundling, he observed, was made for Americans; the "coldness and gravity of their faces proclaim that this sport suits them perfectly." What's more, a couple could play this game for five or six years or longer before deciding to marry, without committing finally to wedlock. If a girl was seduced and had a child, it was not she who was disgraced, but the man. Respectable houses were closed to him, and he could not marry into one of the better families.

A married woman, he continued, was very faithful to her husband, even though she might have led "a most licentious life" in the years before marriage. Men didn't seem to mind this; they were not fussy and believed a girl should be free until she was married. If a married woman committed adultery, the husband announced his wife's "delinquency" and published it in the papers, stating that he would neither pay her bills nor be liable for her debts. Yet even if the situation deteriorated to that stage, adultery was no excuse for dissolving a marriage—the laws did not permit it, and husbands were quite patient about waiting for their wives to repent.

★ ★ ★

ONE OF THE high points of autumn for the French visitors was a visit by "several savage tribes" of Indians of the Six Nations. General Philip Schuyler had arranged this with an eye to favorable propaganda. The English, it seemed, had been assiduously informing the Indians that the French were not allied with the Americans, and Schuyler believed it would be very effective to have some of the natives see at first hand the French army and navy in Newport to give the lie to that talk. So he had directed James Dean, the agent for

Indian affairs, to accompany them and introduce them to Rocham-beau and others.*

By all accounts the visit was a huge success. Nineteen of the Indians were received by Rochambeau, who had some of his regiments parade for them, go through the manual of arms, and fire muskets and cannon—which "alarmed them no end." The Duc de Lauzun's hussars delighted them, as did a tour of the mighty ships in the harbor. Craftily, the Indi-ans informed Rochambeau through an interpreter that they had cho-sen him to lead them in war. They regretted that some of their people had gone over to the English, they added, and gave the reason: "[The English] have such good *tafia*, such good rum! Besides, they give us gunpowder to go hunting [and] by all these things we are often seduced and brought over to their side." Rochambeau got the point and told them at once that the king "thanked them and would not let them lack for spirits." Then he presented them with a medal struck with the arms of France, swords, shirts, blankets, and other gifts, including rouge, which they immediately combed into their hair and daubed over their shirts, blankets, and the rest of their bodies.

If the Indians were fascinated by the French, the reverse was cer-tainly true. Jean-Baptiste-Antoine de Verger described in detail how they oiled and then rouged their bodies, red being their favorite color. "They slit the lobes around the edges of their ears until they hang down to their chins, weighed down by various small ornaments." They pierce the cartilage of the nose and attach more baubles, pull out the hair at the nape of the neck and attach small locks of it to the top of the head. When young, he discovered, they cut designs on their face.

He was particularly impressed with their dancing. After removing their outerwear of animal skins, revealing well-proportioned bodies oiled and rouged, some of them danced with swords in their hands while their comrades intoned a monotonous chant. They danced

---

*Dean was a native of Groton, Connecticut, who had lived as a boy among the Oneidas and become fluent in the Iroquois languages. A protégé of Eleazer Wheelock, the president of Dartmouth, he had graduated from the college before his employment as an agent of Congress.

"with great strength and agility, assuming various postures symbolizing a man in combat and breaking out from time to time into war-cries or dirges so piercing and violent that they filled one with terror." He had seen much and learned something very important: "They prefer rum above all things, and when drunk they are very dangerous."

Quite another kind of discovery for these French Catholics was an introduction to Quakers, of whom many lived in and around Newport. The men, they found, were extremely grave in their dress and manner, very temperate, and inclined to talk little. Unlike a majority of Americans, they did not permit slavery in their society; they never took an oath (since they had no faith in the word of man), refused to pay tithes, and had neither priests nor ministers. The sexes were separated in their meetinghouse on Sundays, with men on one side, women on the other, and complete silence was observed. Only when one of them felt inspired did anyone speak, and the speech was often accompanied by convulsive movements, a twitching of limbs.

It was a rigid sect, to be sure. "Quakers allow themselves no pleasures beyond conversation and meditation; they are forbidden to sing and dance." And the women, Clermont-Crèvecoeur observed, were not only very pretty but "more inclined to pleasure than other sects. . . . They detest their religion [and] If the Quaker men are even more solemn than those of other sects, one finds that Quaker girls balance the score by being much gayer and more playful. They love pleasure but are always held back by the fear of displeasing their parents."

Having said that, he noted, "Their wedding feasts are terribly dreary, since nobody speaks. You may imagine how much fun that would be!"

Of considerably more importance for the Frenchmen's mission here was the acquisition of knowledge about the two sides in America's revolution. In a passage that could have been written by a rebel propagandist, Clermont-Crèvecoeur wrote in his diary, "This country is divided between two parties called Whigs and Tories," adding that the former were the "good Americans," fighting for the freedom of their country and against the unjust laws the English wanted imposed on them, while the others, known as "royalists," remained attached to the king. He and his countrymen had been here long enough that they could "define and analyze the character of these Tories," he said confidently. The majority of them were cowardly and cruel, while some, undecided about whether to take sides, appeared to be waiting for "some happy event to indicate in which direction their interest lay." Still others pretended to be on the side of the Americans but were in fact spies paid by the English to betray their compatriots, and great numbers of them, lured by money and permission from the English, had pillaged and sacked the homes of their fellow citizens. From someone he had heard that three-quarters of the inhabitants were Tories, that you could not travel in safety "for fear of these brigands." What seemed to make the strongest impression on him was that when the French first gave balls the Whigs refused to come to a house to which Tories had been invited. Later, since the latter were so numerous in Newport—especially their ladies—the French never lacked for dancing partners, and "all was smoothed over in the end; the women all danced regardless, and everything went beautifully." In fact, when George Washington came to Newport in March and "[the French] generals gave fêtes and balls in his honor . . . he danced indiscriminately with everyone. He was honored and esteemed even by his enemies."

Washington had other matters on his mind besides dancing. He was there to discuss plans for the coming campaign and spent eight days in talks with Rochambeau and his aides before returning to the Hudson Highlands.

★   ★   ★

IN DECEMBER NEWS reached the Americans that Sir Henry Clinton had dispatched Major General Alexander Leslie to the Chesapeake. He was to make a diversion in favor of Cornwallis, who was

thought to be "acting in the back parts of North Carolina," by proceeding up the James River as far as possible and seizing any magazines
the rebels had in Petersburg and Richmond. The British had recently
captured a quantity of mail from American officers which revealed that
morale among those men had hit rock bottom, giving Clinton every
reason to hope he might be able "to increase and accelerate the confusion which began everywhere to appear in the rebel counsels."

Included in the American officers' correspondence captured by
the British was a letter signed by three generals (Greene, Knox,
Glover) and others, who had written to their respective states saying
that American officers could no longer continue under the present
circumstances.

> An army consisting of a few inadequate thousands, almost desti-
> tute of every public supply, its officers, whose tables once
> abounded with plenty and variety, subsisting month after month
> on one bare ration of dry bread and meat, and that frequently of
> the meanest quality, their families looking up to them for their
> usual support, their children for the education to which they
> once had a title—our enemies know human nature too well to
> apprehend they shall have to contend long with an army under
> such circumstances.

Another purloined letter, from Alexander Hamilton to the former
Son of Liberty Isaac Sears, noted that Clinton was said to be detach-
ing a substantial force to the South, prompting Hamilton to comment
ruefully, "My fears are high, my hopes low."

From yet another source came a particularly bad piece of news:
Henry Laurens had been captured at sea by a British vessel. Laurens,
who had been president of the Continental Congress in 1777 and
1778, was a prominent merchant and planter from Charleston and,
acting for Congress, was on his way to Holland to negotiate a treaty
of commerce and friendship, plus a loan of $10 million. The British
not only sent Laurens to the Tower of London, where he was impris-

oned until the end of 1781, but used certain of his papers as justification to declare war on Holland on December 20, 1780.

Rochambeau had departed from Newport on December 11, headed for Boston, and no sooner arrived there than he was called back because of the sudden death from asthma of the Chevalier de Ternay. On Christmas day a terrible storm with claps of thunder and violent flashes of lightning hit the city, which seemed all of a piece with the terrible weather that had begun in August with hurricanes in the Caribbean and made its way north, overturning almost all the camp tents, sinking a British frigate with all hands in Hell Gate, near New York, and shrouding the Northeast in thick fog.

At about this time Washington set in motion a plan that was certain to raise the rebels' morale if successful. He gave secret orders to Lieutenant Colonel David Humphreys to take a small group of men down the Hudson at night, rowing with muffled oars in the darkness, and, after landing on Manhattan behind the house occupied by General Clinton, to surprise and seize the sentries, break into the house, and capture Clinton and whatever papers they could find. Simultaneously, another party was to abduct General Wilhelm von Knyphausen, commander of the German troops. The kidnappers set out on Christmas night, shortly after Arnold had sailed for the Chesapeake, but unfortunately high winds drove the boats out into New York Bay, well beyond the city.

Nothing more is known of the plot, but it is clear that George Washington was hoping to pull off a coup that would offset any possible advantage the British had gained by the treason of Benedict Arnold.

★　★　★

IN THE AMERICAN army's camps, sinking morale produced a crisis. From Morristown, Brigadier General Anthony Wayne sent a dire message dated January 2, 1781, to the commander in chief: "The most general and unhappy mutiny took place in the Pennsylvania line about 9 o'clock last night [and] a great proportion of the troops, with some artillery, are marching toward Philadelphia. The men seized several field pieces, resisted the officers who tried to restore order, killed one captain, and wounded several others." Approximately half of the soldiers had defied their officers, he estimated, and "how long it will last, God knows. . . ." Fortunately, no officer had joined the mutiny.

The unhappy soldiers had appointed a committee of sergeants to act on their behalf, and they insisted that the enlistments of those who had signed up for "three years or the war" had terminated on the last day of 1780 and that they were eligible for discharges. They demanded the back pay and clothing to which they were entitled and stipulated that participants in the mutiny not be punished.* It turned out that civil authorities—the Council of Pennsylvania—had been brought into the dispute. That was something the council had a right to do, but Washington feared that a civil settlement would be more lenient by far than the disciplinary action the military would require. Nor was that his only worry. The worst was that other units—quite possibly the entire army, as far as he could tell—would follow suit and bring about the end of the war for independence. Once again, the survival of America depended on bread, meat, and clothing for its armed forces, and he wrote for help to the New England governors, telling them that the army simply could not be held together much longer under the appalling conditions that confronted it. Unless the men received three months' back pay, in currency that was truly worth something, and unless they were properly clothed and fed, "the worst that can befall us may be expected."

The main army was far too weak to march against the Pennsylvanians, and in any case, who knew if the troops around headquarters would remain loyal? At this point it was impossible for Washington to

---

*One reason they wanted discharges was that new recruits were being given cash bonuses for signing up. The only way the veterans could collect any money was to get a discharge and re-enlist.

assess the temper of these soldiers, to determine whether he could rely on them. West Point must be held at all costs (and the only way to ensure its safety was to call on the New York militia if it proved necessary); Wayne and his officers must keep the mutineers south of the Delaware River, lest they go over to the enemy; and Congress simply must not flee Philadelphia.

The General was sorely tempted to ride at once to Morristown to face the mutineers, but recognized that in doing so he risked losing the support of other units. "God only knows what will be the consequence, or what can be done in this critical dilemma. All reason, authority and personal influence seem to be lost on them," he wrote. The shattering of discipline seemed the final straw, on top of a worthless currency, failure to obtain the long-term enlistments the army needed so desperately, and the shocking indifference of civilians to the plight of those who were doing the fighting for them. He could not help being reminded of the darkest days of December 1776 and wondered if these past four years of fighting and suffering had achieved anything.

At that time he had had to contend with General Sir William Howe. Now Sir Henry Clinton faced him, and he received the disturbing news that the British commander in chief had sent one or more emissaries who were offering the Pennsylvania troops money and provisions.

Sir Henry had received word of the mutiny on the morning of January 3, as did Washington—about eighteen hours after it began. Clinton was already well aware of the Continental troops' grievances, which the Congress lacked the ability or resources to resolve, and he quite rightly concluded that in the current situation "the least wrong step taken by the rebel rulers on such an emergency might be the means, with proper encouragement, of driving the mutineers in to us." Obviously, Washington was taking pains to avoid that wrong step, but it was going to be touch-and-go.

To ensure that he could take advantage of any change in the situation, Clinton ordered the commander of the British elite troops,

Major General William Phillips, and the officers in charge of the Hessian grenadiers and jägers to proceed by ferry to Staten Island, where they were to await further orders. Meanwhile, he dispatched three messengers to the mutineers by different routes, carrying offers of protection and pardons, with no conditions attached other than allegiance and submission to the British government, while assuring them that they would be under no obligation to serve in the British army and would receive all the back pay due them. Clinton admitted that this was in the nature of an experiment, worth trying, at least. He anticipated that the defectors might march into Pennsylvania, picking up other disaffected troops along the way, and could then be persuaded to move toward the Chesapeake, where Arnold would be waiting to lead them.

While Washington continued to debate whether he should go to the scene of the mutiny, news reached him that the committee of sergeants had refused to negotiate with one of Clinton's emissaries who arrived and had, instead, turned the man over to Wayne. That was good news, if true, but it was soon followed by contradictory word that the mutineers had not, in fact, delivered the emissary to Wayne but were holding him. Then, on January 15, Major General John Sullivan wrote to the commander in chief, "We are happy to inform your Excellency that the terms offered to the Pennsylvania troops are at length finally, and, as we believe, cordially and satisfactorily agreed on; and tomorrow we expect the Pennsylvania Line will be arranged in its former order."

As welcome as this news was, it came at a terrible price. The mutineers agreed to lay down their arms and deliver the British agents to Continental officers, but in return they had been given a number of financial concessions, while half of the men were discharged and the others furloughed until April. That meant the departure of many experienced veterans the army could not afford to lose, and, for the present at least, the Pennsylvania line was no more. The beleaguered General could hardly help wondering if other units would not follow suit, and if the Continental Army itself might cease to exist. Yet he wrote to Rochambeau in Newport, reporting on the mutineers, "It is somewhat extraordinary that these men, however lost to a sense of duty, had so far retained that of honor, as to reject the most advantageous propositions from the enemy."

Then the other shoe fell. In the third week of January Colonel Israel Shreve wrote Washington to say that the New Jersey soldiers in Pompton had mutinied and were marching toward Trenton. This time the General was determined that the matter be settled by the army, not by civilian authorities, and decided on drastic measures. He ordered the West Point garrison to be ready to march at once, had the Jersey militia assemble, told Sullivan to urge Congress not to intervene, and made the same request to Governor William Livingston of New Jersey. He intended to compel the mutineers to submit, for "Unless this dangerous spirit can be suppressed by force, there is an end to all subordination in the Army, and indeed to the army itself. The infection will no doubt shortly pervade the whole mass."

In late January, with two feet of snow in the mountains west of the Hudson, a detachment of New England troops, under the command of Major General Robert Howe, surrounded the huts of the mutineers and ordered them to come out without their arms. When they did, Howe asked for the names of the three chief ringleaders. They were sentenced to death. Then he called out the names of twelve men who had been the most prominent supporters of the chief conspirators, sent them to get their muskets, brought out the three ringleaders, had them kneel before the firing squad in front of all the other mutineers, while three of their supporters were ordered to shoot at the head, three at the heart, and if the victim still struggled, the remaining six should finish him off. As a finale, Howe spoke to all the men by platoons, telling them the seriousness of their guilt and the outrage their actions represented to the civil authority to which they owed obedience. After that was done, he stated, "I think I may pledge myself for their future good conduct."

★　★　★

IN THE EARLY days of the war, as the British groped for a grand strategy that would win it, they had begun by moving against New England, that hotbed of sedition. When that failed, they transferred operations to the middle states, where capturing Philadelphia was expected to be a sure route to victory, but possession of a single city in the great American landmass achieved little. Then the planners figured that seizing the Lake Champlain–Hudson River waterway would cut off the New England states from those to the south, ending the rebellion, but this was foiled by the disastrous defeat and capture of General John Burgoyne's entire army at Saratoga in 1777. Now, British leaders concluded, if they subdued the southern provinces—where loyalist strength was believed to be strongest—the North would eventually tumble into their hands through isolation and attrition. To date, Savannah had fallen, then Charleston, more recently Camden, and prospects were looking up.

The war in the North was finally sputtering out, but in the South the fighting not only continued but surpassed in savagery what had gone on in most areas. From the autumn of 1775 on, Tories and patriots had been at each other's throats, cousin against cousin, with blood feuds exacerbated by the bitter arguments over one's loyalty. The first significant engagement in North Carolina, for example, was at Moore's Creek in February of 1776, when a group of Highland Scots and the so-called Regulators led by Brigadier General Donald McDonald fought the patriot militia. McDonald had fought at Culloden and was a cousin of Allan McDonald, whose wife, Flora, had helped Bonnie Prince Charlie escape after his last battle. This internecine conflict had continued for a long time and was not easy for the British to comprehend or manage.

Oddly, Charleston had been the scene of Sir Henry Clinton's

worst fiasco as a general as well as his greatest triumph. In 1776 he and his opposite number in the navy botched a joint effort by failing to plan and cooperate and by attacking an island in the harbor instead of the city. Yet four years later his reduction of Charleston was brilliantly handled. (When the British were besieging Charleston, a shell fired from a battery on James Island screeched across the Ashley River, up Meeting Street past St. Michael's Church, and into the intersection of Broad Street, where it slammed into the statue of William Pitt commissioned by the colony fourteen years earlier. As the ultimate irony, the ball broke off the Great Commoner's right arm and shattered the hand that held a copy of the Magna Carta.)

After defeating Benjamin Lincoln there in what was the most complete British victory of the war, with more than four thousand Americans killed or captured, Clinton returned to New York, leaving Charles, Earl Cornwallis, his second in command, to secure and enlarge the conquests already made. Sir Henry, who wanted in the worst way to be relieved of his command, yet perversely did *not* want that to happen, remarked after he arrived in New York, "I am by no means the fashion here with civil or military. . . . My successor, if I am permitted to resign the command, will start fair with both."

The British commander was a short, dumpy man with a plain, round face and bulbous nose. Waspish, forever on the alert for a slight and more often than not detecting one, he had a monumental sensitivity to criticism. A loner since the death of his wife, a blow from which he never recovered, he was aloof, resentful, and self-reproachful. He had few friends other than John Jervis, later first lord of the Admiralty and Earl of St. Vincent, and William Phillips, Burgoyne's artillery officer, who was to die of typhoid fever on the Chesapeake in 1781. And in what was to prove fatal in the campaign about to begin, Clinton was disastrously at odds with the two men who were his assigned colleagues: Lord Cornwallis and the aging, irritable Admiral Marriot Arbuthnot. Clinton well knew how important it was to have a naval commander who would act in harmony with him and had, in fact, given Lord Sandwich at the Admiralty the names of five men with whom he could serve comfortably. But Arbuthnot was allowed to stay on as naval chief, and the inevitable trouble followed.

Cornwallis was a man of a different stripe. He was descended from an old, distinguished family that had played a significant part in English history for centuries. A short, thickset officer with graying hair and a cast in one eye—the result of a sports injury at Eton—he had the look and manner of an affable, agreeable fellow, which he was, except for the frequent occasions when he had fits of bad-tempered sulking.

Before he was eighteen he became an ensign in the Grenadier Guards, had a splendid record in Europe during the Seven Years' War, and was present at the fateful battle of Minden. By twenty-one he was a captain, later a lieutenant colonel of his regiment, and upon the death of his father became a member of the House of Lords. As a Whig, he voted consistently against the government's American policy but managed to remain a favorite of the king. In fact, the reason George III approved his assignment to the colonies was his belief that Cornwallis would remain loyal, despite his political views—and he was right. In America his record was spotty, with good performances at Long Island and Fort Lee, and a major failure when Washington's army eluded him and won the battle of Princeton, prompting Henry Clinton's acid comment that Cornwallis was guilty of "the most consummate ignorance I ever heard of [in] any officer above a corporal." Subsequently, Cornwallis fought at Brandywine and Germantown and after returning to England, where his wife was dying, came again to America—this time to hold the South after the surrender of Charleston in May of 1780.

In sharp contrast to his superior, Sir Henry Clinton, Cornwallis was aggressive and eager to put down the rebels in North Carolina while holding on to the huge area of Georgia and South Carolina. Unfortunately for his relations with Clinton, he arranged to communicate directly with Lord George Germain in London, going over his superior's head. That, plus their mutual dislike, boded ill for the command system. Yet relations between him and Clinton were typical of the trouble that was endemic at British headquarters throughout the conflict—bad blood between the commander and his second in command. The latter had considerable latitude in advising his superior officer, but in the case of Clinton and Cornwallis (as with Sir William Howe and Clinton formerly) the man in charge usually rejected the advice and went forward with his own scheme. In the nature of things, the subordinate was ready and waiting if the plan should fail, in which case his views would be vindicated and, as likely as not, his own reputation enhanced. It goes without saying that this situation made for animosity and mistrust between the top men of the command.

Clinton's idea was for Cornwallis to use Charleston as a base, invade North Carolina, and systematically overrun all the American posts between South Carolina and the Chesapeake. He and Admiral Arbuthnot, in one of their few agreements, concluded that the two of them and their commands should remain in New York, ready to meet the French threat, which meant that Cornwallis would be in active command in the South. Meanwhile, after the French arrived in Rhode Island, Clinton drew up three plans and sent them to Arbuthnot for his opinion on which was feasible. Typically, the admiral was evasive and ignored the general's ideas, whereupon Clinton communicated his grievances to London, requesting that he or Arbuthnot should be removed. His complaints were also ignored, with the result that he and the admiral remained locked, all but incommunicado, in a state of paralysis for months on end.

Not only was the British leadership divided and flawed; the army itself was no longer a single fighting force but comprised three commands: one in New York, another in Charleston, and another that was created when Cornwallis departed Charleston and took off to invade North Carolina. Worse yet, Clinton had recently set in motion a fourth command on the Chesapeake, led by Benedict Arnold.

Adding to this dangerous division of the army was the naval situation, with an unreliable Arbuthnot expected to deal with a superior

French fleet, whenever and wherever it appeared. Yet Clinton based his planning on the dubious assumption that Britain would always have control of the coastal waters.

Although neither Clinton nor Cornwallis realized it, the two of them were operating on entirely different premises. Clinton assumed that Cornwallis's offensive would come northward in deliberate stages and eventually merge with his chief's own operations on the Chesapeake. Above all, Charleston was to be secured before that occurred. Cornwallis, on the other hand, with an astounding victory at Camden under his belt, was confident that he could now move to the north, figuring that the South Carolina backcountry was secure enough to warrant Charleston's safety. Clinton had urged him to advance by way of Cape Fear and travel along the coastline, but the earl regarded that area as too unhealthy for his army and chose instead to travel by the highlands—a grievous error.

By doing so, he lost touch with the navy, which could have kept him reasonably well supplied. Instead of remaining long enough in any one place to capitalize on whatever loyalist support existed there, he had to keep moving, living off the land, unable to maneuver the enemy into a decisive battle. To cap it all, from January until late April of 1781 no direct message from Cornwallis ever reached Clinton. It was as though the two generals were fighting separate wars on different continents.

★   ★   ★

WASHINGTON HAD A hunch that Clinton would soon "detach to the southward to extend his conquests," and the American commander was far from sanguine about the rebels' ability to resist him. Sure enough, it was only a few days after Washington reached that conclusion that Sir Henry ordered General Alexander Leslie, with 2,200 men, to the Chesapeake, instructing him to proceed as far as possible up the James River, where he was to seize or destroy any magazines the Americans had in Petersburg or Richmond. Finally, he should establish a post on the Elizabeth River and await orders from Cornwallis.

The rebels' discovery of the Arnold-André plot wrote finis to Clinton's plan to move up the Hudson and seize West Point, but the arrival of an English fleet with the recruits he had been promised permitted Clinton to send Leslie's force south; they had no sooner arrived than Cornwallis ordered them to join him in the Carolinas. That in turn triggered Clinton's decision to dispatch Benedict Arnold's new command to Portsmouth, Virginia, at the mouth of the Chesapeake, though he could "ill spare it."

Virginia's governor, Thomas Jefferson, in a broadside sent to all the towns, warned them to have their militias ready, with every man to put his gun "into the best order, a bayonet fitted to it, a bayonet belt, cartouche box, canteen with its strap, tomahawk, blanket, and knapsack," adding that militia captains should consider sending a wagon with every seventy-five men. If this suggests that Virginia was woefully unprepared, that was indeed the case, and much of the blame was attributable to Mr. Jefferson, who had done little to prepare against invasion. As William North reported to Lewis Morris in January 1781, "if the head is in trouble, the members cannot enjoy themselves" and "this state has everything in its power but does nothing." Arnold, regrettably, "has not been molested. His troops . . . are infamous beasts [and] march'd through the settled part of Virginia 100 miles."

Arriving in Virginia, Arnold wasted no time in lashing out at the rebels. His first target was the James River valley, but he had his eye on other opportunities, made possible by the Royal Navy's unopposed support that enabled him to ascend navigable rivers and destroy supplies vital to the American army in the South. Testifying to the effectiveness of his campaign, Baron von Closen noted in his diary, "All the letters from Virginia [to Newport] are full of lamentations over the horrors and depredations that Arnold's detachment is committing there. . . ."

Quite apart from General Washington's intense desire to capture the traitor, he would have given a lot to remove Arnold from a position that cut the southern army's communications from the north. As matters stood, Arnold had the ability to send some of his troops against the rebels from the north while Cornwallis closed in on them from the south—all of this possible because the British navy dominated the waters off Chesapeake Bay.

More than anyone else, Washington realized the imperative need for a fleet—a French fleet, obviously, since the Americans had nothing worth the name. To John Laurens he wrote, "How loud are our calls from every quarter for a decisive naval superiority, and how might the enemy be crushed if we had it." He was, as before, thinking of New York and how it could be besieged by a French naval force, and of course there was Charleston, which could also be recaptured with adequate sea power.

★　★　★

THANKS TO THE catastrophe at Camden, Gates's army was shattered, the militia gone beyond recall, and the Continentals reduced to remnants, totaling no more than twelve hundred men. And in late September of 1780 Cornwallis was on the move, readying his force for a full-scale invasion of North Carolina. His right wing was heading toward Wilmington and the Cape Fear River; the center, under his personal command, was bound for Hillsboro, not far south of the Virginia border; and his left, composed of loyalists commanded by Major Patrick Ferguson, was operating in the foothills of the hostile backcountry, planning to rendezvous with the main army at Charlotte.

This Ferguson was a first-rate soldier, with experience on the Continent and four years in the American war, and his slight build and long, gentle-looking face belied a fearlessness and tenacity that caused fellow officers to call him "Bull Dog." He had invented what he called a "rifle gun," a breech-loading weapon that could be fired from a prone position with accuracy and speed (five or six shots a minute, or about twenty-five times that of a muzzle-loading gun with a fouled barrel), and he had the reputation of being one of the best marksmen in the army.

The story was told that Ferguson, at the battle of Brandywine, had George Washington in his sights without knowing who he was and refused to fire because the man's back was turned toward him. In that same engagement a musket ball shattered his right elbow, leaving the arm useless. Now he commanded his own corps of seven loyalist battalions, amounting to about a thousand men, and they had reached the village of Gilbert Town between the Broad and Second Broad rivers when his spies alerted him to the gathering of several thousand over-mountain men, moving toward him through a gap in the mountains. Ferguson issued a broadside, warning residents of the area to beware these "back water men . . . a set of mongrels," and led his force to a more secure location on Kings Mountain. This stony spur of the Blue Ridge Mountains had a narrow plateau on its summit, about 600 yards long and 70 to 120 feet wide. It averaged about 100 feet in height above the surrounding land and was a perfect campsite, where Ferguson settled down to await the rebels.

In late September the over-mountain men began to gather, and a curious lot they were. Most were North Carolinians: Colonel Isaac Shelby with 240 men from Sullivan County; Colonel John "Nolichucky Jack" Sevier with 240 from Washington County; and Colonel Charles McDowell with 160 from Burke and Rutherford counties; plus Colonel William Campbell, leading 400 men from Washington County, Virginia. They made their way through snow in the gap and on the bank of the Catawba picked up Colonel Benjamin Cleveland and his 350 men from Wilkes and Surry counties. Shelby was there for a good reason: Ferguson had sent a patriot he took prisoner to tell Shelby if he did not surrender, Ferguson planned to cross the mountains and burn his whole county.

These frontiersmen from the Watauga settlements in what is now Tennessee did not take that sort of threat lightly. They were acutely aware of what the enemy had done at the Battle of the Waxhaws, where Lieutenant Colonel Banastre Tarleton attacked Colonel Abraham Buford's Virginia Continentals, rode them down, and massacred his command even though they had surrendered. As an American wrote, "The demand for quarters . . . was at once found to be in vain . . . for fifteen minutes after every man was prostrate they went over the ground plunging their bayonets into every one that exhibited any signs of life. . . ." Only Buford and a handful of other mounted men escaped from the battlefield, and the man who defeated them was known thereafter as "Bloody Tarleton," and "Tarleton's Quarter" became a rallying cry for the rebels.

Most of the over-mountain irregulars were Scotch-Irish hunters and Indian fighters—big, tough men who had learned combat in the no-quarter warfare of the southern frontier—and they were out to get Ferguson and his Tories after he sent a warning that he planned to hang their leaders and lay waste their homes and settlements. They were deadly shots with their long-barreled rifles, and they traveled light, on horseback, with not much more than a blanket, hunting knife, and a pouch full of ground parched corn sweetened with maple syrup. They were in North Carolina because they preferred to have the fighting here, rather than back home on their farms, near their wives and children.

As Shelby remembered the little army of which he was a part, it "accidentally collected without a head [and] was a mere confused mass, incapable of performing any great achievement." The officers recognized that they needed a commander, but Charles McDowell, the senior man present, was "too slow" and there was too much rivalry between these local warlords for any one of them to be chosen. So they appointed a committee to decide on tactics and asked William Campbell, who had the advantage of being a Virginian, to serve as officer of the day and see that the committee's plans were executed. As an afterthought they sent McDowell to fetch Daniel Morgan or William Davidson— both generals—to see if one of them would take overall command.

The committee's first decision was to track down Ferguson and "pursue him unremittingly" with as many men as had horses and firearms, leaving the others to follow. Just over nine hundred men set out at daylight on October 6, 1780, and at the Cowpens, a place where a local woman named Hannah had pastured her cows, they met up with Colonel James Williams of South Carolina and four hundred men and pushed on that night and the next day through heavy rains. Sixteen-year-old James Collins wrote that each man slept in his blanket and ate whatever he could lay hands on—usually raw turnips and a mess of parched corn. With that and two or three spoonfuls of honey, washed down with a good draft of cold water, he said, a man "could pass longer without suffering than with any other diet he could use."

October 7 was gray and overcast, with a scrim of rain, and the men reached Kings Mountain after noon, dismounted, secured their loose gear to saddles, and hitched their horses before falling in behind their officers. Ferguson, they heard, had announced that "he defied God Almighty and all the rebels out of Hell to overcome him," and Collins recalled that each colonel delivered a short speech to his men, telling those who might be frightened to clear out at once. The teenager said, "I would willingly have been excused, for my feelings were not the most pleasant," but after giving it some thought, "I could not swallow the appellation of coward. . . ." About three o'clock the rebels moved to the attack in four columns, and as they reached the foot of the mountain two columns deployed to the right, two to the left, so that they eventually surrounded the enemy. Each man put three or four musket balls in his mouth to prevent thirst and to be ready to reload in a hurry.

The loyalists' position, which Ferguson had thought impregnable, proved to have its disadvantage: the summit was bare ground, while the slopes of the mountain below were covered with trees, affording the attackers good cover. Another piece of luck for them was that when the enemy opened fire from the heights above them, they aimed too high, as is often the case in such circumstances, and the over-mountain men continued to climb. When they came out in the open, Campbell was heard shouting, "Here they are, boys! Shout like hell and fight like devils!" A charge from Ferguson's troops drove them back, but the determined rebels were coming on fast, moving from tree to tree, in a tactic that won the battle; one defender believed that Ferguson's position on top of the mountain would have enabled his men to oppose a much superior force successfully, but the rebels took shelter among the trees and fought in their favorite manner, dodging behind cover, firing, and running quickly to another tree before anyone could draw a bead on them. Another sixteen-year-old private, Thomas Young, was barefooted and found himself out between his regiment and the loyalist lines. Behind him he could see the rebels with white paper stuck in their hats; ahead were the Tories, with pine knots in their headgear for identification.

In the thick of the fight he saw Colonel Williams charge by at full speed. Near the summit a ball hit the officer's horse below the jaw, and the animal began stamping as if it had fallen into a yellow jacket's nest. Williams threw the reins over the horse's head, leaped off, and dashed ahead. Within minutes Young heard someone shout that the colonel was shot, and he ran up the hill to help him, "for I loved him as a father. He had ever been so kind to me and almost always carried a cake in his pocket for me and his little son, Joseph." Someone sprinkled water on Williams's face and revived him. His son Daniel was holding him in his arms, and the mortally wounded Williams called out, "For God's sake, boys, don't give up the hill!"

Over the roar of battle, the shouting, and the racket of men crashing through the underbrush, both sides could hear the piercing shriek of the silver whistle Patrick Ferguson used to maneuver his men. Mounted on a clever little white horse, he seemed to be everywhere, wearing a checkered hunting shirt over his uniform, the whistle in his teeth, and a sword in his left hand. Suddenly, the whistle was heard no more. Ferguson drooped over the horse's neck with a rifle bullet in his body, his sword broken, his face bleeding badly, and one foot caught in a stirrup. His men lifted him from the horse and propped him against a tree, where he died. At that, the fight went out of his men, and his second in command, Captain Abraham DePeyster, known as "the Bull Dog's pup," ordered a white flag shown. Ferguson had been the only British soldier in the battle; all the rest, on both sides, were Americans.

At the moment of Ferguson's death Colonel Shelby gained the eastern summit and drove the defenders along the ridge until they were forced down the western end, where their comrades had been fighting Cleveland's and Williams's men. Terrified, the loyalists hunkered down behind their wagons and continued to fight until Shelby ordered them to throw down their arms. But there was no staying the rebel militia, who continued to shoot, yelling, "Buford! Buford! Tarleton's Quarter!" Two men who came out carrying white flags were shot dead despite Campbell's cry, "For God's sake, quit! It's murder to shoot any more!" Finally the carnage ended, but the overmountain men stood in a circle four-deep, glowering at their prisoners, calling out the names of those who were known for atrocities. When the fight finally ended, the Tories were found to have lost 157 men killed, 163 wounded, and 698 taken prisoner—every single man of Ferguson's command—against rebel losses of 28 killed and 62 wounded. The battle had taken less than an hour.

As darkness fell over the field, the cries of dying men were terrible to hear, for they had neither medical aid nor water. The next morning James Collins was witness to a pitiful scene: wives and children of the Tories came in great numbers to seek out their husbands, fathers, and brothers in the heaps of dead or among the wounded. The burials were badly handled, Collins later recalled; the bodies were thrown into piles and covered with logs, bark, and rocks, but without proper covering they were prey to a large number of wolves, hogs from the neighborhood, and ravenous dogs that persisted even though many of them were shot.

On the evening of the battle the rebels distributed the plunder by lot, and Collins and his father "drew two fine horses, two guns, and some articles of clothing with a share of powder and lead." Afterward, when the rebel combatants returned to their tents or homes, "It seemed like a calm after a heavy storm . . . and for a short time every man could visit his home or his neighbor without being afraid."

The end of the battle brought no respite to the defeated Tories. Hundreds of them were marched off toward the main patriot army, which was then in Hillsboro, but despite Colonel Campbell's general orders to officers of all ranks to "restrain the disorderly manner of slaughtering and disturbing the prisoners," the furies had been set loose and these rebels wanted revenge against their former loyalist neighbors. Men were beaten, slashed with swords, and after a committee of colonels passed judgment on some of them for "breaking open houses, killing the men, turning the men and women out of doors, and burning the houses," nine were executed. En route to Hillsboro a good many prisoners escaped, but enough were left that Governor Thomas Jefferson of Virginia was asked to help in disposing of them.

When George Washington learned of the victory, he observed, "This advantage will in all probability have a very happy influence upon the successive operations in that quarter." Happy it proved. The loyalists were by then too dispirited to turn out in support of Cornwallis. The British general had ordered Tarleton to take his light infantry and his legion to aid Ferguson, but on the way news of that officer's "melancholy fate" reached him, and when he reported this to headquarters he was recalled immediately. Lord Cornwallis's hopes for conquering all of North Carolina were dashed, and October 14 found him retreating to the south.

To add to the earl's woes, the weather turned foul in anticipation of winter; heavy rains, changing the red clay roads to vast slimy mudholes, slowed his army to a creep. With rebel militia harassing his march and stealing horses, wagons disappearing and food along with them, hundreds of men took sick, many of them from sleeping on the cold, wet ground without tents. Cornwallis himself was laid up with a fever and confined to a cheerless, comfortless hospital wagon to contemplate his plight and reckon with the certainty that his plans for a winter campaign were entirely upset. As he wrote to General Clinton, he could no longer count on assistance from loyalists in and around Ninety-Six:* they were "so totally disheartened by the defeat of Ferguson that, of the whole district, we could with difficulty assemble 100 [men]; and even those, I am convinced, would not have made the smallest difference if they had been attacked."

---

*Ninety-Six was an important post, so-named (erroneously) because it was thought to be ninety-six miles from Fort Prince George. In fact, the distance was sixty-five miles or so, but the name remained.

5

A LITTLE PERSEVERING
AND DETERMINED ARMY

❦

Nathanael Greene had suffered one disappointment after another, having anticipated seeing his beloved wife, Kitty, after their long separation, only to be ordered to the South before they could meet. In a parting letter to her from Fishkill, he wrote, "I am at this moment setting off for the southward, having kept expresses flying all night to see if I could hear anything of you—I have been almost distracted, I wanted to see you so much before I set out." But he was out of luck, and after leaving Philadelphia on November 2 he conferred with Washington, Knox, and other old comrades-in-arms in Preakness, New Jersey, before heading south with the feeling of going to his doom, so dire was most news from his destination.

The situation in the southern department was truly disheartening. Writing to François Barbé-Marbois, secretary to France's ambassador, Alexander Hamilton pulled no punches: "The want of money makes us want everything else, even intelligence," adding, "I confess I view our affairs in a gloomy light." He understood that a congress of neutral powers would meet during the coming winter to "mediate a peace." If so, "God send it—we want one."

Greene reached what was left of Gates's army in Charlotte a month later, having stopped on his long journey to visit the Maryland and Virginia assemblies and beg their support. Though they promised what help they could find, it was clear that not much would be forthcoming, since both state treasuries were so impoverished "they could not furnish forage" for Greene's horses.

Bitterly, he wrote a friend that along the way he had seen people "engaged in pursuit of pleasure, almost regardless of their danger, public credit lost, and every man excusing himself from giving the least aid to Government, from an apprehension that they would get no return for any advance."

Greene, who was to end the war with a military reputation second only to Washington's, was born near Warwick, Rhode Island, in 1742. One of six sons of a well-to-do Quaker preacher who owned an ironworks, Nathanael lost his mother when he was eleven. He grew up working on the family farm, schooled by an itinerant tutor, but only briefly, because his father was prejudiced against book learning. Not until he was seventeen or eighteen did he discover the world of books, and from then on he was seldom without one. In 1770 his father died, and he and his brothers continued to operate the ironworks, which became one of the state's largest businesses.

The onrush of events in the worsening quarrel between Britain and its colonies soon tested Greene's belief in the pacifist teachings of the Society of Friends, and he was read out of the church for failure to conform to its principles. Recently married to Catherine Littlefield, known as Kitty, he organized a military unit called the Kentish Guards, but was not elected an officer because he walked with a pronounced limp from a stiff knee, which some thought unbefitting for a military man. Greene was sensitive about his affliction, which had been with him since childhood, but he swallowed his pride and settled for the rank of private at a time, ironically, when the state assembly chose him to serve on a committee that was revising the military laws of the province. He traveled frequently to Boston, where he spent hours watching the redcoats drilling on the Common, examining the British fortification of Boston Neck, and whiling away what leisure time he had in Henry Knox's London Bookstore, purchasing military manuals and discussing military science with the proprietor, who would become Washington's artillerist and Greene's lifelong friend.

Greene was a husky man of above-average height, whose portrait by Charles Willson Peale shows his friendly face, a broad, high forehead, somewhat narrow, penetrating eyes, a thin nose, and large, sensuous mouth. The Quaker's knowledge of military matters and his perceptive, analytical mind impressed everyone with whom he came in contact, and Rhode Island selected him to command its armed force, giving him the rank of brigadier general. During the 1775–76 siege of Boston he played a valuable role in organizing the raw troops, and when George Washington arrived to take over the newly christened Continental Army, he and Greene hit it off at once. Washington considered Greene's soldiers the best officered of all those around Boston; certainly they had the highest morale, and many officers, including Henry Knox, regarded Greene as nothing short of a military genius.

In less than a year, he was in charge of the troops on Long Island, a key to the defense of New York, and Washington's aide Alexander Hamilton observed that the commander in chief's discerning eye "marked him out as the object of his confidence. . . . He gained it, and he preserved it, amidst all the checkered varieties of military vicissitude." In assigning him to the southern command, Washington knew that Greene would be up against just about every vicissitude a military man could face, but he was utterly confident in him, knowing that he was a good manager of men, extremely intelligent, patient, resourceful, and without question the best man for the onerous task ahead.

Greene reached Charlotte and Gates's former command, only to find a ghost of an army with "the appearance of the troops . . . wretched beyond description," suffering—as the army did everywhere—from an appalling lack of food and clothing. Gates had lost the confidence of his officers; the troops were undisciplined and were so accustomed to plundering as to be a terror to the local inhabitants. Summing up the deficiencies in a letter to Joseph Reed, a former aide to Washington, Greene said, "The wants of this army are so numerous and various that the shortest way of telling you is to inform you that we have nothing. . . ." He was doing everything in his power to bring order to the army, "but it is all an up-hill business." As in the North, the militia here, "like the locusts of Egypt, have eaten up everything, and the expense has been so enormous that it has ruined the currency of the State."

It was especially discouraging to note that in a state so large the powers of government were so weak that everybody did pretty much as they pleased. Greene believed the strength and resources of the region were greatly overrated, and observed that large numbers of the inhabitants were moving away, with the army forced to exist on charity and daily collections, mostly consisting of Indian meal and beef. Politically, the people were divided, with Whigs and Tories pursuing each other with "savage fury." By contrast with the back-country people, who were bold and daring, those in the tidewater region were sickly and, unfortunately, made indifferent militia. Greene noted that Daniel Morgan was in the area of the Broad River "with a little flying army," while Colonel William Washington was not far from Morgan and had just defeated a party of Tories. He had plans for both those officers, and as for his own position, Greene described it as "a camp of repose, for the purpose of repairing our wagons, recruiting our horses, and disciplining the troops."

On December 20 Greene made the risky decision to divide his small army, ignoring the military axiom that splitting an inferior force when faced with a superior one is to hazard having the enemy destroy one and then turn on the other. Yet Greene, as always, had thought through his dilemma and his options. In no way could he stand up to Cornwallis in a pitched battle, nor did he dare give the enemy or the Carolinians—or his own troops, for that matter—the impression that he was retreating. By sending his left wing west of the Catawba River, he would improve his chances of provisioning both wings of his army while their presence would protect and encourage the local folk.

The man to whom he gave command of the left wing, composed of his light infantry, was as close to being a legend as the Continental Army possessed. Daniel Morgan, who had spent most of his forty-five years on the rugged Virginia frontier as a farmer and teamster, drawing freight between the isolated mountain communities, was a six-foot, two-hundred-pound, barrel-chested giant, with a big smile on his friendly face and a famous temper. He carried a personal grudge against the king of England that went back to the French and Indian War, when he made the mistake of hitting a British officer who had slapped him with the flat of his sword. For this he was sentenced to receive 500 lashes on his broad, muscled back, and he liked to boast that the redcoats still owed him one, for he bore only 499 stripes—someone had miscounted. In addition to those scars, he had lost all his teeth on one side when an Indian bullet went through his neck and mouth, leaving an ugly scooped-out scar.

The old wagoner had been with General Edward Braddock's doomed expedition in 1755, along with a host of other now-famous individuals such as George Washington, General Thomas Gage, Greene's first cousin Daniel Boone, and others. He was a born leader and was his Virginia county's unanimous choice to lead their riflemen to Boston in 1775, after which he fought with Arnold in the attack on Quebec and was taken prisoner and later exchanged. In 1777 he was detached with his corps of riflemen to join Gates and was instrumental in the defeat of Burgoyne at Saratoga. Like Benedict Arnold, Morgan resented being passed over, denied the rank he felt he had earned, and was so crippled by arthritis and sciatica that he returned home to Virginia. But he could remain there no longer when he learned of Cornwallis's devastating victory over Gates at Camden. Belatedly, Congress made him a brigadier general, and now he was preparing for the battle of his life.

When Cornwallis had recovered from his fever and heard that Morgan was threatening his post at Ninety-Six, he immediately detached Colonel Banastre Tarleton with 750 men and a pair of three-pounders to push Morgan "to the utmost," forcing him to fight or withdraw. Both Greene and Morgan got wind of this, and the former sent a message to the old wagoner: "Colonel Tarleton is said to be on his way to pay you a visit. I doubt not but he will have a decent reception and a proper dismission."

The infamous Banastre Tarleton, a stocky redhead whose very name was anathema to southern patriots, came from a wealthy Liverpool family and was educated there and at Oxford, after which a cornet's commission was purchased for him in the king's Dragoon Guards in 1775. His unsavory reputation grew in 1780 after a series of victories that earned him the names "Bloody Tarleton" and "Butcher" for his savage attacks. When the hard-driving Tarleton came close enough to Morgan to ferret out his movements, he realized that the American was in no position to menace Ninety-Six and ordered his lieutenant to forward his baggage—"but no women"—while notifying Cornwallis that he planned to destroy Morgan or drive him in the direction of Kings Mountain. That way, if Morgan escaped, Cornwallis would have an opportunity to head him off.

Meanwhile, Morgan's scouts had tracked the British cavalryman, and the American was reacting with moves of his own—first to Thicketty Creek, then, on the evening of January 16—raw and cold at sundown—he reached Cowpens. This was where Morgan decided to stand and fight, and he chose the position "at the risk of its wearing the face of a retreat" though it provided security in case he "should . . . be unfortunate."

In the fading light of day, Morgan and some of his officers rode back and forth across the pastures, and he liked what he saw: a long, wide opening with some scattered trees, sloping upward, then a dip, then another upward slope to a ridge, behind which was a grassy swale, deep enough that riders on horseback could not be seen from the approach below.

Five miles behind the site was the Broad River, and the old wagoner sent his baggage there. He had no boats, so crossing the river was out of the question; his militia would have to fight, and he had in mind a very important and unorthodox role for them. During the night he went from one group of volunteers to another; one of them recollected:

> [Morgan] helped them to fix their swords, joked with them about their sweethearts, told them to keep in good spirits, and the day would be ours. And long after I laid down, he was going about among the soldiers encouraging them and telling them that the old wagoner could crack his whip over Ben [Tarleton] in the morning, as sure as they lived.
>
> "Just hold up your heads, boys, three fires," he would say, "and you are free, and then when you return to your homes, how the old folks will bless you, and the girls kiss you for your gallant conduct."
>
> I don't believe he slept a wink that night.

The sign and countersign for the next day were "Fire" and "Sword," with a suggestion that the Lord was on the rebels' side, and during the night hours small parties of militia arrived in camp, bringing tales of Tarleton's cruelty and boasting of how they would stop him.

Tarleton had bivouacked for the night about twelve miles from Morgan's position, and an hour before daylight American scouts reported him within five miles, coming on fast. Although Morgan was suffering such pain that he could hardly sit his horse, he was moving among his men, telling the militia again that all he wanted was a couple of good volleys, after which they could fall back to the next line. The undergrowth on the battleground had been cropped short by grazing cattle, and the trees—mostly red oak, hickory, and pine—were scattered so they offered little hindrance to his infantry's movements. Morgan was sufficiently confident of his plan that he posted militia in the front line, but the men he chose were all good riflemen from North and South Carolina and Virginia, and they were commanded by a superb fighter: Andrew Pickens, the South Carolina guerrilla leader. A taciturn, homely man, Pickens was a staunch member of the Presbyterian Church who was described by a contemporary as a fellow who would "first take the words out of his mouth, between his fingers, and examine them before he uttered them."

Morgan told Pickens's men to take shelter in or behind trees and "Shoot for the epaulets, boys! Shoot for the epaulets!"—picking off every British officer they could before falling back to the line behind them. There, spread out in a line about three hundred yards wide, were his least experienced troops—militiamen from the Carolinas, who had been ordered to hold their fire until they could see the buttons on the redcoats' uniforms and then to shoot three times, aiming low, before they filed off to the left and took shelter behind a small hill.

In a third line, on rising ground, were three hundred Maryland and Delaware Continentals with fixed bayonets—Morgan's best troops—bolstered on either side by seasoned militiamen from Virginia and Georgia, many of them former Continentals who had reenlisted and returned. These men—all of them under Lieutenant Colonel John Eager Howard—had strict orders not to fire until Morgan gave the word. To their rear, behind another hillock, were Colonel William Washington's cavalry and some mounted infantry under Lieutenant Colonel James McCall.

While his men waited in various stages of nervousness, slapping their hands together to keep warm in the bitter cold, Morgan rode slowly through the lines, telling them to sit down and "ease your joints" to calm them. He knew how to talk to soldiers, Morgan did, and it was said that he visited every unit in his thousand-man force, explaining to them exactly how they were going to beat "Benny" Tarleton. Shortly after sunrise the enemy force came into view, and as they hurried to form a battle line they shed their gear, prodded by Tarleton, who wanted immediate action. "It was the most beautiful line I ever saw," said the sixteen-year-old private Thomas Young, who remembered that the redcoats sent up a shout.

At that, Morgan yelled to his men, "They give us the British halloo, boys. Give them the Indian halloo, by God!" That produced a series of loud war whoops, and the old wagoner trotted along the lines, bucking up the men, reminding them not to fire at the redcoats till they could see the whites of their eyes. Tarleton had sent fifty of his three hundred cavalrymen to probe the American position, judging from past experience that the untrained rebels would run, but the riflemen behind trees opened fire on the advancing British horsemen and emptied fifteen saddles. When the other riders saw that, they reined in their mounts and galloped back to Tarleton's lines. Seeing those empty saddles convinced the commander that this was not going to be as easy as he had thought, but at the sight of Morgan's first line retiring toward the second, as if retreating, he deployed his infantrymen in formal battle formation, with his two small fieldpieces in the center and two hundred cavalry and the kilted Highlanders in reserve.

These British had had little sleep the night before. They began their march at 3 A.M., and for the next five hours were slogging through the darkness, on sodden roads, into swamps, streams, and rough terrain until they finally came in sight of the Americans. They were tired and had barely formed up when their impetuous commander ordered them to move forward. Stepping off as if on a parade ground, they were an impressive sight—the red-coated British regulars, Tarleton's British legion in green, bayonets and cavalry sabers glinting in the rising sun. As Tarleton said later, "the animation of the officers and the alacrity of the soldiers afforded the most promising assurances of success."

Facing them were some 450 militiamen in buckskin or homespun, for most of whom a formal battle like this was a wholly new and terrifying experience. But the moment for which Morgan had planned so carefully was upon them, and the old wagoner continued to ride back and forth behind them, telling them again and again not to fire. On the British came, closer and closer, and Pickens's men took careful aim with their rifles or muskets, and when the oncoming bayonets were a hundred yards away they got the signal they were waiting for and let loose a deadly blast, reloaded, and fired again, killing most of the British who fell in battle that day. There were great gaps in the British line, but they kept moving forward while Pickens's troops, according to orders, ran across to the American left, where the Continentals waited. For soldiers on the right, it was a long way to run, and fifty British dragoons were thundering down on them, racing in for the kill.

Suddenly, seemingly out of nowhere, Washington's and McCall's horsemen appeared, sabers waving in the air, and charged into the flank of Tarleton's cavalry, who were outnumbered at this moment almost three to one. In moments ten British dragoons were dead or wounded and the rest fled, while the American militiamen who had come so near destruction were still intact, off on one side of the hillock.

Convinced that the rebels were retreating, the British infantry came on at a run but they were now confronted by veterans—the three hundred Continentals and former Continentals, who made up the main American line. Kneeling for greater accuracy, they aimed low, exchanging volley after volley with the redcoats in a firefight that continued for half an hour. At that point Tarleton called on his reserve, the Highlanders, and ordered them forward on his left. With bagpipes keening, they advanced toward the side of the hill where the Continentals were engaged. Seeing that he would be outflanked, John Eager Howard ordered the company on his extreme right to wheel about so as to face this new threat, but somehow the order was misunderstood and the men began heading for the rear. Other soldiers, seeing this, assumed that an order to retreat had been given, and followed them.

Morgan confronted Howard, demanding to know what was going on, and when Howard convinced him that the men were not retreating, the commander told him that he would pick a place where they could establish a new line.

Tarleton was certain that the rebels were on the run now and decided to throw everything he had at them, including the legion cavalry, who were not yet committed. Infantry and cavalry alike, eager to be in at the kill, began racing up the slope in complete disorder, and William Washington, who was out in front of the American lines and off to the right, could see the confusion of the British and sent word to Morgan that the enemy was behaving like a mob. Give them one fire, he proposed, and he would charge them. Morgan received this message just as Pickens's riflemen, who had, incredibly, made a complete circuit of the entire battlefield, suddenly appeared on his right. That was all he needed to make his decision. He gave an order to the Continentals: "Face about, give them one fire, and the day is ours!"

By this time the British, running forward wildly, as if every man wanted the honor of winning this fight, had appeared on the crest of the slope and were pounding downhill in a mad rush, about fifty yards from the Americans, when Morgan's order was obeyed. The whole line of Delaware and Maryland Continentals, plus the riflemen at the ends of their line, faced about and fired in a burst of flame and blinding smoke, shooting from the hip at the onrushing redcoats, who were stopped dead. From the right side, Pickens's men were firing, Howard yelled, "Give them the bayonets!" and the startled British, in complete disarray, broke ranks, threw down their weapons and cartouche boxes, and made for the wagon road. The elated Thomas Young said it was "the prettiest sort of running."

Lieutenant Roderick Mackenzie of the Highlanders, who was wounded in the battle and was extremely critical of Tarleton's decisions, described the chaos. When the British fell back, it "communicated a panic to others, which soon became general: a total rout ensued. Two hundred and fifty horse which had not been engaged, fled through the woods with the utmost precipitation, bearing down such officers as opposed their flight. . . ."

Although it was clear that the British were defeated, Tarleton chose to attack with no more than fifty horse against Washington's cavalry, who were supported by Continentals, and his entire force was repulsed. Before it ended, the hundred Highlanders fought on until nine of their officers were dead or wounded, and then surrendered.

One of them, a Major McArthur, spoke with Colonel Howard, who expressed surprise at the precipitate manner in which Tarleton sent his troops into battle. Nothing better could be expected, said the major, "when troops were commanded by a rash, foolish boy." The defeat of the cocky young cavalryman at Cowpens, with the loss of many fine officers and veteran troops, released a lot of pent-up anger of senior military men in the British army—enough that Tarleton submitted his resignation, which was rejected by Cornwallis.

Colonel Howard also talked with Captain Duncanson of the British First Grenadiers, who handed him his sword and stood there, pulling at Howard's saddle. The colonel was annoyed at this and asked what he was doing, to which the Briton replied that they had orders from Tarleton to give no quarter and he feared the rebels would treat him accordingly. Howard reassured him. As Morgan was to say, in contrast to "Tarleton's Quarter," "Not a man was killed, wounded, or even insulted after he had surrendered."

When the fighting ceased, the extent of Morgan's victory could be seen. The British lost 110 men killed, including 39 officers; 229 were wounded and captured, and 550 others surrendered. The stunning defeat cost Cornwallis nearly one-fourth of his entire army in the South. In addition to the prisoners, the booty included the two three-pounders, 800 muskets, 100 horses, 35 wagonloads of baggage, 60 black slaves, enormous quantities of ammunition, and "all their music"—their prized band instruments. Against this, Morgan, who had gone into battle with 800 men—two-thirds of them militia—lost 12 killed and 60 wounded against Tarleton's 1,150 veterans.

Tarleton and some fifty mounted men were the only British to escape, and they were hotly pursued by William Washington, who rode well ahead of his own cavalrymen in his eagerness to take the man known as the "Butcher." He caught up with the enemy, and Tarleton and two other officers turned suddenly and came at him with sabers. Washington lashed out at one and broke his own sword in half when their blades met. The other officer with Tarleton raised his saber, but fortuitously Washington's senior sergeant galloped up, parried the blow on his own weapon, and then wounded the man in his sword arm. Tarleton headed for Washington, swung his saber, which the American managed to ward off with his broken sword, and with other rebel cavalrymen almost upon him, Tarleton fired his pistol at Washington but missed the American and wounded his horse. Then the Green Dragoon raced off.

Morgan's stunning victory was cause for rejoicing and celebration by patriots everywhere—"a healing cordial to our drooping spirits," as Congressman John Mathews wrote to Nathanael Greene. It was not only a tactical masterpiece, but astonishing in that a majority of Morgan's outnumbered force consisted of untrained militia, who had overcome Tarleton's veterans. Best of all, the most despised British officer in America had been defeated and humiliated—an achievement not lost on the British at home. Gloomily, Horace Walpole wrote, "America is once more not quite ready to be conquered, although every now and then we fancy it is. Tarleton is defeated, Cornwallis is checked, and Arnold not sure of having betrayed his friends to much purpose."

For Lord Cornwallis, it was a body blow. He had been confident that Tarleton would destroy Morgan's force handily, and was obviously undone when the cavalryman reported to him the day after the battle. An eyewitness said that the earl "leaned forward on his sword as he listened to his subordinate. Angered by what he heard, he pressed so hard that the sword snapped in two, and he swore loudly that he would recapture Morgan's prisoners no matter what the cost." Later, writing to Lord Rawdon, whom he had left behind in Camden, he confided, "The late affair has almost broke my heart."

In Greene's camp at Cheraw the electrifying news was delivered to the general by an excited Major Edward Giles, Morgan's aide, and the troops went wild. Giles wrote Morgan to say, "We have had a feu de joie,* drunk all your healths, swore you were the finest fellows on earth, and love you if possible more than ever." He added that victory

---

*The military's way of celebrating good news: the troops lined up and fired their muskets into the air in sequence, from one end of the line to the other.

had been celebrated with what were undoubtedly generous portions of spirits known as cherry bounce.

★   ★   ★

DANIEL MORGAN WAS acutely aware that he had no time to celebrate. His position was precarious, to say the least, since he didn't know where Cornwallis was—only that he would be on the march as quickly as possible, determined to pounce on the rebels and liberate their prisoners. Within two hours after the last shot was fired at Cowpens, the exhausted old wagoner, in such agony that he could ride only at a walk, set his face to the north.

When Cornwallis learned to his dismay of Tarleton's defeat, he was about twenty-five miles to the south, waiting for Major General Alexander Leslie to arrive with reinforcements from New York. He decided to pursue Morgan immediately, but the army was not ready to march until two days later, the 19th of January. Figuring that Morgan would stay near the Broad River or perhaps attack the garrison at Ninety-Six, Cornwallis marched in a northwesterly direction, hoping to cut him off. However, Morgan had headed on another tangent, and when Cornwallis, realizing his mistake, arrived at Ramsour's Mills, it was to learn that his foe had passed that way two days earlier and by now had crossed the Catawba, putting two rivers between them. On that same day Cornwallis wrote to Lord Rawdon, "My situation is most critical. I see infinite danger in proceeding, but certain ruin in retreating. I am therefore determined to go on." What he did not say was that he had burned his bridges behind him, by destroying the fortifications in Charleston and taking with him all the matériel he was to need during the campaign.

Realizing that the only way he could possibly catch up with Morgan was to lighten the loads his soldiers were carrying, he made the decision to destroy all extraneous baggage—burning the men's tents, all the wagons and their contents except for ammunition, medical supplies, hospital stores, and salt, even food that could not be carried in the men's haversacks and, unkindest cut of all, the rum. While anguished troops looked on, casks were stove in and the liquor was poured out on the ground. The earl tried to set an example by consigning the headquarters baggage to the flames, but that carried little weight with some men; significantly, many of his Hessian troops and some of the British—perhaps 250 in all—deserted after these extreme economy measures.

At Gilbert Town Morgan had detached Pickens and most of the militia, plus some of William Washington's cavalry, to march the prisoners to a ford across the Catawba, whence they were to be sent to Virginia. The old wagoner and his Continentals rested at their camp until February 1, when Pickens rejoined them, and in the meantime Greene, having learned about Morgan's plans on January 25, could see how desperate the situation was and dispatched a courier to Lieutenant Colonel Edward Carrington, his quartermaster general, telling him to assemble boats on the Dan River to ferry the entire army across. The race for the Dan was on.

That river, which was now the goal of both armies, lay along the boundary between North Carolina and Virginia. Greene put his army under the command of Brigadier General Isaac Huger and ordered him to move up the Pee Dee and the Yadkin (which were the same river) as far as Salisbury, North Carolina, where Morgan would rendezvous with him. Meanwhile Greene, with an aide, a guide, and a handful of dragoons, set off through Tory-infested country on a 125-mile ride. When Greene arrived at Morgan's camp, the two had a heated discussion over their next move: Morgan arguing for a retreat into the Blue Ridge Mountains where the troops would be safe, Greene with another scheme in mind. When Morgan informed him that Cornwallis had destroyed his baggage and probably intended to march north, Greene was elated. "Then he is ours!" he exclaimed.

Greene wrote at once to Huger, describing Cornwallis's plan as a "mad scheme of pushing through the country," moving farther and farther from his supply bases. Behind the American general's confidence was the belief that he could keep just far enough ahead of

Cornwallis to tempt him to follow along, day after day, ever hopeful of catching up and forcing the rebels to fight. It was a huge risk he ran, and Morgan told him so, saying he would not answer for the consequences if the plan failed. "You won't have to," Greene replied, "for I shall take the measure upon myself."

This was orange-clay country, broken by the S-curves and oxbows of the winding Yadkin, with visibility that was often poor on account of heavy fogs. The river, like so many other streams, was a deep-brown color from the clay of the banks, and it was bordered by fertile bottomland and low-lying hills. At the Catawba River crossing, where the British hoped to outflank Morgan, they were delayed by high water and rebel militiamen, but persevered and reached the other shore without great loss, only to discover that Morgan had marched all night and part of the next day, reaching the Yadkin, thirty miles away. The experience, one of his men observed, was "very unpleasant . . . it having rained incessantly all night, which rendered the roads almost inaccessible." Meanwhile Greene waited until midnight for the militia at the appointed rendezvous, and upon learning that those troops had been hopelessly dispersed, he rode on alone to Salisbury. There he dismounted at Steele's Tavern and was greeted inside by an acquaintance.

"What? Alone, Greene?"

"Yes," the general replied, "alone, tired, hungry, and penniless."

He was overhead by Mrs. Steele, who brought him breakfast and two small bags of hard currency, saying he needed them more than she did. Indeed he did. Mrs. Steele could not have known it, but those two bags contained all the money that was possessed just then by the army of the southern department of the United States of America.

★ ★ ★

AS NATHANAEL GREENE wrote the commander in chief, Huger was prevented by "heavy rains, deep creeks, bad roads, [and] poor horses" from reaching Salisbury in time to meet Greene and Morgan, so he was instructed to rejoin the old wagoner at Guilford Courthouse. Morgan's men were on short rations but made a forced march through driving rain and sleet toward their new destination. When they reached Guilford, they had marched forty-eight miles in the past forty-seven hours, in what could only be described as abominable conditions. At Guilford Huger and his ragged, emaciated soldiers, most of whom were barefoot and were sharing a single blanket for every four men, met them, and with the Dan still seventy miles distant Greene was faced with a new dilemma. Daniel Morgan was simply unable to continue; the agony of his sciatica was complicated by such painful hemorrhoids that he could no longer sit a horse, and he wanted to head for home. Reluctantly, Greene gave him a leave of absence, and General Morgan, who had rendered invaluable service to the cause from 1775 to 1781, from Boston and Quebec to South Carolina, now vanished from the scene of action.

In his place Greene put another experienced, dependable man: Colonel Otho Williams from Maryland, who had begun his military career at Boston in 1775 as a lieutenant in the Franklin County rifle corps. He was another of the hard-core cadre who had started at the beginning and was still fighting six years later, having been with the unlucky Canadian expedition and at Fort Washington, where he was captured. After being exchanged, he marched to South Carolina with Baron Johann Kalb and was one of the last Maryland Continentals to leave the field at the disastrous Battle of Camden. Another welcome addition to the army was Colonel Thaddeus Kosciuszko, a Polish volunteer and engineer who had selected the site and supervised the building of fortifications at Saratoga.

In charge of the light troops and cavalry, which now included Henry Lee's legion, Otho Williams headed out on February 10 as if bound for the upper fords of the Dan, but this was a feint planned by Greene, who believed that was the direction Cornwallis would take, rather than crossing the river below, where he would have to have boats. Greene, of course, had already arranged for boats to be at the lower ford, ready for his army. One reason he chose that location was its proximity to more populated areas of Virginia, where reinforcements could join him; another was that if Benedict Arnold planned to join Cornwallis, that was the route he would probably take, and nothing would please Greene more than to be there to greet him.

The march to the Dan was a nightmare—day after day of rain, turning the red clay roads into slippery troughs. To keep from freezing, both armies had to have fires, and the men slept in the open since the only tents were used to keep provisions and powder dry. Greene's soldiers had nothing but rags for clothing; hundreds were without shoes and suffering in agony from lacerated, half-frozen feet. Unhappily, only 200 of the expected reinforcements from Virginia turned up, and as he took stock of his force, Greene could count on a few more than 2,000, of whom 1,426 were reliable Continentals, in contrast to Cornwallis's 2,500 to 3,000 veterans.

Williams and the light troops had turned right and were following Greene's men on a parallel road, ready to swing into action if the British came too close. He kept just far enough ahead of Cornwallis so the latter could not get between him and Greene, and to do so he kept half his men on patrol at night while the others slept, then he got them marching at 3 A.M. to get far enough ahead to cook the meal that had to last until the following morning. Even so, Cornwallis's vanguard was almost always in sight, though never close enough to bring on a fight.

What was at stake here was of enormous importance to the rebel cause, for if Greene's small army were destroyed, Cornwallis would unquestionably join forces with Generals Arnold and William Phillips—a tough career officer who had been Burgoyne's artillerist in the Saratoga campaign and who, with General Friedrich Riedesel, had been exchanged for General Benjamin Lincoln. Cornwallis could then release all the prisoners surrendered by Burgoyne at Saratoga, who had been incarcerated in Virginia, plus those captured at Cowpens, and the war in the South would be all but over except for some partisan fighting. Virginia, the Carolinas, and Georgia would be securely in enemy hands.

One evening, just after dark, Williams's men glimpsed a row of campfires ahead of them and assumed it must be Greene's men, which meant they would have to fight the British pursuers to give Greene's troops a chance to flee. Fortunately, what they saw proved to be campfires lit by Greene's soldiers two nights earlier, which had been kept burning by volunteers in the hope that Williams's men could use them while they rested. But there was no rest in store for these fellows; the redcoats were hot on their trail. A messenger from Greene rode up and handed Williams a note, stating that the general had arranged for his baggage and stores to be ferried across the Dan. Meantime, the message continued, "The North Carolina militia have all deserted us, except about 80 men. . . . You have the flower of the army, don't expose the men too much, lest our situation grow more critical." That was easier said than done, for Williams and his 700 soldiers, consisting of the light troops and Light-Horse Harry Lee's cavalry, were a long way from the Dan, a troop of Tarleton's horse was on their heels, and the rest of Cornwallis's force was only four miles away.

At midnight Williams had his men on the march again, having heard from Greene: "4 o'clock. Follow our route. I have not slept four hours since you left me, so great has been my solicitude to prepare for the worst." After a brief halt, they were on the move once more, half frozen, shuffling along the cold, muddy roads, when a courier rode up with yet another message from Greene: "Irwin's ferry, twelve past 5 o'clock. All our troops are over and the stage is clear. . . . I am ready to receive you and give you a hearty welcome." The word was passed down the ranks, and Williams's entire command shouted for joy at the top of their lungs. General Charles O'Hara, riding at the head of Cornwallis's vanguard, which was now well behind their prey, heard them and knew what the cheering meant. Williams detached Lee's cavalry to delay the British while he marched his troops to Irwin's ferry. They arrived as the sun was setting on February 14, having traveled forty miles in sixteen hours under all but impossible conditions.

It was dark when Lee's exhausted horsemen finally arrived at the south bank of the Dan between eight and nine o'clock, just as the boats returned from delivering Williams's infantrymen to the Virginia shore. Lee's men clambered aboard the boats, the horses swam alongside, and they reached the opposite bank just as the British van appeared. The water was too high for the enemy to cross without boats, and there were no boats. The rebels had won the race, thanks to the herculean efforts of a Rhode Island ironmaker and a ragged band of southern rebels who didn't know the meaning of the word *quit*.

★   ★   ★

ON DECEMBER 20, 1780, Benedict Arnold, commanding some seventeen hundred men, had embarked for Chesapeake Bay with a fleet of forty-two sail. He had orders to fortify Portsmouth, the town that commanded entry to the bay from the sea. Accompanying him were his own American legion, which had been beefed up by the addition of numerous loyalist volunteers, along with Lieutenant Colonel John Graves Simcoe's Queen's Rangers, a loyalist regiment of horse and foot whose bridles were adorned with black and white feathers, memorializing Simcoe's closest friend, the late John André. Without this outfit it is doubtful that Arnold would have had a command, but these troops graciously agreed to serve under him despite his reputation as the man responsible for André's death. He also had a company of Hessians, a regiment of British regulars, and an extremely reluctant soldier in the person of John Champe, formerly sergeant major in Lee's Light-Horse Corps, who would now be compelled to fight against his own country. If captured by the Americans, he faced execution unless he could somehow get word to Light-Horse Harry, the only man in the southern army who knew the circumstances of his "desertion." If captured as a deserter by the British, he would surely be hanged. Sometime during the coming months, no one knows how, Champe deserted from the British camp and found his way through the backwoods to Lee's legion's campsite on the Congaree River. To

keep him from being hanged by the enemy if he were captured in battle, Lee gave him an honorable discharge and sent him to Loudoun
County, in Virginia, where he sat out the rest of the war for independence.*

When Arnold reached Hampton Roads on December 30, he
learned immediately how easy the conquest of Virginia was to be when
his scouts reported that the road to Richmond was open. Except for
the burning of Norfolk in 1776 and a 1779 raid by British, Hessian,
and loyalist troops that laid waste towns, plantations, and huge quantities of tobacco in the same area, eastern Virginia had been virtually
untouched by war. The consequence, regrettably, was a certain amount
of apathy, and now, for reasons known only to himself, Governor
Thomas Jefferson had ignored George Washington's warning that the
British were preparing to invade the state and waited three days before
calling out the militia. Light-Horse Harry Lee, who was no friend to
Jefferson, remarked that the governor, who was a gentleman "highly
respected for his literary accomplishments, and as highly esteemed for
his amiability and modesty," had done nothing to prepare the state,
leaving it vulnerable to attack by a relatively small force. "The government which does not prepare in time, doubles the power of its adver-
sary," he observed, "and sports with the lives of its citizens. . . ." In this
instance, nine hundred British troops, led by the traitor Arnold, had
dared leave their ships and march twenty-five miles to Richmond. "It
will scarcely be credited by posterity," Lee went on, "that the governor
of the oldest State in the Union . . . was driven out of its metropolis,
and forced to secure personal safety by flight, and that its archives, with
all its munitions and stores, were yielded to the will of the invader. . . ."

Arnold struck quickly and ferociously, overrunning American
forts, raiding supply depots and magazines, torching plantations, villages, and iron foundries, and destroying Virginia's state papers

---

*Despite the hazardous mission he had undertaken so courageously, Champe never did get the
promotion he had been promised. In 1837 his needy widow was granted $120 a year as the
relict of a Revolutionary veteran; by then the former sergeant major was long dead.

before returning to Portsmouth, where his troops went into camp for the winter.

At the same time that he learned from British intelligence agents that the Marquis de Lafayette was assembling a substantial force in Maryland to move against Portsmouth, Arnold had fallen out with his opposite number in the navy, Captain Thomas Symonds, over their joint division of prize money. It was the usual Arnold story—haggling over money, in this case the value of prizes taken on the James River, which the two had agreed to share. When Symonds's officers argued that the navy should get all the money, Arnold appealed to Sir Henry Clinton in so offensive a manner that Symonds refused to take his ships up the Chesapeake to attack Lafayette's transports. To make matters worse, the American traitor accused Symonds of cowardice for keeping his ships in shoal water: "I believe he is heartily inclined to do [so] whenever he thinks there is danger."

During March and April the vindictive Arnold was virtually unopposed while burning thousands of hogsheads of tobacco and military stores near Petersburg despite a valiant attempt by militiamen under General Muhlenberg to hold them off. One by one the vital stores of weapons, food, and clothing desperately needed by Greene's army were being seized or went up in smoke, along with Virginia's great cash crop—tobacco.

Arnold, of course, was fighting for his life—in the sense that he *had* to win the laurels that would bring him the respect and renown he craved so badly as payment for his treason. To Lord George Germain, secretary of state for the colonies and George III's chief adviser on the American war, he had written suggesting that Washington and his army must be forced into a decisive battle—exactly what the American commander in chief had been trying to avoid for years. He also urged Germain to consider offering every rebel soldier who deserted his entire back pay. The sum of the Continental troops' arrears, Arnold suggested, would not cost Britain as much as continuing the war for a few months, and each soldier "taken from the rebel army and added to ours is as two men imported from Europe." All this was a cogent argument at a time when British military sources were stretched dangerously thin.

Money, he believed, would "prove a more formidable argument than arms," and he even urged Germain to consider offering a title to George Washington: the sort of award that "might not prove unacceptable." As for himself, the turncoat requested promotion in rank to major general and a command in which he would be able to prove his worth to His Majesty.

The fact was that Arnold was restless and bored with the slow pace of his work in Virginia. Just then he was building fortifications at Portsmouth, preparing for a siege, and writing to Sir Henry Clinton, asking that he be ordered back to New York, "as a life of inaction will be very prejudicial to my health." Clinton reacted to his appeal for relief by sending another detachment from New York, headed by Major General William Phillips, with orders to supersede Arnold.

In a letter to his old friend Phillips, Cornwallis conveyed his thoughts, reflecting his anger and contempt for Clinton.

> Now, my dear friend, what is our plan? Without one, we cannot succeed, and I assure you that I am quite tired of marching about the country in quest of adventures. If we mean an offensive war in America, we must abandon New York and bring our whole force into Virginia; we then have a stake to fight for and a successful battle may give us America. If our plan is defensive, mixed with desultory expeditions, let us quit the Carolinas (which cannot be held defensively while Virginia can be so easily armed against us) and stick to our salt pork at New York, sending now and then a detachment to steal tobacco, etc.

Since no orders had arrived for Arnold, leaving him without an assignment, he tagged along with Phillips on yet another foray up the James River. On their return, after seizing rebel shipping and destroying more mills and warehouses, orders came from Cornwallis, directing them to join him in Petersburg. His army was in a "very critical situation," he wrote, and they should collect supplies for his men—an enterprise they undertook vigorously during the next two weeks, raiding what rebel storehouses remained along the river and prompting Henry Lee to say of their operations: ". . . the restrained licentiousness of the unprincipled burst out, and shocking outrages were committed upon our unprotected fellow-citizens—disgraceful to British arms, and degrading to the name of man."

When the two generals returned to Petersburg in early May, Phillips rode in a carriage, critically ill with a fever that killed him on May 13, before Cornwallis arrived. Arnold was himself in such a bad way, with gout in his hands and feet that kept him in agony, that he was put aboard a vessel bound for New York, where he found Clinton in a foul humor. The reasons were several, but not least was that the general had learned of a letter from Arnold to Lord George Germain criticizing Sir Henry's management of the war.

★   ★   ★

CORNWALLIS'S CHARACTERIZATION OF his army as being in a "very critical situation" had to do, ironically, with two victories he claimed to have won. After losing the race to the Dan River, he paid dearly for destroying all his supplies and had to return to Hillsboro. To prevent the British from picking up Tory recruits in the area, Greene recrossed the Dan, doing his best to harass the enemy, not giving them an opportunity to fight for three weeks. Then, having received some reinforcements from Virginia—enough so he finally outnumbered the British—he moved to Guilford Courthouse and laid out his battle plan, following the pattern used with such success by Morgan at Cowpens. In an engagement on March 15 that was "long, obstinate, and bloody," Greene said his troops were "obliged to give up the ground and [we] lost our artillery, but the enemy have been so soundly beaten that they dare not move towards us since the action, notwithstanding the artillery, they have gained no advantage.

On the contrary, they are little short of being ruined. The enemy's loss in killed and wounded cannot be less than between six and seven hundred, perhaps more."

Greene had been certain of victory but his hopes were dashed by the failure of the North Carolina militia, who "had the most advantageous position I ever saw, and left it without making scarcely the shadow of opposition." Many of the men threw away their weapons and fled even before a gun was fired at them. In fact, not a man was even wounded. Greene was elated with the performance of the Virginia militia and Lee's cavalry, which "performed wonders": "Indeed, the horse is our great safeguard, and without them the militia could not keep the field in his country." Then, appraising his small force, he added: "Never did an army labour under so many disadvantages as this; but the fortitude and patience of the officers and soldiery rise superior to all difficulties. We have little to eat, less to drink, and lodge in the woods in the midst of smoke. Indeed, our fatigue is excessive. I was so much overcome night before last that I fainted."

Cornwallis had a narrow escape in the battle. His horse had been shot, so he took one of the dragoons' mounts and didn't notice that the saddlebags were hanging under the animal's belly. The underbrush here was thick and greatly slowed his movement, but the general was unconscious of his danger. At this point Sergeant Roger Lamb of the Royal Welsh Fusiliers caught hold of the horse's bridle and turned his head while warning Cornwallis if he had pursued the same direction he would have been surrounded and perhaps cut to pieces or captured. Lamb ran alongside with the bridle in his hand until the earl reached the 23d Regiment at the edge of the woods. Before the battle ended, the British were in such a bad way that Cornwallis took the desperate measure of firing grapeshot into a tangled crowd of men, killing his own men as well as Americans. While he proclaimed "a compleat Victory" because he occupied the field of battle, he had lost a quarter of his army, including some of his best officers, leading Charles James Fox of the opposition in Parliament to suggest, "Another such victory would destroy the British army." And that, of course, was precisely the objective of Greene's campaign.

Immediately after the battle, Cornwallis raised the royal standard in Hillsboro and issued a proclamation calling on "all loyal subjects to stand forth & take an active part in restoring good Order & Government." How many North Carolinians responded favorably is not known, but Cornwallis's diminished force was so worn out that he was forced to retire to the coast to refit and lick his wounds.

After Guilford Courthouse each of the opposing commanders had a major decision to make: which direction to take that would do the most damage to the enemy. For his part, Greene admitted to Washington that he was "at a loss what is best to be done," yet he had decided to carry the war back to South Carolina. This move would be "critical and dangerous, and the troops exposed to every hardship," but it had the advantage of forcing Cornwallis to follow him or to give up his posts in that state. Greene recognized that Lafayette, in Virginia, could count on support from Washington, and his proposal appeared to have no negative ramifications except for the strain on his men. He would share their troubles with them, he added, and had no doubt that they would "bear up under it with that magnanimity which has already supported them, and for which they deserve everything of their country." He expected to be able to march in about five days, and since the move would be unexpected by the enemy, he would keep it secret as long as possible, so the element of surprise would work in his favor.

It was not an easy choice, but it was typical of Nathanael Greene, the studious onetime Quaker who had resigned himself to being a private in a Rhode Island militia company six years earlier because his members were ashamed to have an officer who limped. Now, as before, necessity obliged him to commit himself to chance, and, he said, "I trust my friends will do justice to my reputation if any accident attends me."

As for Cornwallis, he had no qualms about moving his force to Virginia. Writing to Clinton on April 23, 1781, he told him, "My present undertaking sits heavy on my mind. I have experienced the distresses and dangers of marching some hundreds of miles, in a country chiefly hostile, without one active or useful friend; without intelligence, and without communication with any part of the country." In a letter written to his superior two weeks earlier he had given him a veritable catalog of disaster. He had been unable to follow up on his "victory" at Guilford for lack of provisions and other necessities. He had remained on the battlefield for two days before marching to a town that was supposed to contain the greatest number of Tories, and most of them rode into camp, shook his hand, said they were glad to see him and hear that he had beaten Greene. Then they rode home again. "I could not get 100 men in all the Regulators' country to stay with us, even as militia."

What Cornwallis did not say was that the past months' actions had earned him a reputation not unlike that of Tarleton. "Cornwallis is the scourge—and a severe one he is," wrote Richard Henry Lee to Arthur Lee. On their march toward Virginia the British had shown little mercy: " 'Tis said that 2 or 3000 Negroes march in their train, that every kind of stock which they cannot remove they destroy—eating up the green wheat and by destroying of the fences expose to destruction the other growing grains. They have burnt a great number of warehouses full of tobacco and they are now pressing on to the large ones on Rappahanock and Potomac Rivers and the valuable iron works in our northern parts."

Yet in spite of Cornwallis's efforts to provide for his men, a third of his increasingly depleted army was sick or wounded, the rest without shoes and worn down with fatigue. Since January 15, he had lost 1,501 of the 3,224 men he had then. Proceeding to Cross Creek, he found to his mortification that it was impossible to obtain provisions or forage for his horses. Navigating the Cape Fear River was impracticable ("and the inhabitants on each side almost universally hostile"), so now he was looking impatiently for the expected reinforcements from Europe, trying to find supplies of all kinds, hoping "to preserve the troops from the fatal sickness which so nearly ruined the army last autumn." He was in the dark, he told Clinton, as to plans for the summer's campaigns, but he had to say he hoped the Chesapeake would become the seat of war. Until Virginia was subdued it would be difficult to hold the Carolinas, and the rivers of Virginia are advantageous to an invading army. And for emphasis he added that "North Carolina is, of all the provinces in America, the most difficult to attack . . . on account of its great extent, of the numberless rivers and creeks, and the total want of interior navigation." Furthermore, no material assistance could be expected of the inhabitants, as he well knew from experience. Indeed, the North Carolina Tories, on whose support Cornwallis had counted, failed him completely, he told Germain. "Our experience has shown that their numbers are not so great as had been represented and that their friendship was only passive."

Cornwallis didn't mention it, but what was happening in North Carolina beyond the actions of the two armies was real civil war, conducted in the main by Francis Marion, Andrew Pickens, and Thomas Sumter.

Among those who were caught up in this struggle was a young lad named Andrew Jackson. Not yet fourteen years of age, Jackson was in the home of a patriot fighter when some of Tarleton's men broke in and began smashing the furniture. As Jackson told the story, the British officer tried to make him clean his boots and Jackson refused, saying he was a prisoner of war and should be treated as such. The officer, infuriated, swung his saber at the boy, who broke the blow to his head with his left hand. However, the gashes on his head and hand formed scars the future president of the United States would carry to his grave, along with a hatred for the British, who not only kept him in jail at Camden for two months but, he said, "starved me nearly to death and gave me the small-pox." His brother, who had also been captured, died, and when Jackson was released after his mother pleaded with his captors for leniency on account of his youth, he was "a skeleton—not quite six feet long and a little over six inches thick!"

Francis Marion, who had begun life as a baby "small enough to be put into a quart mug," had been a frail child but grew up farming the family lands and joined a militia company in 1761. When organized resistance in the South was put down by the British, he put together his own partisan brigade and began guerrilla operations, which were so successful that the British sent several task forces to take him, but failed. After Marion—known as "The Swamp Fox"—and his brigade had fought regulars and Tories in at least nine operations between January and mid-July of 1781, Greene wrote him a letter of thanks.

> no man has a better claim to the public thanks or is more gener-ally admired than you are. . . . Surrounded on every side with a superior force, hunted from every quarter by veteran troops, you have found means to elude all their attempts, and to keep alive the expiring hopes of an oppressed militia, when all succour seemed to be cut off. To fight the enemy bravely with a prospect of victory is nothing; but to fight with intrepidity under the con-stant impression of a defeat, and inspire irregular troops to do it, is a talent peculiar to yourself.

For Nathanael Greene, who had succeeded in maneuvering the British from most of their positions in South Carolina and all of them in Georgia, General Washington had high praise: "I confess to you that I am unable to conceive what more could have been done, under your circumstances, than has been displayed by your little persevering and determined army."

6

OUR DELIVERANCE MUST COME

Far to the north of Virginia, Washington's army had been idle since November, unable to do more than survive. But if the fledgling United States were to outlast the British, that force would have to be strengthened or supported in such a way that it could win this war. In a January letter carried to the Comte de Vergennes by Colonel John Laurens, the new military envoy to France, the Marquis de Lafayette had written, "With a naval inferiority it is impossible to make war in America. It is that which prevents us from attacking any point that might be carried with two or three thousand men. It is that which reduces us to defensive operations, as dangerous as they are humiliating." But so far the court at Versailles was doing nothing to satisfy that crying need.

George Washington wrote to Laurens on April 9, explaining the necessity for the French to act at once if the dream of independence was to be realized.

> If France delays a timely and powerful aid in the critical posture of our affairs it will avail us nothing should she attempt it hereafter. We are at this hour suspended in the Balance; not from choice but from hard and absolute necessity; and you may rely

upon it as a fact that we cannot transport the provisions from the States in which they are assessed to the army, because we cannot pay the teamsters who will no longer work for Certificates. It is equally certain that our troops are fast approaching Nakedness, and that we have nothing to clothe them with, that our hospitals are without medicines and our sick without nutriment except such as well men eat; and that our public works are at a Stand and the artificers disbanding.

But why need I run into detail, when it may be declared in a word, that we are at the end of our tether, and that now or never our deliverance must come.

Sir Henry Clinton, in New York, was reported to have more than ten thousand men, while Washington's force, in posts along the Hudson near West Point, had fewer than half that number. As the American commander confided to his journal, his army lacked storehouses filled with provisions and arsenals with military stores; it had neither the means nor the money to obtain transport; the General even had to suspend the regularly scheduled expresses between his headquarters and Rochambeau's for lack of funds to pay the riders. Scavenging for foodstuffs had oppressed the local people, "souring their tempers and alienating their affection"; worse, almost none of the states had produced as many as one-eighth of the number of soldiers expected of them, indicating that no prospect of "a glorious offensive campaign" was in the army's future, but rather "a bewildered and gloomy defensive one." Not only were the people tired of the war; they were beginning to be apathetic about the eventual outcome, eager to have it over with on almost any terms so they could get back to some sort of normal life. The economy was in a shambles, the Congress was regarded as inept and incapable, and the future looked bleaker than ever.

Now another spring was here, and the Hudson, awesome in full flood, raced toward the ocean with millions of tons of meltwater from the Catskills and Adirondacks, bearing the message that it was time for the army, such as it was, to be on the move.

Six months earlier, the Comte de Rochambeau's son, Donatien-

Marie-Joseph de Vimeur, Vicomte Rochambeau, had sailed for France on the frigate *Amazone*, taking advantage of a northeast wind and thick fog to slip through the British blockade, and though pursued by an enemy ship, the frigate barely managed to escape in a gale. After landing at Brest, the young man had gone immediately to Versailles to present "suggestions" from his father and General Washington to Louis XVI's foreign minister, Charles Gravier, Comte de Vergennes. The suggestions were not welcome. This was, after all, the fourth campaign that would have to be supported by France, and where, the minister asked, would it end? It was impossible for the king to satisfy these insatiable demands for money, for "if he did so he would surely ruin France." He pointed out that the king was under enormous financial pressures and had expected, at the very least, that the Americans would cover the expenses of their own military force.

At this point Benjamin Franklin stepped in, writing a masterful letter that appears to have mollified Vergennes and helped persuade him and the king to agree to send ships and financial support to America. Franklin had said he was growing old, enfeebled by illness, and did not have long to be concerned with these affairs, adding that the present junction was critical, that Congress might lose its influence over the people if it failed to attract the support needed to carry on the war. Shrewdly, the old man reminded Vergennes that if the English were to recover their former colonies, an opportunity like the present one might not recur, while possession of the vast territory and resources of America would afford the English a broad basis for future greatness, ever expanding commerce, and a supply of seamen and soldiers that would make them "the terror of Europe."

The result of deliberations at the court of Versailles was that the Americans received their long-awaited reply on May 8, 1781, when the French frigate *Concorde* docked at Boston and Vicomte de Rochambeau, bearing orders from the court, debarked with Jacques-Melchoir Saint-Laurent, Comte de Barras, who was replacing the late Ternay as commander of the fleet, plus several officers who were to join the Comte de Rochambeau. The news brought by young Rochambeau was stunning. "We learned that M. [François Joseph Paul] de Grasse had left Brest March 22, with 26 ships of the line, 8 frigates, and 150 transports; that their destination was unknown; that it was believed that the ships, 4 frigates and most of the convoy would sail to the Islands [i.e., West Indies]." Of equal importance, the young man brought with him 6 million livres "to supply the needs and upkeep of the American army."

Although de Grasse's ultimate destination was indeed a secret, the fact that an important French fleet was under way to American waters was cause for immense joy by French and American commanders alike. Immediately, Washington called for an operations planning conference with Rochambeau and the Chevalier de Chastellux in Wethersfield, Connecticut, which the French—always interested in the aesthetics of a place—declared charming, saying, "it would be impossible to find prettier houses and a more beautiful view."

With winter only a bleak memory, Washington was still eager for an opportunity to attack New York, believing a coup there to be "the most capable of striking a deathblow to Britain's dominion in America." Clinton had reduced his garrison by sending troops to the South, but if threatened he would certainly have to recall some of them, which in turn would reduce the pressure on Greene and Lafayette. Another factor favoring New York was Washington's certainty that he could neither locate nor afford the means of transporting the allied armies to Virginia. Everything, of course, depended on the arrival of a superior French fleet in American waters.

Rochambeau, seemingly agreeable and as friendly as ever, possessed certain knowledge he was unwilling to share with Washington. He knew, for instance, that the main French fleet was sailing directly to the West Indies, but did not reveal how long it would be there; nor did he divulge the fact that de Grasse had orders to sail north in July or August. When he asked Washington how he proposed to capitalize on the possible presence of a superior French fleet, the American commander replied that it was difficult to say until they knew the size of the naval force, but in any case it could be used profitably in an operation against New York, or then again, in circumstances as yet unknown. (In fact, as both Washington and Rochambeau were aware, a French squadron would have a difficult time forcing the bar at Sandy Hook.)

What the Wethersfield discussions came down to was that Rochambeau preferred to focus attention on the Chesapeake Bay area, while Washington wanted a campaign in the South to be an alternative, to be undertaken only if the allies proved incapable of taking New York. Although Rochambeau was too diplomatic to say so in so many words, he was unalterably opposed to a strike against New York and began writing letters to see that the momentum went in the direction he desired. In the meantime, the conferees concluded, until word was received from de Grasse, the French army—minus several hundred left behind to guard the heavy artillery—would march to the Hudson and join the Americans in an operation against New York.

To be certain he got what he really wanted, Rochambeau sent a dispatch to de Grasse reporting the result of the conference, noting his own opposition to the conclusion and urging the admiral to sail not to New York but to Chesapeake Bay. He requested that de Grasse respond immediately because he wanted to "take the earliest opportunity to combine our march with that of General Washington, so as to proceed by land as expeditiously as possible, and join him at any stipulated part of the Chesapeake."

When the Wethersfield meetings broke up, Washington had his aide Tench Tilghman send off renewed appeals for troop levies to the New England governors before the General rode to New Windsor to begin planning for the joint operation. Meanwhile Sir Henry Clinton was of course aware of the Wethersfield conference and knew the desperate state of Washington's army, but he and Cornwallis were engaged in their usual bickering and Clinton, who had received word that the Americans and French were planning a strike against New

York, ordered Cornwallis to send him "with all possible dispatch" all the troops he could spare.

★ ★ ★

WHETHER WASHINGTON ADMITTED it even to himself, he was somewhat out of his depth in these dealings with French officers. The Virginia planter was a successful farmer without much in the way of formal education—with no knowledge at all of the French language—and while much of his adult life had been spent in military activities, he was often hard put to deal diplomatically with these proud, often touchy Frenchmen. Not only did these men have differing ideas as to how the war should be run, but each of them had allies in high places in France who could throw their weight around. Washington's initial move, as a means of solving the language difficulty, had been to inform Rochambeau that he would communicate with him through the Marquis de Lafayette, "a friend from whom I conceal nothing. . . . I entreat you to receive whatever he shall tell you as coming from me." This arrangement had been altered at Rochambeau's urging, and, especially since the conference in Wethersfield, the American commander had found no need to rely on an intermediary other than Tilghman, who was proficient in French thanks to his education at the Philadelphia College and Academy established by Benjamin Franklin.

During their close association, Washington and Rochambeau did their level best to provide the public with the impression of Franco-American unity, but beneath the surface were many tense moments. The Frenchman was not an easy man to deal with, as his subordinates knew. Comte Fersen observed that he distrusted some of them "in a way that is disagreeable and indeed insulting," and Claude Blanchard, Rochambeau's commissary in chief, had many uncomfortable set-tos with him, complained of frequent "reproach and suspicion," and went on to say, "He mistrusts every one and always believes that he sees himself surrounded by rogues and idiots. This character, combined with manners far from courteous, makes him disagreeable to everybody."

Two other figures in the bizarre cast confronted by Washington were the Chevalier de Chastellux and the Chevalier de La Luzerne. Chastellux, third in command of the French army in America, was not only a prominent soldier but a famous philosopher and author, who was now traveling the United States collecting material for a book on the country. A dark-haired man with a long, rather solemn face and small green-brown eyes, Chastellux was immediately taken with George Washington, whom he characterized as "the greatest and the best of men." In his book he provided a superb picture of the American general—one that was to influence contemporaries and generations to follow. The General's strongest characteristic, he said, was "the perfect harmony which reigns between the physical and moral qualities. . . ." He was "Brave without temerity, laborious without ambition, generous without prodigality, noble without pride, virtuous without severity. . . ." He was, in short, a very paragon of a man whom history, Chastellux predicted, would honor not because of any particular virtue but because, "at the end of a long civil war, he had nothing with which he could reproach himself."

One of Washington's skills that most impressed Chastellux (as it did many another contemporary) was his superb horsemanship. Washington's horses, which he broke and trained himself, were universally admired, as was the way he always rode at a gallop, even when he had no special reason to hurry. "He is a very excellent and bold horseman," the Frenchman wrote, "leaping the highest fences and going extremely quick without standing upon his stirrups, bearing on the bridle, or letting his horse run wild."

(Chastellux was nothing if not candid in his observations of the American army. Speaking of medical treatment, he remarked, "the distinction between surgeon and physician is as little known in the army of Washington as in that of Agamemnon.")

La Luzerne, a friendly, worldly-wise, thirty-six-year-old, spoke almost no English when he appeared on the scene to become minister to the United States, but this did not deter him from becoming a man of enormous influence. Unlike La Luzerne, most of the French were no more comfortable dealing with their opposite numbers than the Americans were. Even Lafayette, who had come to know these new allies better than most others, observed, "I cannot deny that the Americans are somewhat difficult to handle, especially for a Frenchman."

★   ★   ★

WASHINGTON, LIKE ROCHAMBEAU, was determined to persuade de Grasse to sail to American waters—and soon—and he dispatched a trusted officer named Allen McLane, a daring cavalryman who had served brilliantly in numerous battles, to see de Grasse and provide him with full details on the military situation in the states. The American commander was beginning to have misgivings about the attack on New York and wanted to keep open the possibility of action in the Chesapeake, so in early June, McLane, appearing as a marine captain on the privateer *Congress*, sailed for the islands hoping to meet with de Grasse. On the way they spoke a French frigate, learned the location of de Grasse's fleet, and McLane was soon aboard the French admiral's flagship.

At that moment, de Grasse and his officers were considering an attack on the island of Jamaica but interrupted the discussions to hear McLane's news from America. As McLane described his historic mission in his journal with tantalizing brevity, "Visited Cap François [now Cap Haitien] in July, was examined by Count de Grasse in Council of War aboard the *Ville de Paris*, gave as [my] considered opinion that Count de Grasse could make it easy for Genl Washington to reduce the British Army in the South if he proceeded with his fleet and Army to the Chesapeake." Whether it was McLane's persuasiveness or the written recommendations de Grasse received from

Rochambeau and Washington at this time, the die was cast. De Grasse would sail for America.

★ ★ ★

O N J U N E 1 0 the first brigade of French troops stepped off on what proved to be a 756-mile march to the South, in a departure from Newport that could only be described as an emotional spectacle. It was a sad occasion for the French, most of whom agreed with Jean-Baptiste-Antoine de Verger, who said, "there are few places or indeed none in the world, where the [fair sex] is so beautiful and so amiable," and for the townspeople, who had thoroughly enjoyed the presence and impeccable behavior of these troops and were sorry to see them go. As the brilliantly uniformed troops dressed ranks, crowds lining the streets waved their hats and cheered and threw kisses as they began to march to the docks, where they embarked for Providence.

Apparently, a legion of officers regretted acutely that they would not see again a young Quaker woman named Polly Lawton (pronounced "Layton"). Her favorite pastime was teasing the visitors about their profession, which she called immoral, but that did not deter one French count from pronouncing her "a nymph rather than a woman," whose eyes reflected "the meekness and purity of her mind and the goodness of her heart . . . if I had not been married and happy I should, whilst coming to defend the liberty of the Americans, have lost my own at the feet of Polly Leiton." The Prince de Broglie wrote, "Suddenly the door opened and in came the very goddess of grace and beauty. It was Minerva herself, and her name was Polly Lawton," whose costume had the effect of giving her the air of the Holy Virgin.

Unlike his love-struck officers, Rochambeau, after all the frustrations of prolonged inactivity, could hardly wait to leave Newport, knowing he had the honor of leading the cream of the French infantry—the Soissonnais and the Bourbonnais regiments, with which he had fought in the Seven Years' War—along with the Saintonge and Deux-Ponts, two equally distinguished units.

Providence, where the army stayed for eight days, was a rather pretty town, according to one of the officers, well built and thickly settled, but it seemed deserted, with little commercial activity. None of the streets were paved and the town was surrounded by woodlands, but the air was pure and healthy.

Leaving Providence on June 18, the army was ordered to march in four divisions, which were led by Rochambeau, Baron de Vioménil, Comte de Vioménil, and Comte de Custine, whose second in command was Louis-Alexandre Berthier (later marshal of France and Napoleon's chief of staff). The going was difficult, especially for the artillery, and because of the roads, which were described successively as very poor, very bad, frightful, and execrable, it took almost two weeks to reach East Hartford. Upon arrival in Hartford, the army set up camp and stayed for two days to rest and make repairs to the artillery.

It is not clear how he knew this, since he had seen only Rhode Island and Massachusetts, but Clermont-Crèvecoeur pronounced Connecticut "unquestionably the most fertile province in America, for its soil yields everything necessary to life." The pasturage was good, the cattle of excellent quality, and the poultry and game exquisite. The woods abounded in walnut trees ("the nuts are quite good, but you lose patience trying to eat them"), whose wood was used to make wheels and shafts of incredible lightness—unlike the carriages of France, which were so heavy they ruined the roads. Clermont-Crèvecoeur was so captivated by the lush orchards and apple trees that he got to thinking how unfortunate it was that the Americans did not make their own wine and substitute it for the cider they produced in such great quantity. Since the country had such a healthy and salubrious climate, he concluded that "the Americans' laziness doubtless prevents them from making the effort."

Such thoughts led him to ponder the people the French troops had seen. Among them were elders of both sexes who enjoyed perfect health at a very advanced age and were gay and amiable, "not at all

burdened with the infirmities that are our lot in our declining years."
The people, though hardworking, "do not labor to excess as our peas-
ants do. The sweat of their brow is not expended on satisfying the
extravagant desires of the rich and luxury-loving; they limit themselves to enjoying what is truly necessary."

Only one dark spot marred his idyllic picture of Connecticut:
"You often encounter Tories here. This country is unfortunately
swarming with them, and the harm they have done to the inhabitants
is incredible."

Moving on, the French army camped in Farmington, where
crowds turned out to hear their regimental bands play and watch their
generals and colonels dance with the local girls.

Several days later, after an otherwise uneventful trip, the troops
stopped at Newtown, New York, a desolate place with ruined fields
and houses, and much poverty, which the French were convinced was
the capital of Tory country. The loyalists usually strike by night, they
heard, when they travel in packs, attack an isolated post, then retire to
the woods where they bury their arms. Although the French were on
guard against these marauders, none appeared; the troops probably
suffered greater psychological damage when their campsite in a stony
field proved to be "infested with snakes and adders."

They spent two days in Newtown and planned to stay longer, but
a message arrived from General Washington, saying he was on the
march and hoped Rochambeau would join him soon. To facilitate
matters, one of Washington's aides, Colonel David Cobb, met them
here and remained with them, since he knew the country well and
could help plan their marches. He brought with him Sheldon's dragoons, "who are incontestably the best troops on the continent,"
according to Clermont-Crèvecoeur.

Washington wanted Rochambeau's first brigade to be in Bedford
by the evening of July 2; from there, the armies would proceed immediately to King's Bridge, fifteen miles from New York. On the march
through western Connecticut the French noted the devastation of the
villages, and in North Castle "Everything has been either destroyed or

burned by the British." Several attempts were made to find and attack Oliver DeLancey's loyalist corps in this vicinity, but they failed. (Success depended on surprise, and the enemy could hardly be unaware of the allies' movements.) By July 6, when they marched from North Castle to Philipsburg at White Plains, the troops had been on the road since 3 A.M. with nothing to eat; they found nothing to drink; and the heat was unbearable. They had to make frequent halts, and more than four hundred soldiers dropped by the roadside because of fatigue. That same evening a French officer, bedded down in a meadow, saw that the top of the grass was covered with sparks and, looking closer, discovered that these were generated by "a fly that imitates our glow-worms." He had just seen his first fireflies.

On July 7, the moment arrived when the French and Americans actually camped cheek by jowl, separated only by a small stream near Dobbs Ferry. The next day La Luzerne, the French minister, arrived in camp, and Rochambeau put on a review for him and Washington and his officers. Washington had seen the French troops in Newport, Baron Closen said, so the spectacle "could not have made as much of an impression on him as on the other American officers, who were especially taken with Lauzun's legion and its lancers."

Twenty-four hours later the American contingent—some four thousand strong—had its chance, and the French headquarters staff was invited to see it pass in review. Astonishingly, "the whole effect was rather good," Closen wrote, but when Clermont-Crèvecoeur had his first opportunity to view the American camp, he was struck at first, not by the army's smart appearance, "but by its destitution: the men were without uniforms and covered with rags; most of them were barefoot. They were of all sizes, down to children who could not have been over fourteen. There were many negroes, mulattoes, etc. Only their artillerymen were wearing uniforms." He realized that these men and boys were "the elite of the country and are actually very good troops, well schooled in their profession. We had nothing but praise for them later," he added, especially for the officers, who had good practical experience. A few of the American regiments had white uniforms: coat, jacket, vest, and trousers of white cotton, buttoned from the bottom to the calves, like gaiters. Several battalions wore little black caps with white plumes, and Washington's mounted guard wore hard leather helmets with horsehair crests. Sheldon's legion had large caps with bearskin fastenings. Three-quarters of the Rhode Island regiment, he said, "consists of negroes, and that regiment is the most neatly dressed, the best under arms, and the most precise in its maneuvers."

On that same day Rochambeau wrote to Barras, informing him that the French troops had arrived safely and asking him to apprehend "ten love-stricken Soissonnais who returned to see their mistresses in Newport." Then, writing to the minister of war in Versailles, he reported that his army had marched 220 miles in eleven days, finding or supplying their own rations, and whatever expense they had incurred "has been essential to our American allies." Before concluding, he pleaded, "For heaven's sake, Sir, do not forget our money and real funds for the month of October; our neighbors lack everything, and the subsidy which they can draw on in letters of exchange will soon discredit this currency."

★ ★ ★

THE CLOSER THE French and American armies came to New York City, the more frequent the skirmishes—some with British or Hessians, others with loyalists of Oliver DeLancey's corps—and the more devastation they saw. As Louis-Alexandre Berthier wrote:

> This whole country gives evidence of the horrors of war. The inhabitants here are in communication with the English and are pillaged by American raiding parties. All the Whigs have abandoned their houses. Among them are some very handsome ones, deserted, half destroyed, or burned, with untended orchards and gardens filled with fruits and vegetables, and driveways overgrown with grass 2 feet high. Only along the borders of the Sound is there less devastation, since there the inhabitants have changed sides whenever it has proved expedient.

For a month and more, while playing cat and mouse with Clinton's defense forces, Washington and Rochambeau made a careful study of the area—sometimes spending twenty-four hours at a time in the saddle. On one occasion, after mounting at five in the morning, they crossed to an island between the mainland and Long Island, and, while the engineers were taking some measurements, the generals lay down in the sun and fell asleep. The Frenchman awoke first, called Washington at once to say the tide was coming in, and they returned quickly to the little causeway on which they had crossed to the island, only to find it under water. Someone found a few boats, into which they threw their saddles and bridles, and two American soldiers went ahead, leading by the bridles two horses that were good swimmers, and some ninety other horses followed. This entire operation took about an hour, and fortunately the enemy never knew the predicament in which the supreme commanders of the American and French armies found themselves.

In the third week of July they made a reconnaissance in force, screened from the enemy by five thousand troops, and wisely concluded that an attack on Manhattan was impossible—too risky by far. To oppose about five thousand French troops and somewhat fewer Americans, Clinton now had as many as fourteen thousand veteran soldiers behind well-fortified lines, protected by the East and Hudson rivers patrolled by British ships. During these weeks, seeing the rebel army at close quarters, Closen's admiration for them continued to grow: "It is incredible," he wrote, "that soldiers composed of men of every age, even of children, of whites and blacks, almost naked, unpaid, and rather poorly fed, can march so well and withstand fire so steadfastly." As for Washington, "He is certainly admirable as the leader of his army, in which everyone regards him as his friend and father."

★   ★   ★

WHEN THE ARMIES were traveling over "execrable roads" on the way to King's Bridge, the French artillery somehow lost its way, and

Rochambeau sent Berthier out in the night to locate it. In the pitch dark, all alone in completely strange country that was crawling with loyalists, he followed one road after another, dismounting at every crossroad to feel the road for tracks made by the heavy guns. Finally, after doing this for several miles, he located where the artillerymen had made a wrong turn, galloped after them, and managed to get them on the right road so that they caught up with Rochambeau by daybreak.

Later that day the two generals, with their aides, engineers, and Berthier, reached Morrisania and surprised a corps of some twenty loyalists. Washington ordered eight dragoons to charge them, and five French officers went along, galloping up in hopes of taking prisoners; but just as they arrived, the loyalists took refuge in a house and greeted the allies with musket fire. The horsemen surrounded the house, calling on the Tories to surrender or they would burn the building. That threat was enough and out they came, but as they did they saw about two hundred men gathered across the river to support them, firing muskets and fieldpieces loaded with grapeshot. One of the loyalists, armed with a brace of pistols, rushed up to Berthier, shouting, "Prisoner!"; fired on him at a range of five paces, yelling, "Die, you dog of a Frenchman!"; and as he was about to fire his other gun, Berthier "got ahead of him by putting a ball through his chest, which killed him on the spot." Berthier and his colleagues "sabered, shot, or captured the rest," taking ten men and seven horses.

Baron Closen was part of this escapade and estimated that he and his cohorts had drawn two hundred musket or pistol shots and about twenty rounds from the cannon, the only casualty being a horse ridden by the Comte de Damas. But Closen himself came close to death. As he pursued some loyalists through an orchard, his hat caught on a branch and then fell to the ground. Without thinking of the danger from the intense gunfire, he reined in his horse, dismounted, and picked up the hat. By the time he climbed back on his horse, the other officers had disappeared, and when he rejoined them where the generals were waiting, they said they thought he had been killed, all because of his "excessive pride."

★　★　★

ON JULY 8 de Grasse sent word to Rochambeau that he would sail from Santo Domingo for the Chesapeake on August 13, just over a month hence, with twenty-five or twenty-nine ships of the line, bringing some three thousand troops of the Gâtinais, Agénois, and Touraine regiments, plus artillerists, cannon, and a hundred dragoons. Once in the Chesapeake he planned to stay until October 15—no longer—when he would have to return to the West Indies with his troops. It was clear at once to Rochambeau and Washington that they had a window of opportunity of four or five weeks at most in which to make use of the French fleet—*if* the British navy did not interfere.

Washington wrote in his diary on August 1 that he could no longer see any grounds for continuing preparations against New York City, "and therefore I turned my views more seriously than I had before done to the operation to the southward." Soon he was investigating whether there were any "deep-waisted sloops and schooners proper to carry horses" on the Delaware and the Chesapeake. From a joyful Lafayette he learned that Cornwallis was taking up a strong position at York and Gloucester, sealing himself off from rescue if the British fleet should not be on hand to protect him. York, the marquis wrote, "is surrounded by a river and a morass . . . Gloucester is a neck of land projected into the river and opposite to York"—both of them tempting, vulnerable targets. One man in the young Frenchman's army considered the situation and concluded that Cornwallis's "single tour to Virginia has cost the King more money by the loss of forts, men, cannon, stores, magazines, and supposed Carolina territory, than it would have cost the whole nobility of England to have made the tour of the world."

On August 14 Washington received what was unquestionably one of the most important letters of the war. Barras wrote from Newport, having heard from de Grasse that he was definitely sailing for the

Chesapeake, bringing twenty-nine warships and more than three thousand troops. As Washington now knew, he had barely two months in which to concentrate the allied armies in Virginia, at least six hundred miles from Newport, and he wrote, "Matters having now come to a crisis and a decisive plan to be determined on, I was obliged, from the shortness of Count de Grasse's promised stay on this coast . . . and the feeble compliance of the States to my requisitions for men . . . to give up all idea of attacking New York. . . ."

On August 15 the General instructed Lafayette to position his force in such a way as to prevent Cornwallis from returning to North Carolina, and at the same time ordered General William Heath to remain behind with a regiment of artillery, Sheldon's dragoons, and a number of understrength infantry regiments to safeguard the Hudson River posts. It was by no means enough, but it was all he could possibly spare. At the same time, since the crucial need was to convince Clinton that an attack was to be made on New York, rumors were spread that de Grasse was expected imminently, while the allied troops began crossing the Hudson near King's Bridge. Knowing how vulnerable the armies were at that point, a French officer was astonished at Clinton's inactivity. "An enemy, a little bold and able," he wrote, "would have seized the moment of our crossing . . . for an attack. His indifference and lethargy at this moment is an enigma that cannot be solved by me." What the Frenchman did not know was that one more worry had been added to General Clinton's list of woes, leading him to be more cautious than ever. Prince William—George III's son—had arrived in New York, seeking a bit of adventure. Now here was a young man the Americans would dearly love to capture, and Clinton had no intention of doing anything that would expose him to danger.

From King's Bridge, the allied armies moved to New Jersey as if they were to assault Staten Island, and to preserve the fiction, Washington brought along some landing craft capable of ferrying troops across to the island and the French built some bake ovens as though they were planning for a long stay.

Apparently, the American commander had enough money by then

to pay for express riders to carry his messages to Congress. A British spy (who signed himself "A Gentleman of Philadelphia") informed his contact, a Captain Beckwith, that he was unlikely to send more information on the "Force and Situation" of Washington's army, because the General now sent messages by different routes and "in as secret a way as possible." All of which suggests that the spy had been intercepting Washington's reports with some regularity. That aside, the "Gentleman" was able to give Beckwith a full account of all vessels that had sailed from Philadelphia's port, including details concerning their cargoes and destinations.

★　★　★

AS HE HAD demonstrated on so many occasions during this long war, George Washington was a gambler—he had to be, given the paucity of his resources and the odds against him. Now, with recruiting almost at a dead end and his army dwindling day by day, he had no choice but to head for Virginia, hoping against hope that de Grasse's fleet would materialize on schedule.

It was a formidable challenge—one on which the future of Washington's army and the newborn United States depended—and the operation was fraught with uncertainties and potential problems. First and foremost: what if the French naval squadron did not show up? Allied cooperation had failed before: in 1778, in an abortive campaign at Newport; in 1779 at Savannah; and in 1780 when the French fleet had been cooped up by the British at Newport. Another possibility was that the French fleet might be driven off by the British, in which case the allied armies would be stranded between New York and Virginia and the forces of Clinton and Cornwallis. A further uncertainty had to do with Barras, who was then in Newport with his squadron. He had to be persuaded to abandon his proposed attack on Newfoundland in order to carry Rochambeau's heavy cannon to the Chesapeake, along with a large quantity of salt provisions Washington had laid aside for just such a purpose. Barras was actually senior to de Grasse and had no wish to serve under him. To compound the difficulties, Barras would have to sail past New York and on to the Chesapeake in the face of a likely encounter with a superior British naval force—quite possibly the fleet under the formidable Sir George Rodney that was rumored to be en route to New York from the West Indies.

It is hard to conceive the difficulties of timing inherent in the scheme. Here you had one fleet sailing north from the West Indies and another coming south from Newport, both subject to the vagaries of wind, the possibility of severe storms, and the likelihood that they would be intercepted by British warships. And these two fleets were expected to meet on schedule.

Then, rendezvousing with them would be some nine or ten thousand troops from two armies that could scarcely communicate with each other, soldiers who had to march hundreds of miles to their destination over poor or nonexistent roads, uncertain weather conditions, and the possibility of attack by General Clinton's forces.

And—the all-important fact—these disparate allied forces had to come together at precisely the same moment. All things considered, it appeared that only a miracle could make it happen.

★   ★   ★

AS WASHINGTON'S AND Rochambeau's armies made their way south, Lafayette was about to get some help from the Pennsylvania line, which began arriving in Virginia in early June. In late March Anthony Wayne had promised Lafayette a thousand men, and on May 7 the Frenchman sent him a message, writing on the outside, "This letter being of grim importance must be forwarded day and night." Even though the plea for help was slow in arriving, it was no easy matter for Wayne to fulfill his earlier promise. His men were in no mood to travel anywhere unless they were paid in something other than the hopelessly depreciated Continental currency. Writing from Philadelphia, Colonel William Grayson reported, "Wayne, with a thousand men, can't move a peg at present for the want of cash. . . ." (In addition, his soldiers hated the idea of marching south, where the very air was regarded as unhealthy by northern troops, who were certain it caused ague and fever. Lafayette had been warned that since his hair was thin and he wore no wig, he might suffer death in the southern sun.) So angry were the Pennsylvanians over the lack of real money that another mutiny broke out, which was put down by the most draconian measures. Twelve ringleaders were sentenced to death, and when the firing squad shot, seven men fell, six of them dead. The seventh was bayoneted, with Wayne pointing a pistol at the executioner to ensure the deed was done. After the other five men were hanged, the Pennsylvanians marched, "mute as fish."

So, at the same time the combined forces of Washington and Rochambeau were heading south, soldiers in the Pennsylvania line were marching in the same direction. One of the Pennsylvania officers, whose name has been lost to history, kept a journal, recording the daily events common to all armies on the march, with comments on the weather, which had so much effect on their spirits and comfort level (or lack thereof), along with departures from the norm. His first entry notes that the officers were sick from "excess of drinking." The next day they were under the weather for the same reason, this time with some suffering fits. Then they had to spruce up—wash their clothing and burnish their weapons—for a review by the governor of Pennsylvania and his lady. Crossing a river, a boat carrying ammunition sank, injuring a sergeant, while three men and two horses drowned.

They slogged through rainwater "half a leg deep" before reaching Virginia, about which the writer had little good to say: "Nothing but Negros and Indian Corn, the soil being in Genl. very poor and the Timber chiefly Pine." Several days later they arrived at their destination, joining Lafayette's command, and for the next two weeks marched and countermarched at all hours of the day and night, hoping to meet the enemy on favorable ground, but not until the end of June—on a "day the hotest I ever felt"—did they see any action. They tried to intercept Lieutenant Colonel Simcoe's cavalry, but Lafayette ordered them to withdraw, fearing that "the Whole British Army would come in pursuit" of them.

One man was shot for desertion; their regimental doctor and two soldiers drowned. Then they had a skirmish on July 6 near Jamestown, where the British again outnumbered them, costing the Pennsylvanians 24 killed, 107 wounded, and the loss of two six-pounders. During this period they visited Richmond, where they found much of the city destroyed by Arnold and great numbers of slaves with smallpox who were dead or dying. They also encountered Baron Steuben, who gave them a lesson in maneuvers to be employed in a siege.

During the ninety-eight-day period between May 26 and September 1, they had spent sixty-seven days marching, traveling at least 735 miles (an average of nearly 11 miles a day).

★   ★   ★

ONE MAN WHO kept his finger on the pulse of the constantly changing situation in Virginia was George Mason, squire of Gunston Hall in Alexandria. This former delegate to the Continental Congress had one son, William, who had just returned from militia service in South Carolina, and another, Thomson, who was recently back from a tour of duty on the James River, so their father had up-to-date information on the state's militia when he wrote on June 3, 1781, to his eldest son and namesake in Paris.

An enemy fleet commanded Virginia's shores and was able to move British troops "from place to place, where they please, without opposition, so that we no sooner collect a Force sufficient to counteract them in one part of the Country, but they shift to another. . . ." He informed young George of Lafayette's whereabouts, and his reinforcements from Pennsylvania. Greene was in South Carolina and had taken all the enemy's posts there except Charleston; General Phillips had died recently; Arnold succeeded him but was soon superseded by Cornwallis, who was now in overall command of the enemy army in Virginia.

British forces were rampaging through the state, burning tobacco warehouses and plundering the country. If only the French fleet would arrive, Mason added, it would immediately change the face of affairs, "but it has been so long expected in vain, that little credit is now given to reports concerning it." As George Mason, Jr., knew, his family's part of Virginia was a Whig stronghold, "well affected to the french alliance, yet they grow uneasy and restless & begin to think that our Allies are spinning out the war, in order to weaken America, as well as Great Britain & thereby leave us, at the End of it, as dependent as possible upon themselves." Perhaps this was an unjust opinion, but it was natural that it was held by many farmers and planters, heavily burdened with taxes, whose sons were frequently taken from their families for military duty. Those people saw readily enough how the British fleet could move troops hither and yon around the continent and how a strong French fleet would have prevented this from happening.

Mason did not know how much longer Americans could hold out against the unequal opposition of Great Britain. France clearly wanted the states separated from England, but "by drawing out the thread too fine & long, it may unexpectedly break in her hands."

In conclusion, he wrote, "God bless you, my dear Child! and grant that we may meet again, in your native country, as Freemen; otherwise, that we may never see each other more, is the prayer of your affectionate Father, G. Mason."

★　★　★

WHILE THE ALLIED generals had their own concerns, Sir Henry Clinton was reckoning with the threat that he might be attacked. He was well aware of the movement of the allied troops, since most of their line of march from King's Ferry on the Hudson to the Delaware lay along a route he took to be an operation against Staten Island. He was also receiving accurate data from his network of spies and alert patrols. After the Wethersfield conference General Chastellux had written to La Luzerne to say that despite Rochambeau's opposition, he had persuaded the latter to attack New York, and at the same time Washington wrote to Major General John Sullivan with roughly the same message. Both letters were intercepted by Clinton's men, and the British general—eager to spread discord—gleefully sent Chastellux's letter to Rochambeau under a flag of truce, saying that he "ought to be on guard against his associates." Rochambeau, in a frosty reply, requested Clinton to refrain from sending him further flags of truce "because they would no longer be received, since General Washington was the commander-in-chief of the combined army." At the same time Rochambeau summoned Chastellux, asked if he recognized the letter, and when he admitted that he did gave him a dressing-down, adding that "Although he would not have expected such conduct from him, to show him . . . that he did not wish to report it to the court, he was burning his letter, hoping that this lesson would be sufficient." These letters and, especially, the presence of the boats Washington had brought along as props strengthened Clinton's belief that Staten Island was an allied objective.

Understandably, Rochambeau was increasingly disturbed by what he perceived as Washington's indiscretion, but in this instance there is strong reason to believe that the American commander wanted the information leaked to the enemy. Whatever the truth of the matter, Clinton sent Cornwallis a copy of Washington's letter along with an order to send two thousand of his troops to him at once and to take a defensive position at Williamsburg or Yorktown.

When the allied forces appeared on the east side of the Hudson near King's Bridge, just fifteen miles from lower Manhattan, it became clear to Clinton that he was threatened and would have to have reinforcements from Cornwallis in order to defend New York. Upon hearing that the two hundred jägers plus loyalists posted at King's Bridge had skirmished with the enemy, he was apprehensive that a full-scale attack was imminent and rode to the scene immediately to size up the situation. Seeing that nothing could be attempted without bringing on a general action—which he was not prepared to do—he took heart from Washington's withdrawal to White Plains and figured his advanced post in Westchester was adequate as long as the allies made no further moves against it.

In the meantime he kept turning over in his mind the possibility of launching an attack on Philadelphia. He and Cornwallis had been arguing over this by mail, Clinton taking the position that the city contained the rebels' "principal depots of stores for the campaign, an immense quantity of European and West India commodities, and no inconsiderable supply of money, which their uninterrupted trade and cruisers have lately procured them." Furthermore, he argued, bitter experience had convinced him (and should convince Cornwallis) that no possibility existed of reestablishing order in any rebellious province "without the hearty assistance of numerous friends. These, My Lord, are not, I think, to be found in Virginia. . . . But I believe there is a greater probability of finding them in Pennsylvania than in any except the southern provinces." The earl, he pointed out, had tried to find the purported Tory strength in the Carolinas and had failed. The only remaining source of loyalist support lay in and around Philadelphia, and as long as he remained in command, he intended to exploit the situation there.

★   ★   ★

WORD ARRIVED AT allied headquarters that Barras would sail from Newport to Virginia on August 21. This welcome news meant that de Grasse's fleet would be beefed up, making it superior to anything the British could muster, but even so, questions remained. The allied generals now knew when and where they would march, but the fiction of an attack on New York had to be maintained lest Clinton assail them while they were on the move, and at a certain moment the British general would know with certainty that they were bound for the South. To date, even the men in Washington's army had to guess what was happening: as Surgeon Thacher wrote, "Our situation reminds me of some theatrical exhibition, where the interest and expectations of the spectators are continually increasing, and where curiosity is wrought to the highest point."

A message from General David Forman, who was at a lookout post near Sandy Hook in New York harbor, produced a flurry of excitement and suspense. He reported eighteen large British ships of war off the Hook; if these were added to those formerly under Arbuthnot, it would give the British twenty-nine—possibly a few more than de Grasse had. The next day Washington, who had passed through Princeton to Trenton, heard again from Forman. This time the news was more encouraging. The fleet he had spotted consisted of only fifteen ships of the line and four frigates. Whether they were under Rodney or Admiral Graves could not be determined, but it meant that the British strength was not twenty-nine but twenty-two, at most.

One group of French officers took advantage of their stop in Princeton to examine the terrain and replay the battle Washington had won there in 1776. All of them had studied military history and battlefield topography as part of their education, and this was too good an opportunity to be lost. At a relaxed moment they gathered around a table covered with maps showing the evacuation of Boston, Burgoyne's surrender, and one based on the engraving by William Faden, showing the surprise of Trenton and the march on Princeton. On a visit to the French camp Washington passed the tent of these officers, looked in and saw what they were studying, and "Despite his modesty . . . seemed pleased to find thus assembled all the successful and pleasant events of the war." He joined them at a tavern and had some Madeira and punch, after which they all mounted horses and escorted him back to his camp.

On August 30, after learning that Rochambeau had heard from Lafayette that Cornwallis had retired to York and entrenched his army, it dawned on the junior officers that they were headed for Virginia to confront the British general and his army.

7

A PARTIAL ENGAGEMENT

From Chatham, New Jersey, on August 27, General Washington wrote to Governor Thomas Nelson of Virginia, who had succeeded Thomas Jefferson in June, telling him that plans had changed, that the combined armies were heading south to join a formidable fleet and land forces under Admiral de Grasse to "strike a blow at the Enemy in Virginia." In order for this operation to succeed, it was imperative that the state of Virginia supply the allies with salted provisions,* beef cattle, forage, and teams of horses with wagons. He was confident of victory over Cornwallis but could not emphasize enough the need for Virginia to cooperate. "Let me entreat your Excellency that every exertion may be made to feed and supply our army while we have occasion to continue in the State." That put it squarely up to the governor, who in fact had just issued a broadside announcing the arrival of the French fleet and calling for "Vigorous exertions" to ensure the conquest of the British. He urged all militiamen to turn out "with a gun of any sort," and everyone was asked to supply flour

---

*Washington had set aside a considerable store of salted provisions in Rhode Island but feared they would not arrive in Virginia in time to feed the army.

and spirits in particular, plus cattle, wagons, and horses. "Not a moment is to be lost in the Execution of this Business," he added.

Passing through Trenton, Washington proceeded toward Philadelphia in company with Rochambeau, Chastellux, and a host of French officers, and on the outskirts of the city they were met by members of the City Guard, who escorted them into town. The American commander met a number of old friends and then rode to the home of the financier Robert Morris, where he set up headquarters. He paid a visit to Congress, which was in terrible straits: in recent months as many as five states were sometimes unrepresented; it had no credit and was attempting to hold off creditors; while members were working on a treaty with Holland, trying to determine the borders of Vermont, and endeavoring to patch up the weak Articles of Confederation. But as far as taking action went, Congress, to all intents and purposes, was impotent.

Following the generals, the French and American armies marched south, with the French continually enthralled by the countryside—especially the fertile New Jersey farmland and the charm of Trenton, with its many handsome buildings. En route through Pennsylvania they commented on the "rich and large villages" and the fine countryside that had escaped the ravages of the British when they abandoned Philadelphia. Even Baron Closen's disappointment at finding no good Rhine wine in the vicinity was somewhat mollified when he tasted a pear cider, which he declared delicious.

On August 30 the French officers traveling with the army entered Philadelphia and made their way to the assembly hall, where the generals and local notables awaited them. After downing a rum punch, they went to La Luzerne's residence, where "Rochambeau and his staff were housed like princes," and dined that evening at financier Robert Morris's home, where they had "all the foreign wines possible with which to drink endless toasts" to the kings of France and Spain, the United States, and the speedy arrival of the Comte de Grasse, while in the city's harbor several vessels fired salutes in honor of the occasion. Later the city was illuminated in tribute to Washington,

who strolled through some of the principal streets surrounded by
enthusiastic admirers. He can hardly have been in the mood for
toasts; he was writing Lafayette to say, "I am distressed beyond
expression to know what is become of the Count de Grasse, and for
fear the English fleet, by occupying the Chesapeake (towards which
my last accounts say they were steering) should frustrate all our flattering prospects in that quarter." It was no easy time for a man whose
heart was set on the success of a plan of enormous complexity. As
soon as Lafayette had news of any kind, he was to send it *on the Spur
of Speed*, for I am almost all impatience and anxiety. . . ."

On the afternoon of September 2 the American army made its
appearance but did not halt; thanks to the hot, dry weather the troops
marched through town and raised a cloud of dust "like a smothering
snow-storm," according to Surgeon James Thacher, who found it
embarrassing "as the ladies were viewing us from the open windows
of every house as we passed through this splendid city." The line of
march was a good two miles long, and "The general officers and their
aides, in rich military uniform, mounted on noble steeds elegantly
caparisoned, were followed by their servants and baggage." Behind
each brigade came several fieldpieces and ammunition wagons, and
the soldiers, he reported, "marched in slow and solemn step, regu-
lated by drum and fife."

Certainly, no private soldier in the ranks wore a "rich military uniform" comparable to those of the officers, and it came as a shock to
Philadelphians lining the streets to see these dirt-caked, threadbare
men who made up the army of the United States. Nor did the troops
look to be enjoying themselves despite the cheers from the crowd.
Some two thousand of them—Colonel Alexander Scammell's Continental light infantry, the Rhode Island and Moses Hazen's regiments,
two regiments of Continentals from New York, John Lamb's
artillerymen, light infantry from Connecticut and New York, plus
sappers and miners—a mixed bag, to be sure, were thoroughly unen-
thusiastic about heading south into what they regarded as an
unhealthy climate, far from home. More to the point, they had

received no pay and were not about to embark on a new adventure without some of that money in negotiable coins in their pockets. The impasse was resolved when the obliging Rochambeau loaned Washington twenty thousand dollars so the Continental Army could continue south.

Few of those men looked forward to the road that lay ahead, for these marches were exhausting, even under ideal circumstances. Private Joseph Plumb Martin wrote years after the war, ". . . I have felt more anxiety, undergone more fatigue and hardships, suffered more every way, in performing one of those tedious marches than ever I did in fighting the hottest battle I was ever engaged in. . . ."

For the young men and boys who had rarely, if ever, been away from home and were every day more distant from their loved ones, the longing for families could be painful, and Francis Barber meant to see that his wife wrote him regularly and kissed their children, George and Polly, over and over again for him. In mid-July he sent off a letter numbered 6 and said how anxious he was because only that day had he received a message she wrote on June 1. That said, he proceeded to lecture her sternly on how often he wished she would write, and at what length. He did not want apologies about how she was in a hurry or that it was too late at night to write fully. Think how you would feel, he said, if after four weeks of anxious waiting for a letter one was handed to you "written on the quarter of a sheet of paper; your last, my dear Nancy, comes under [that] description."

He was enjoying "uninterrupted health," he told her, despite the hardships of their march, which had "robbed me of all my fat" and made him "the colour of an Indian." The letter was signed, "I have the happiness to be, dear Nancy, your most faithfull and affectionate husband, F. Barber." Under the date on the letter someone has written in pencil, *"Killed at Yorktown."*

On the same day the Americans paraded through Philadelphia, General Sir Henry Clinton sent a message to Lord Cornwallis: "By intelligence which I have this day received, it would seem that Mr. Washington is moving with an army to the southward, with an appearance of haste; and gives out that he expects the cooperation of a considerable French armament. Your Lordship, however, may be assured that if this should be the case, I shall endeavour to reinforce your command by all means within the compass of my power. . . ." Whether Cornwallis realized it or not, this meant that he was going to be dependent on the navy to bring him reinforcements or, if necessary, remove his army from the peninsula he had chosen to occupy.

★ ★ ★

ON SEPTEMBER 3 the real show began in Philadelphia with the appearance of the first French brigade. As Chastellux put it aptly, "The arrival of the French troops . . . was in the nature of a triumph." The soldiers had halted about a mile outside the city, where they "spruced up," powdering their hair and donning dress white uniforms so they were "dressed as elegantly as ever were the soldiers of a garrison on a day of royal review." With flags unfurled and drums beating and a cannon at the head of each regiment, with slow match lighted, they followed Lauzun's chasseurs down Front Street and up Vine to the Commons at Centre Square with brass bands playing, the crowds wild with enthusiasm, as "the ladies appeared at the windows in their most splendid attire. All Philadelphia was astonished to see people who had endured the fatigues of a long journey so ruddy and so handsome." Perhaps nothing emphasized the dramatic difference from their American allies so much as the runners who carried orders from one command to another wearing short, tight-bodied coats, rich waistcoats with a silver fringe, rose-colored shoes, cap adorned with a coat of arms, and a cane with an enormous head. Word went through the crowd that all these young fellows were princes (they looked it but were not).

At the last they passed in review in single file before assembled congressmen and the president of that body, who was "wearing a black velvet coat and dressed in a most singular fashion," past the commanding generals and the French minister, and then went into camp on the large plain near the river. For the American onlookers, the spotless, colorful uniforms of the French were like nothing they had seen: all were white, but the different regiments could be identified by the different colors of their lapels, collars, and buttons. The Bourbonnais had crimson lapels, pink collars, and white buttons; the Soissonais, who put on a brilliant exhibition of the manual of arms a day or so later for some twenty thousand spectators, wore rose-colored lapels, light blue collars, and yellow buttons, plus white and rose-colored feathers in their grenadier caps. The climactic moment came when Lauzun's cavalry clattered into view—German, Irish, and Polish mercenaries, many of them—wearing sky-blue jackets with white braid, yellow trousers, sashes with scarlet and yellow stripes, black boots, and towering black fezzes. Even their horses had saddle blankets of white sheepskin trimmed in light blue. It was not lost on the Philadelphians that many of the young officers came from old titled French families, and to cap it all, the Duc de Lauzun, the only duke to fight in America, rode at the head of this extraordinary procession. It was an experience that was remembered for years in great detail by Philadelphians and passed along to succeeding generations as one of the most memorable moments in the city's history.

The Comte de Clermont-Crèvecoeur and several friends paid a call on two of the city's prominent scientists: Pierre Eugène du Simitière and Dr. Abraham Chovet. The former showed them his museum of natural history, as yet unfinished, and later they looked with wonder at Dr. Chovet's life-size wax figures of a man and a woman, with removable organs, which he used in teaching anatomy. It was impossible to behold these, the count wrote, "without shuddering."

What struck the French visitors about Philadelphia was its cosmopolitan character. While the Quakers outnumbered other religions, the city "probably contains every religious sect in the world. Freedom of conscience is tolerated here," one of them wrote, and "Little by little this superb city has been settled from every country in Europe and has become quite a commercial center. Since the war this seems to be the only city in America whose trade has not declined; in fact, the war seems to have made it even more prosperous"—a phenomenon that owed a lot to the extremely large Quaker population. He went on to say that the Philadelphians seemed to take little interest in who was winning the war. They were almost all merchants, and several told him that they didn't want peace—it would only hurt their trade.

Everywhere the French went, they discovered something about Americans that surprised or sometimes shocked them, and Philadelphia was no exception. In that city, they learned, young people received as fine an education as they could obtain in Europe, and their schools offered every type of instruction, which led Clermont-Crèvecoeur to speculate on the class system in Philadelphia. While neither rank nor distinction existed among ordinary citizens—all of whom believed themselves equal, enabling a cordwainer, a locksmith, or a merchant to become a member of Congress—"The rich alone take precedence over the common people." One effect of this was to create a scramble for lucrative jobs, which were usually bestowed on the wealthy because they could make "their alleged talents shine in the light of their gold," letting the right people know they had money. To put it another way, Americans considered themselves equals but showed a certain deference to those with money, "who associate only with one another."

He saw poor families whose daughters "could not be better dressed. They would rather dress well and look rich than eat better food," and while the wardrobes of these girls were not large, "One sees no girls here in town or country whose hair is not dressed in the French fashion. Those who cannot afford jewelry make up for it by substituting ordinary ribbons and feathers . . . and nature's richest ornaments—flowers." On the other hand, Americans had an unrivaled casualness, and anyone who tried to instill in them a taste for the social life comparable to France's was wasting his time and trouble.

Once again Clermont-Crèvecoeur took a swipe at bundling—this time, at the habit of girls and young women who visit a female friend for five or six days at a time. What can one make of this? he asked. "Certainly nothing favorable to these belles. Do they not bundle with one another? This is what many people think. One dare not state it as a fact. But their attitude towards men, their conduct when in their company, the disappearance of the lilies and roses of their youth at the age of twenty to twenty-eight, and their distaste for bundling with men are all good reasons for believing that one is not mistaken."

Officers in Rochambeau's army were astonished to find a low regard for the military profession in America. While high-ranking officers were held in esteem, lieutenants were "virtually scorned," and an American general would never invite a lowly lieutenant to join him at a meal. The difference, of course, was that every commissioned officer in the French military had to produce proof of nobility, so that a lieutenant, for example, might enjoy the same social status as a general. But they gradually became adjusted to the American attitude. "Since the two armies are now joined, the same rules had to apply to both. For a long time we were unhappy about this situation, but after a while no longer thought about it."

★   ★   ★

ONE OF THE many rivers that flows into Chesapeake Bay is the Elk, and Washington planned to load his troops for embarkation at what was called Head of Elk. On September 5 he said farewell to Rochambeau—who wanted to travel from Philadelphia to Chester by water—and rode southward while the count and his staff drifted down the Delaware in a small boat and had a memorable trip. "It would be difficult to have a more beautiful sight than that of Philadelphia as one leaves it by water," one of them wrote, before they passed by some of the landmarks of the 1777 campaign: Mud Island, Red Bank, and Billingsport.

Downriver, approaching Chester, the French officers could see an American officer dancing up and down, waving his hat with one hand and a handkerchief with the other. At first they thought it might be Washington, but that was impossible; the behavior of His Excellency, the Comte de Deux-Ponts knew, was "of a natural coldness and a noble approach." But Washington indeed it was, and Deux-Ponts said, "his features, his whole bearing and deportment were now changed in an instant." Suddenly, he was "a citizen happy beyond measure at the good fortune of his country." The Duc de Lauzun, who was also there, wrote, "I never saw a man so thoroughly and openly delighted."

"I caught sight of General Washington," Rochambeau recalled, "waving his hat at me with demonstrative gestures of the greatest joy. When I rode up to him, he explained that he had just received a dispatch . . . informing him that de Grasse had arrived." Then, as Baron Closen wrote, "MM. De Rochambeau and Washington embraced *warmly* on the shore" (surprising Closen, who had been troubled earlier by the obvious coolness between the two over the question of attacking New York). Rochambeau must have felt enormous satisfaction that his plans were coming to fruition, the baron observed, noting that "The soldiers from then on spoke of Cornwallis as if they had already captured him; but one must not count his chickens before they are hatched. It is true that he will be taken soon."

★   ★   ★

AS EAGERLY AS Washington and others looked forward to the arrival of de Grasse's fleet, the brief history of relations between America's army and France's navy hardly inspired confidence or enthusiasm. Colonial suspicion of the French was an old one, of course, dating back to the numerous French and Indian wars, when their neighbors in Canada succeeded in setting the frontiers aflame, with murderous attacks, kidnappings, and the pillage of villages and isolated farms. These savage conflicts were largely quiescent after the peace of 1763, but that was less than a generation ago, and in New England, particularly, dislike of French Catholicism and Bourbon despotism remained a tenet of Puritanism.

So in the best of circumstances a Frenchman arriving in America was greeted with a certain wariness, to say the least. Nevertheless, the alliance with France that came after the rebels' astonishing victory over Burgoyne's army in 1777 not only was welcomed by many Americans but was seen as the avenue to victory and real independence, a view that engendered a great deal of overconfidence. Unhappily, the coalition got off to a very rocky start.

In the spring of 1778, not long after the treaty of alliance took effect, a large fleet under the command of the Comte d' Estaing sailed from Toulon and made an incredibly slow crossing of three months, missing a rare opportunity to catch a British fleet in Chesapeake Bay that was ferrying Clinton's army to New York after the enemy evacuated Philadelphia. By the time d'Estaing arrived at the Delaware capes, he was low on water and provisions and had sick men on board every ship. He sailed north, only to be told by local pilots that the depth of the water at Sandy Hook, at the entrance to New York's harbor, was no more than twenty-one feet at low tide, and his ships drew twenty-seven feet. The pilots added that they could take him into New York Bay only when a northeast wind coincided with a strong spring tide—which meant that he would have to wait until the following year to make the attempt.

On July 20 he sailed for Newport in response to a recommendation by Congress, expecting to cooperate with Major General John Sullivan's force there to capture the three-thousand-man British garrison. At one point the Americans had an army of ten thousand—most of them militia—greatly outnumbering the British, but through a series of mishaps and misunderstandings the effort turned into a giant fiasco, with a breakdown of communications and Sullivan peremptorily ordering d'Estaing to do this and do that. One of the French officers left a vivid description of the American militia: "I have never seen a more laughable spectacle. All the tailors and apothecaries in the country must have been called out. . . . One could recognize them by their round wigs. They were mounted on bad nags and looked like a flock of ducks in cross-belts. . . . I guessed that these warriors were more anxious to eat up our supplies than to make a close acquaintance with the enemy, and I was not mistaken; they soon disappeared"—five thousand of them in a few days' time. Admiral d'Estaing was gentlemanly enough to ignore Sullivan's criticism, but it was plain to see that the American had created a real rift with the new allies, especially when he implied that they had run from a fight. Then, when d'Estaing's fleet—badly damaged by a storm—sailed off for Boston, leaving Sullivan to fight the British garrison alone, the reputation of the French plummeted. The situation was made even worse when Sullivan and his generals signed a letter saying the French departure was "derogatory to the honor of France, contrary to the intentions of his Most Christian Majesty and the interest of this nation, and destructive in the highest degree to the welfare of the United States of America, and highly injurious to the alliance formed between the two nations." In the aftermath, attempting to ameliorate the effects on the alliance, Washington urged Lafayette "to afford a healing hand to the wound that unintentionally has been made," at the same time appealing to d'Estaing to forgive and forget. Both sides put the ugly incident behind them, but the damage had been done.

★   ★   ★

THE UNHAPPY TALE of the joint effort to take Savannah in 1779 is quickly told. It began in the spring of 1778 when His Majesty George III, who spent a good many waking hours doing his best to micro-manage the war in America, looked at the map, realized how remote the Carolinas and Georgia were from the rest of the states, and decreed that General Clinton's strategy should include an attack "upon the southern colonies with a view to the conquest . . . of Georgia and South Carolina." Once in British hands, those territories would revert to royal colonies and serve as stepping-stones to North Carolina, the Chesapeake, and Virginia. The king decided that two thousand men would be enough to seize and retain Savannah, and, taking another step, he laid out a plan by which Georgia's most important port should be reduced in an operation in which "large numbers of the inhabitants would flock to the King's standard. . . ." Clinton was also instructed to dispatch 3,500 men under Lieutenant Colonel Archibald Campbell to meet General Augustin Prevost, who would bring a detachment from the British garrison at St. Augustine plus a number of Indians. The two of them would converge on Savannah, and Savannah would be in British hands.

In the waning days of December Campbell, without waiting for Prevost because the number of Americans protecting Savannah was fewer than a thousand men, had an aged slave guide part of his force through the swamps while another approached from the other side. Taken by surprise in front and rear, the Americans lost more than five hundred dead, wounded, and missing, and the few survivors headed for South Carolina.

In the meantime General Benjamin Lincoln, an obese Massachusetts militia officer with an undistinguished record, who was reckoned by Washington to be an "active, spirited, sensible man," had been named commander of the southern department and reached Charleston early in December. Lincoln had some eight hundred Continentals in Charleston, and he and John Rutledge, the South Carolina governor, had written to Admiral d'Estaing urging him to join them in an operation to retrieve Savannah from the British. Suddenly, early in September 1779, they received word that d'Estaing was actually off the coast of Georgia with four thousand men and could stay no longer than two weeks, since the hurricane season would soon be upon them. Lincoln collected every soldier within reach, sent out a call for South Carolina and Georgia militia, and took off through the piney woods to Georgia, arriving there to join d'Estaing on the 16th of the month. It turned out that the count—without waiting for Lincoln—had told Prevost to surrender but then, instead of storming the city with his superior forces, had done nothing. The Briton took advantage of the lapse by increasing his numbers with the garrison from Beaufort and strengthening his defenses so that by the time the allies had their batteries ready to lay siege to the town, the British were ready for them.

When days and nights of cannonading the town proved fruitless, although almost every dwelling was damaged, d'Estaing and Lincoln were bickering over just about everything (including the quality of meals at the latter's table), and the Frenchman was increasingly anxious about heavy weather in the offing. At his insistence, they made a direct assault on the enemy's works. It was the worst decision that could have been made; within an hour the British ditch "was filled with dead" from the allies' army, "many hung dead and wounded on the abatis," and beyond the defense perimeter "the plain was strewed with mangled bodies," according to an Englishman. D'Estaing himself was badly wounded, and the American and French casualties were more than eight hundred to the enemy's loss of fifty-seven.

D'Estaing, with his crews dying from scurvy and fever, and his ships threatened by the onset of hurricane weather, was determined to leave at once despite the pleas of the Americans, and a badly disappointed Lincoln reluctantly led his shattered army beyond the Savannah River as the French disappeared over the horizon. The cost of this failure was enormous. Their successful defense of the town had given the British a vital foothold from which they could move north, just as George III had in mind, with the strong possibility of reducing the Americans' hold on all the southern states. Thanks to the failure of allied arms, the enemy had an entirely new and promising field of operations.

★   ★   ★

EARLY IN 1780 the inept, hapless d'Estaing returned to France, where he was influential in persuading the government to send Rochambeau with an army to America,* but regrettably, the sour taste of the admiral's failures had so poisoned the attitude of the rebels that news of yet another French fleet on its way was greeted with little enthusiasm by the general public.

---

*After the war d'Estaing went into politics, became commandant of the National Guard, and was appointed admiral by the National Assembly. But he remained loyal to the royal family, testified in favor of Marie Antoinette, and was sent to the guillotine in 1794.

The successor to d'Estaing was another count—François-Joseph-Paul, Comte de Grasse, a giant of a man, six feet two inches tall, heavyset, extremely handsome, and a member of one of France's oldest aristocratic families. Now fifty-nine years old, he had attended naval school at the age of eleven, served in several campaigns against the Turks, and fought in the War of Jenkins's Ear in 1740, when he was taken prisoner by the British. Held for three months, he profited from the experience by making a number of English friends and collecting invaluable information about their navy. After serving in the Indian Ocean, West Indies, and Mediterranean, he took command of the seventy-four-gun *Intrépide* in 1778, the same year he became a commodore. Subsequently, he served with d'Estaing in the West Indies and was present at the action at Savannah. After a spell of bad health when he remained in France, he was promoted to rear admiral and sailed from Brest with twenty ships of the line—all carrying seventy-four guns or more—three frigates, two cutters, several heavy freighters, and a convoy of 150 vessels for the West Indies. At the same time he was given the rank of lieutenant general, which made him senior to all the other French general officers (including Barras, who accepted reality and served under his orders until the War for Independence ended).

De Grasse's flotilla set sail on March 22, 1781, with a favorable wind that continued until they were south of Madeira nine days later. On the 25th of the month they reached the area of the trade winds, and finally sighted the island of Martinique in the Lesser Antilles at dawn on April 28. From the governor general of the Leeward Islands they learned that an English fleet of eighteen ships of the line, under Admiral Sir Samuel Hood, had blockaded the entrance to Fort Royal, the capital of Martinique, for almost two months and was still waiting for the French to appear. At daybreak the following day, de Grasse deployed his fleet in line of battle and, keeping to windward, sailed off to meet the British, sighting the enemy about eight o'clock.

When the two fleets met, it was clear that the British ships were better sailers, and those vessels maintained excellent order, while the

French center and rear squadrons were badly scattered. The skirmish continued through the day until ten o'clock at night, with the French *Vaillant* the principal casualty after being shelled continuously by four enemy ships for almost two hours.

The next day was spent with the two fleets attempting to outmaneuver each other. On May 1 de Grasse discovered that Hood was withdrawing and tried to overtake him, but only one frigate had enough speed, and after sending two broadsides through the English admiral's cabin windows, the frigate and the rest of the French ships retired and headed for Martinique. Anchoring there on May 6, de Grasse summoned all his captains and "with the sharpest reproaches" let them know how dissatisfied he was with the performance of some of them, especially in obeying signals and acting accordingly.

★ ★ ★

ONE OF THE men who sailed with de Grasse was a young Swedish naval officer, Carl Gustaf Tornquist, who was filled with enthusiasm for the American cause. Tornquist had obtained leave to travel to Paris, where he volunteered for service, and was accepted and assigned to the ship of the line *Vaillant* in the admiral's fleet. Like so many European visitors to the new world, he was fascinated by what he saw. Martinique, he discovered, had one of the best harbors in the West Indies, situated to the lee of the island and from twenty to fifty fathoms deep. It was large enough to accommodate sixty warships plus merchant vessels, while the repair wharf there was suitable for the largest ships of the line. One of the best features of the harbor was that ships were safe during hurricane season—between the end of July and the beginning of October—when the storms struck "with such violence that no ship can possibly keep to the sea, much less lay at anchor."

Fort Royal, with its abundant source of freshwater from two rivers, looked more like a village with many small stone houses, dominated by Government House and the large hospitals. St.-Pierre, the second city on the island, he described as "one of the prettiest, adorned with beautiful houses and orchards." That, too, had a large open roadstead and a splendid freshwater supply, which was piped out to ships in the harbor. The inhabitants, he went on, were generally well-to-do, thanks in large part to the intensive trade in sugar, cotton, coffee, tobacco, and Martinique liqueur, which Tornquist declared "the best in the whole world."

International trade was the lifeblood of the eighteenth century, and the West Indies was at the heart of it, thanks in no small part to the prevailing ocean currents. In the Atlantic, the Canary current off the Azores runs south and southeast along the west coast of Africa, then turns west to become the North Equatorial current that were followed by vessels bound for the Windward and Leeward islands. From here, off Venezuela to the east coast of Florida, what was known as the Spanish Main was the breeding ground of pirates who lurked in bays and inlets, lying in wait for Spanish ships loaded with treasure from Peru or an unsuspecting merchantman or slaver bound for America. From the Leeward Islands the Antilles current flows northwest to the Bahamas and Charleston, where it is picked up by the Gulf Stream and turns northeasterly and then east, heading back to Europe. In this great oval-shaped bowl formed by the Atlantic currents, trade that was absolutely vital to the American revolutionaries was conducted. Since Britain had prevented its colonies from developing the production of weapons or gunpowder and America lacked the raw materials and skills that were essential to their manufacture in large quantities, ammunition shipped from Europe was the Continental Army's sole source of supply, and the essential providers, or middlemen, were the neutral Dutch. Their town of St. Eustatius, or Statia, as it was called, was the wealthiest port in the Caribbean, and its importance is suggested by the fact that it changed hands more than twenty times in a century and a half.

English and French interest focused intensely on the West Indies because of the wealth produced by sugar and its by-products. Supposedly one-third of France's overseas trade came from the islands, and the British islands sent almost three hundred ships to London in most years—revenues in 1776 alone totaling £4.25 million, compared with £1.25 million from the East India Company. Britain did not really need the output of American farms; those simply duplicated the produce of the home islands, whereas the products of the tropical islands were a much better fit for the British economy. In 1778 Lord George Germain had made clear the need for controlling the West Indies: "Having them in possession, instead of cringing to an American Congress for peace, we shall prescribe the terms, and bid America be only what we please."

★ ★ ★

SAILING FOR TOBAGO, de Grasse's fleet soon sighted nine enemy ships of the line, but those vessels were fast sailers and had the advantage of the wind and eluded them. The same afternoon they captured two merchant vessels loaded with slaves, gold dust, ivory tusks, and whale blubber, cargoes estimated to be worth 600,000 livres. Running in to Tobago, which had been taken by France in June, they received word that enemy ships were in sight, which proved to be twenty-two ships of the line commanded by Rodney. The British admiral, Tornquist wrote, "presumably found our fleet in too good order [and] therefore refused to fight." Whatever the reason, the British sailed away under cover of darkness.

On June 20 de Grasse's fleet anchored off Tobago, where the troops debarked and took on water and food supplies, including the purchase of one hundred oxen for provisions, before beginning to repair all the damaged ships. During the several engagements in the West Indies they had lost 46 dead and 105 wounded, and the latter were taken ashore to a hospital. Two weeks later the fleet hoisted anchor and made for Grenada, Porto Rico, and Santo Domingo, where five ships were detached to look for enemy cruisers. At sunset on July 16 they were in Cap François (later Cape Haitien), a pretty town closed in by high mountain ridges. Here Tornquist was told that in the summer months the land breezes pick up, accompanied by

thunder and hard rain during the night, and last until morning, when the weather becomes beautiful—so that ships had to depart before the sea breeze commenced around 9 or 10 A.M., after which it was impossible to leave. That was only part of the problem; although the harbor was large enough to accommodate 350 sail, only one ship at a time could pass between the shallows and the fort, which was a mere musket shot distant from the channel.

On July 23 the combustibility of a crowded port in hot weather was demonstrated when the ship's clerk of the *Intrépide* began to draw some brandy into a large cask for the crew in the cockpit. The door on a lantern had been left open, and the warm air blowing through it carried the flame and ignited the cask, which burst, and fire spread through the entire after hold. Fortunately, the bulkhead had been laid up with bricks, which gave the captain enough time to have his ship towed away from other vessels and throw overboard as much powder as he could, while pumping water into the powder magazine and cutting holes at the waterline. Even so, the fire spread to the masts and rigging, and the stern of the ship blew up in a huge explosion. Twenty men drowned, and houses in the city were damaged by the blast, with some of the local people injured.

★   ★   ★

WHILE THE FLEET was at Cap François, a frigate sailed into the bay with a letter from New England for Comte de Grasse. This was the communiqué from Rochambeau, detailing the needs of the army and urging de Grasse to sail for the Chesapeake. The admiral immediately set about raising the money requested by Rochambeau. Although he and another French officer pledged their personal properties as collateral, he was unable to acquire sufficient funds locally and sent a frigate to Havana, where the commander of the port informed the principal inhabitants of the Americans' need and succeeded in collecting some 2.5 million livres, chiefly from the women, who produced cash as well as their jewelry as collateral. When de

Grasse's fleet weighed anchor and sailed for Chesapeake Bay on August 5, it carried the money, plus 3,500 men commanded by the Marquis de Saint-Simon—a corps comprising the Agénois, Gâtinais, and Touraine regiments—as well as Lauzun's legion. Along the way the fleet captured three small British warships, including one from Rodney's squadron that had sprung a bad leak and was trying to reach Charleston. Late in the evening of August 22, in calm weather, de Grasse's ships dropped anchor on the banks of the Chesapeake, "5 leagues from land in 13 to 18 fathoms sand bottom."

All in all, the French admiral had twenty-eight ships of the line and four frigates, manned by fifteen thousand sailors, with eight hundred marines and Saint-Simon's regiments. By September 5, a confident General George Weedon wrote Nathanael Greene, "New York will certainly be ours before Xmas, the Business with his Lordship in this State will very soon be at an End, for suppose you know e'er this, that we have got him handsomly in a pudding bag with 5000 Land Forces and about 60 Ships including Transports." Weedon was also delighted with the new governor of Virginia, Thomas Nelson, who, unlike his predecessor, Thomas Jefferson, was a military man. Weedon promised Greene, "nothing will be wanting (that Government can sanctify) to facilitate our plans."

A report from Washington to de Grasse indicated that the British had a fleet of twenty-four ships in the vicinity of Maryland and Virginia. With the stage now set for the allies' joint operation to go into effect, the gnawing question was whether or not that force would intervene.

★ ★ ★

TO WASHINGTON'S HUGE disappointment, the transports he had expected to be waiting for the armies at Head of Elk were so few in number that only two thousand troops could be ferried south to Williamsburg and Yorktown. He had more than one reason to get them moving as fast as possible: the place is so dry, one French officer said, that "one is drowned with dust there," and "Fever is very prevalent." Since the bulk of the allied army would be forced to march as far as Baltimore, at the least, the General set off at a gallop toward that town in search of boats.* As Clinton's ubiquitous spies informed the British general, "all the boats which could be procured in the Chesapeake were pressed [into service], oyster boats and every kind of vessel capable of containing men."

As it turned out, only the grenadiers and chasseurs with small cannon boarded the boats, but when those who went by land heard about the trip by water they were grateful to have traveled the way they did. The weather was terrible, with headwinds so strong that the journey downriver took eighteen days, and the boats, crowded with more than fifty passengers, were so full that no room was left for provisions. The chief commissary, Blanchard, who accompanied the Comte de Custine, described the Chesapeake as "a little Mediterranean," noting in his journal that the vessel was too small to do any cooking so the men had only cheese and biscuits, the officers some cold meat.

When they reached their destination, passengers who had been aboard several badly damaged vessels were unloaded at the entrance to the York River and put aboard warships, where they confidently expected to get a couple nights of decent rest. Unluckily for them, that was the night Cornwallis chose to send fireships to attack them, and all night firebrands rained on the warships, spreading terror among the men. A French lieutenant named St. Exupéry, serving on the *Triton*, wrote in his journal:

> Six ships in flames and proceeding abreast offered a horrible spectacle, when a seventh ship . . . bore down upon the *Triton* and burst into flames at a distance of a pistol shot. This sudden explosion made the sailors on the *Triton* lose their heads. Two hundred

---

*An indication of the intricacies of travel in the eighteenth century appears in a letter from Mordecai Gist to two Maryland gentlemen, requesting fresh horses for Washington to use between Baltimore and Queen Anns, his next stop, and the same number from Queen Anns to the Potomac. Gist said the General would require animals for himself, four aides, and nine servants—fourteen in all, which should be ready "tomorrow morning 10 o'clock."

of them either jumped overboard or into the various boats along-side. . . . Fortunately for the rest of our crew our vessel at that moment swung about and made sail; the fire-ships, whose sails were already consumed, could not follow her. . . . The *Triton*, during this night, lost 17 men, her bowsprit, and her stem.

Although the soldiers traveling overland decided at the end of the journey that they had had an easy time of it, what they confided to their journals was a different story. As one man wrote, the roads were "frightful," the country "abominable, cut by deep ravines and many small rivers, which the soldiers were obliged to ford after removing their shoes and stockings." The next day the roads were "virtually impassable . . . diabolic" and "the [river] bottom so rocky that the horses risked breaking their legs. All the way across we were in water up to our waists, and the horses up to their knees." On that leg of the trip alone they lost several horses, and not until they were on the out-skirts of Baltimore were the roads any better. Unfortunately, although they enjoyed a sojourn in that city, no boats were available and they departed on foot on September 17 in excessive heat, reaching Annapo-lis two days later. There—finally—boats were accessible so they could make the rest of the trip by water with a splendid breeze that followed them for five days to the James River and the French fleet.

For those who came after them, it was not so simple: Baron de Vioménil, assuming the transports in Annapolis would accommodate the Bourbonnais brigade, had an estimate made of the number of men each boat would hold and was told, "it is impossible." A trial was made in several craft, just to see how crowded they would be, and when he saw the result the baron gave the order to march overland. He decided it would be foolhardy to "expose the troops to the torture of such discomfort and restraint for several days and to the great risks we would run in these little boats, shamefully equipped in every respect."

When Verger and others formed up to march to Williamsburg, he was ill from the heat, hunger, and bad water. They had found a well and quenched their thirst, only to discover that the wells in the neighborhood had been poisoned by the British, who had thrown corpses into them. The result was an outbreak of dysentery and several deaths. But further horrors were in store. In Jamestown Verger said he was "nearly an eyewitness to the atrocities committed by the British." He had arrived shortly after the departure of Tarleton's dragoons, who had pillaged a house and

> violated a young woman who was pregnant. After fastening her to a door, one of them split open her belly with a sabre, killing the infant, then wrote over the door the following inscription, which I saw:
>
> > *You dam rebel's Whore,*
> > *You shall never bear enny more.*

The Swede, Carl Tornquist, had witnessed similar atrocities near Hampton. On a beautiful estate he saw a pregnant woman murdered in her bed by several bayonet stabs, her breasts cut open, and a grim sentence scrawled above the bed canopy: *"Thou shalt never give birth to a rebel."* In another room of the house Tornquist and his colleagues found a cupboard containing five decapitated human heads and, in the pastures and barns, horses, cows, and oxen that had been slaughtered. A storehouse that had contained ten thousand hogsheads of tobacco lay in ashes. "Such was our first sight on landing in this unfortunate territory," he wrote.

★   ★   ★

EARLY IN THE morning of September 9 Washington and a single aide—David Humphreys—saddled up, leaving the rest of his staff to follow, and rode off on a trip he had been longing to make for almost six and a half seemingly endless years. Before daylight faded he was determined to cover the sixty miles that led to his beloved Mount Vernon, the great white house with the pillared porch that had been home to him since he was a little child. It was obviously a sentimental journey, but almost certainly he was eager to have the French officers see his Virginia estate and enjoy the warm hospitality it had to offer.

It was still light when he rode through the gates and up the tree-lined road to the doorway where Martha, her daughter-in-law, and four small children he had never seen before awaited him— step-grandchildren who had been born since he left home. The sky was light enough that he could stand at the far end of the center hall and look out at the Potomac, darkening now in the spreading dusk, far below, where the river ran half a mile wide before twisting and turning as it flowed south toward the Chesapeake.

On the way home the General had been distressed to see the condition of the roads—the route over which the allied armies and all their wagons and cannon must pass, along with the cavalry and the cattle for feeding the troops—and that night, as tired as he was, he dictated a letter to his aide Jonathan Trumbull for the officer in charge of the Fairfax County militia to put the men to work on the roads at once, telling him to use an inducement that they could go home as soon as the job was done. The next morning Washington sent off a flurry of letters, most of them dealing with the impending march from the Potomac to the York—instructions to militia brigadiers to repair roads, provision for fresh horses or a carriage for Rochambeau or Chastellux for part of the route and for improvement of fords across rivers. Most of all he wanted news of Barras, whose arrival in Virginia was imperative because it would give de Grasse complete superiority.

Martha, of course, was busily preparing for the arrival of the French generals and her husband's aides. Rochambeau arrived that night; Chastellux was to appear the following day. Trumbull, who was seeing a splendid southern plantation for the first time, described it when everyone arrived: "A numerous family now present. All accommodated. An elegant seat and situation; great appearance of opulence and real exhibitions of hospitality and princely entertainment." Washington's military family reached Mount Vernon at mealtime; when Rochambeau and his aides came that evening, they were shown to the best quarters. The following morning the General had to double as commander and host. He learned that food for his troops was in short supply, as ever, and wrote to the governor of Maryland asking for provisions, since all his men had to eat was green corn, four ears daily per man. He told his servants to leave the next morning at five o'clock for Fredericksburg, to find forage for his party's horses and arrange for lodging at a local tavern. Their master would follow twenty-four hours later.

After spending three nights at Mount Vernon, Washington rode south and on the way saw a rider approaching who turned out to be carrying dispatches for Congress. The man had news for Washington—bad news. De Grasse's fleet had weighed anchor, headed for the open sea, and disappeared from view. Evidently, French lookouts had spotted the white sails of an English fleet heading for the Chesapeake, and de Grasse had gone out to meet them. There was no further word, and Trumbull noted Washington's reaction: "Much agitated."

The General had suffered so many disappointments over the past six years it was natural that he should imagine how this might mean the unraveling of his and Rochambeau's plans. Now, instead of the heady anticipation of victory, there was a distinct possibility of disaster. What if de Grasse had been defeated? What if he had sailed back to the West Indies or was barred by the British from reentering Chesapeake Bay? Washington's immediate reaction was to ensure the safety of the allied troops, and he sent word that the boats from Head of Elk should get their passengers on shore at once and stay where they were, while the marching troops were ordered to halt.

As for the generals and their staffs, they kept riding south, hoping for good news but prepared to hear the worst. It was not an easy trip, and what had begun as a large cavalcade of officers dwindled every day—aides having been dispatched on a variety of errands, with some riders simply unwilling or unable to maintain the pace Washington and Rochambeau set. It was late in the afternoon on September 14—three hard days' ride after leaving Mount Vernon—when the two generals and ten others trotted into Williamsburg, down spacious Duke of Gloucester Street lined with shade trees toward the huge Governor's Palace with rosy brick walls beyond the green.

★　★　★

ONE PUZZLING QUESTION was why Cornwallis had been content to remain in what was obviously a cul-de-sac when he could so easily have had his troops pack up their gear and depart, since Lafayette had insufficient strength and no real hope of stopping him. He could have done that at any time before Washington and Rochambeau and the French fleet arrived, but he was clearly contemptuous of Lafayette (whom he called "the boy") and his small force and serenely confident that he could remain where he was until reinforced or depart by sea in his own good time.

From the time he arrived in Virginia, Cornwallis had done nothing to conquer the place beyond fruitlessly chasing Lafayette and his little army around the state, promising that "The boy cannot escape me." Lafayette recognized the danger he risked, but kept shying away from Cornwallis, teasing him on, and as he told Washington, "Were I to fight a battle, I should be cut to pieces, the militia dispersed, and the arms lost. Were I to decline fighting, the country would think itself given up. I am therefore determined to skirmish, but not to engage too far." As he aptly described his situation, "I am not strong enough even to get beaten." Lafayette's army was so small, in fact (a mere fifteen hundred regulars and precious few militiamen), that he was obliged "to push on as one who had heartily wished a general engagement," while conning Cornwallis into thinking he had eight thousand men.

When the Frenchman learned that the British had settled in at Yorktown, he set up camp on the Pamunkey River—a tributary of the York—near West Point and began calling for cavalry. "Push on every dragoon!" he wrote to Steuben; Tarleton, he added, had arrived at

York and "I dread the consequences of such a superiority of horse," but fortunately Tarleton and Simcoe made no forays out of Yorktown or Gloucester.

In the waning days of August Lafayette learned from Washington what was in the offing—de Grasse's fleet arriving, and the two allied armies coming to Virginia. The commander in chief told him he must keep Cornwallis in the dark about this while taking steps to prevent him from leaving the peninsula if he should realize his danger. Anthony Wayne and his Pennsylvanians were then on the south side of the James River, preparing to join Greene in South Carolina. Following Washington's instructions, Lafayette put a stop to that, explaining the General's plan and ordering Wayne to take a "healthy position" near Westover, collect adequate supplies for his men, and be prepared to stop any attempt by Cornwallis to move south. At the same time, North Carolina's Governor Thomas Burke was asked to destroy the fords and boats on rivers the enemy would have to cross and post militia to delay them.

To keep Cornwallis from moving up the peninsula to cross the James near Richmond, Lafayette met with the Marquis de Saint-Simon as soon as the French fleet arrived and arranged for him to land his troops on Jamestown Island. There Lafayette and Wayne joined him, and the combined force, under Lafayette's command, marched to Williamsburg and took up a strong position across the peninsula. By the evening of September 7, between that force and the fleet, Cornwallis was hemmed in —"in a pudding bag," as General Weedon had said—and it seemed unlikely that he could break out in either direction.

That was the situation when Washington and Rochambeau arrived on the scene a week later. Word of their coming had spread instantaneously through the camp, and drums beat insistently in the several groups of tents. After riding past those of the Virginia militia, Washington stopped west of the College of William and Mary in the French camp, dismounted, and waited, assuming that a ceremonial reception of some sort might be planned. Shortly, Lafayette, who had been in a sickbed, Governor Thomas Nelson, and General Saint-Simon rode up, and the emotional Frenchman, overjoyed to be reunited with the man he considered a father, leaped from his horse and threw his arms around Washington. As St. George Tucker wrote his wife, Lafayette "caught the General round his body, hugged him as close as it was possible, and absolutely kissed him from ear to ear once or twice . . . with as much ardor as ever an absent lover kissed his mistress on his return." Saint-Simon then invited the commander in chief to ride through his camp, where the troops were lining up on both sides of the road.

After twenty-year-old Lieutenant Ebenezer Denny's Pennsylvania brigade was paraded before the General, he could hardly wait to write his wife: "Officers all pay their respects to the Commander-in-Chief. Go in a body. Those who are not personally known, their names given by General [Edward] Hand and General [Anthony] Wayne. He stands in the door, takes every man by the hand. The officers all pass in, receiving his hand and shake. This is the first time I had seen the General. . . ."

That evening, in Washington's honor, Saint-Simon laid on a sumptuous dinner at which "an elegant band of music" played a quartet from Grétry's *Lucille*—an opera "signifying the happiness of the family when blessed with the presence of their father."

Sometime between late night or early morning the best possible news was received. A dispatch from de Grasse reported that he had returned to Chesapeake Bay with two enemy frigates in tow after an engagement with the British fleet led by Admiral Thomas Graves. (Whether Washington had anything to say about the tone of the letter is not known, but it reads as though de Grasse were addressing a subordinate of very little competence. The French admiral was annoyed at the delay in arrival of the troops, he wrote, adding, "The season is approaching when, against my will, I shall be obliged to forsake the allies for whom I have done my very best and more than could be expected.")

Good news came from Barras, who had slipped quietly into the bay during the battle between de Grasse and Graves, bringing the French siege guns and those salt provisions Washington had been hoarding for an emergency and, by adding his ships to de Grasse's, making the combined total thirty-two ships of the line. By eluding Graves, Barras won praise from Closen for pulling off a miraculous escape, but his maneuver was just plain common sense. He had sailed out to sea—far to the east—before heading south and then traveled to the latitude of Albemarle Sound in North Carolina before turning north and following the coastline to the Chesapeake.

★　★　★

WHEN WASHINGTON RECEIVED the message from de Grasse, he characterized the Battle of the Capes as "a partial engagement," as it certainly was. But since it proved to be the naval action that determined the outcome of the Revolutionary War, it deserved to be remembered in rather different terms. The story, which embraces the almost unbelievable pieces of luck—miracles, perhaps—that made possible America's ultimate victory, began in the West Indies.

Early in 1781 Admiral George Rodney, who was cruising in the West Indies, got word that Holland had entered the war against Great Britain, and, shortly after being reinforced by Samuel Hood, he captured the Dutch possession of St. Eustatius,* a tiny island whose guns in Fort Orange had returned the salute of an American vessel, the *Andrea Doria*, as she entered the harbor on November 16, 1776. This gesture infuriated the British because it was the first time the red-and-white-striped flag of the Congress had ever been honored by a foreign nation—a salute, as it turned out, to a new state destined to change the course of history. That moment (commemorating, as it were, America's Declaration of Independence) marked

---

*He also took booty worth several million pounds sterling. Under the rules of warfare his share was worth a fortune, but unfortunately for him much of the goods belonged to English merchants and the ship he sent to Britain with what he had not already auctioned was captured by the French. As a result, he had almost nothing to show for it.

the beginning of what one British diplomat called "the most eventful epoch of European history," during which there was a revolutionary transition of power from the hands of noblemen and monarchs to those of citizens whose power was theirs by virtue of constitutional representation.

Around the same time, Admiral Rodney, who was responsible for neutralizing the French fleet in American waters, sent a warning to Arbuthnot, in New York, so "you may be upon your guard," that a large French squadron was heading west across the Atlantic, adding that if it visited the American coast, "I shall send every assistance in my power." By the time this dispatch reached New York, Arbuthnot had been succeeded by Graves, who ignored the warning and decided to embark on a cruise toward Rhode Island. As a result, he was absent when a second dispatch from Rodney arrived, stating that de Grasse had been seen in Cap François, and Graves should take his fleet to Virginia and have his frigates keep watch for the Frenchmen.

That second dispatch never reached Graves. The captain of a sloop of war carried it to New York but, finding Graves absent, sailed eastward in search of him and, in a stroke of good luck for the Americans, was attacked by three Yankee privateers that forced him to run aground on Long Island. To save the dispatch, he threw it overboard.

In the West Indies, Admiral Sir Samuel Hood was now in command of the British squadron there. He had spent much of his career serving with Rodney, most recently as his second in command; when Sir George fell sick and sailed for England in July 1781, the energetic Hood—who knew that de Grasse was somewhere in the vicinity, but who was unsure whether he had sailed for the mainland or was still in the Caribbean—headed at once for New York with fourteen warships, determined to join Admiral Graves and seek out de Grasse or Barras before they could combine forces.

En route he looked in at Chesapeake Bay, found only several picket vessels on patrol for Cornwallis, and proceeded to New York, where Graves's warships were all at anchor in the harbor. Hood, it turned out, had been in too much of a hurry. De Grasse had left the West Indies almost a week ahead of him but had sailed up the American coast past Charleston, where he captured three British ships, including one on which the ailing Lord Rawdon* was returning to England—all this while Hood, some distance out in the Atlantic and unaware of de Grasse's whereabouts, sped north. Meanwhile de Grasse, hugging the coastline, proceeded to the Chesapeake and entered the bay with the transports and his thirty warships, including the *Ville de Paris*, the largest naval vessel in the world.

When Hood, meanwhile, went ashore in New York, he found General Clinton and Admiral Graves in a leisurely discussion of what they might do next. Indicative of how Graves's mind was working, the last communiqué Hood received from him stated: "No intelligence yet of de Grasse. Accounts say he has gone to Havana to join the Spaniards. A little time will shew us. All the American accounts are big with expectation and the army has lately crossed to the Southward and appears in motion in the Jerseys as if to threaten Staten Island. For my own part, I believe the mountain in labor."

Hood was junior to Graves but didn't hesitate to tell the senior admiral that no time was to be lost, that they should sail immediately. During the evening a message arrived with news that Barras had left Rhode Island and was sailing south—information that finally moved Graves to act. Some delay was caused because five of his ten warships needed repairs, but at last they got under way and headed for the Chesapeake, figuring that the French might be there. Although Graves was hoping "to fall in with one of the enemy's squadrons," his fleet, which then consisted of nineteen ships carrying

---

*According to Closen, a Mr. and Mrs. Doyle were captured along with Rawdon, and "Gossip asserts that this very pretty lady . . . was the Lord's mistress during his campaigns in the South. It is certain that M. Doyle, whom Lord Rawdon made lieutenant-colonel of his regiment, seemed to be a *very easy-going fellow*." Guillaume, Comte de Deux-Ponts, who met the three prisoners while on his way to Williamsburg, reported that Mrs. Doyle seemed pleased with her situation and observed that "the French, even on the sea, were better than her countrymen."

nineteen hundred guns, never caught sight of Barras's much smaller force of slower vessels, which eluded them on the way south.

Arriving off the Chesapeake on the morning of September 5 on a fresh northeast wind, the British squadron was heading toward the bay on a starboard tack with its heaviest ships in the lead when a lookout aboard HMS *Solebay* called out that he saw a forest of masts in the harbor, about ten miles distant. The captain didn't believe him; they must be trees, he said. It was soon apparent, however, that they were not trees but French ships, and they were putting to sea with decks cleared for action. De Grasse had twenty-four ships of the line, carrying seventeen hundred guns.

This was hurricane season along the Virginia capes, and the engagement between the two fleets would be determined in no small part by the quirky winds and currents. De Grasse was in a hurry to get at the enemy, so a number of sailors who were on shore had to be left behind when his ships slipped their cables and sailed out of the harbor on the ebb tide, around noon. This movement, one French officer said, was executed with such precision and boldness, in spite of the absence of some of the best-drilled members of the crews, that the enemy was taken by surprise. For several reasons, the French had to stay on the defensive: the absence of those veteran crew members created difficulties; so did the danger of getting too far from the mouths of the York and James rivers (it was feared that the English fleet, known to be superior sailers, would get between the mouths of the rivers and the French). Even so, around three o'clock the French ships were ordered to run full so the entire fleet could produce the heaviest possible fire when they came alongside the British; about an hour later the action began "at the distance of a musketshot . . . from ship to ship," according to Tornquist.

About five o'clock the wind had shifted so that the French were to windward, and de Grasse signaled his captains to lay on canvas and head after the enemy as best they could. But Graves, whose squadron had been "severely punished," took advantage of the wind and kept his distance from the pursuers until sunset brought an end to the engagement.

Throughout the night the French fleet remained in line of battle with fires lighted, sailing close to the enemy, and the rising sun revealed that the English "had suffered greatly" and been "severely punished." So extensive was the damage to the sixty-four-gun *Terrible* that it had to be blown up three days later, and Graves's flagship, *London*, had lost three masts and was "in a most wretched plight."

On September 6 what little wind there was was feeble, out of the north, until four in the afternoon, and the two fleets spent the day making repairs, while staying in sight of each other. The wind came up out of the southwest in the evening, enabling the French to move toward the enemy, but daylight was dying and it was too late to engage.

The following day the sea was calm, and the English stayed before what little wind there was while doing their best to repair the damage to their ships.

On September 8 the wind shifted in favor of the British, and Graves attacked. Reacting immediately, de Grasse turned and signaled his lead ship to close with the enemy. Seeing his danger, Graves ordered his whole fleet to turn and run before the wind.

On the night of September 9 the British fleet disappeared, and not a single ship could be seen the following morning. By this time both fleets had drifted down to the latitude of Cape Hatteras, about a hundred miles to the south. De Grasse, figuring he could not force Graves to action, and concerned lest a change in the wind might permit the British fleet to get ahead of him and attack Barras, who was carrying the vitally important allied siege artillery, signaled his captains to return to the Chesapeake.

Luck—or Providence—had been with the Americans in every instance that counted. First of all, Graves never received Rodney's warning. Then, inexplicably, the British under Graves failed to attack de Grasse's ships one by one as they emerged from Chesapeake Bay. Another stroke of luck was that the lethargic Graves—not the aggressive Rodney, who would not have let such a rare opportunity slip by—was commanding the British squadron. Yet another was that Barras and his ships made it safely from Rhode Island to Virginia without detection by either Hood or Graves. In the naval engagement that decided the Yorktown campaign, only one ship was lost, and that was scuttled by the British.

8

PREPARE TO HEAR THE WORST

In the normal course of events General Sir Henry Clinton might have been content with his lot. Here he was, commander in chief of British forces in America, surrounded by sycophants, cosseted by his mistress, safe and secure in New York with his army, watched over by a powerful naval force under Admiral Thomas Graves. But these were not normal times, and Clinton was desperately unhappy about the deteriorating situation in the Chesapeake.

He was no man to admit guilt, but he bore a considerable responsibility for the total breakdown in the meeting of minds between himself and Charles, Earl Cornwallis. In fact, both men were equally to blame, but Clinton was, after all, in command and should have made clear to his subordinate exactly what he was to do and when. But he had not. And Cornwallis, who was energetic, ambitious, and strong-willed, had taken advantage of Clinton's lapses and indecision and followed his own path from South Carolina to Virginia.

After defeating the Americans at Camden in 1780, Cornwallis decided that the backcountry was sufficiently secure that he could leave Charleston and march north. Clinton had recommended that he take the coastal route, but Cornwallis, observing that that was too unhealthy, headed for the highlands of North Carolina. It was a costly mistake. Leaving the coast meant leaving the navy behind, so he was constantly short of supplies. Because of that, he could not remain in one place long enough to encourage loyalists to join him, he could hold no territory, and he was unable to engage the rebels in a decisive battle.

Lacking insight into Clinton's plans for Virginia, Cornwallis assumed that the troops sent there by his superior were his to command—an illusion enforced when the soldiers under General Leslie arrived and he promptly summoned them to join him in the Carolinas. From this moment on, relations between the two generals worsened to the point where they barely existed. Cornwallis was capable of great charm, but he had frequent episodes of the sulks and bad temper, which showed in his letters to Clinton, who did not understand them and laid them to ulterior motives on the earl's part.

Clinton was certain that Cornwallis was undermining his authority by writing directly to the ministry in London (which he was), going over Clinton's head and influencing military policy in America. For almost four months between January and late April of 1781, no direct word from Cornwallis reached Clinton, leaving the latter to guess what was going on in the South while making decisions concerning the Chesapeake. Then came a letter from Cornwallis written on April 10, beginning, "I have a chance of sending a few lines to New York," summarizing the battle at Guilford Courthouse and saying that he had been obliged to rest his army—a third of which had been sick and wounded, many without shoes and exhausted—but he had been doing his best to put his men in shape to take the field. Reinforcements would be essential, as would be a return to the high country, to avoid "the fatal sickness which so nearly ruined the army last autumn."

Now he was "very anxious to receive Your Excellency's commands," since he was "totally in the dark as to the intended operations of the summer." The Chesapeake, he added, ought to be the seat of war—even at the expense of abandoning New York. Meantime he was dispatching an aide to London with news of his latest campaign and would send copies to Clinton.

Two weeks later Cornwallis was writing again, angrily this time, to say how disagreeable it was to decide upon vital matters "without an opportunity of procuring Your Excellency's directions or approbation." The delay of conveying letters and not receiving answers had become intolerable, and his present undertaking (whatever that might be, Clinton may have wondered) "sits heavy on my mind." The situation he had left behind in South Carolina was grave, yet he had had to act precipitately since no reinforcements were forthcoming from Europe and the impending return of General Greene to North Carolina would put a junction with Major General William Phillips out of his power.

In one letter, Cornwallis informed Clinton that he had been "uniformly successful" in the Carolinas, ignoring the fact that he had lost three-quarters of his army. His march to the north was made because a return to Charleston had the appearance of defeat, so, leaving behind a garrison to defend itself in South Carolina, he headed for Virginia, which, he told Clinton, should be the focus of their activity.

His letters to Germain and Phillips at this time conveyed his fears for South Carolina and Lord Rawdon, in whose care he had left the post with precious few troops to defend it—an action that smacked of incompetence or very poor judgment. Before Clinton had a chance to stop him, he headed north and reached Virginia by May.

For his part, Clinton was all the more determined to defend New York, where he expected to be attacked in force. In desperation he had written to Germain in late April asking to be allowed to resign if Arbuthnot was not recalled. The admiral, "who from age, temper, and inconsistency of conduct is really so little to be depended on that, was I to continue to serve with him, I should be constantly under the most distressing apprehensions of the miscarriage of . . . enterprises we might be engaged in." Fortunately for Clinton's peace of mind on that count, Arbuthnot finally departed in June. Meanwhile, to forestall an attack on New York, Sir Henry thought of striking at Philadelphia, employing Cornwallis's force in a pincers movement, but the earl was having none of that and said so. Then Clinton thought to have the two armies integrated in the defense of New York, with Cornwallis to remain in Chesapeake Bay while sending most of his troops to Manhattan, and the general ordered the earl to do this in what was a decidedly peremptory tone. Clinton's instructions so infuriated Cornwallis that he marched his army to Portsmouth to sail for New York while asking that he be given permission to return to South Carolina. Clinton, dumbfounded, countermanded the order to move the troops and subsequently ordered Cornwallis to select a post and fortify it.

The letters traveling back and forth between the two generals over which town Cornwallis was to use as his base can only be described as bickering. The earl was against York, saying it "far exceeds our power, consistent with your plans, to make safe defensive posts there and at Gloucester." He favored Portsmouth. Back came a retort from Clinton stating that he and Admiral Graves considered Hampton Roads "the fittest station for all ships" and that York would provide security for Old Point Comfort and Hampton Roads. "You will," he added, "without loss of time examine Old Point Comfort and fortify it. . . ." Clinton went on to tell the earl that "until the season for recommencing operation in the Chesapeake shall return" (whenever that might be), Cornwallis must be content with a defensive posture and not retain any more troops than he considered absolutely essential for that purpose.

The thinly veiled animosity between the two threatened to bubble to the surface, with Clinton's messages becoming ever more complicated and contradictory, Cornwallis's resentful, until neither understood what the other was saying or doing. As an example of Clinton's baffling instructions, while he debated whether to take some of Cornwallis's troops to defend New York or attack Philadelphia, he successively ordered the earl to send some of his men to the latter city, then to New York, then told him to set up a post in York and later in Old Point Comfort, and called for reinforcements to New York at the same time, adding that Cornwallis could keep them in Virginia if necessary.

Meantime, of course, both officers were writing to Lord George Germain; each gave his version of what was transpiring, in letters highly critical of the other. Clinton complained that Cornwallis had frustrated his plan to capture rebel stores in Philadelphia by refusing to send him troops, and went on to remind the secretary of state for the colonies of Cornwallis's statement that subduing Virginia was a top priority, with which Clinton agreed, while saying that "Conquest alone will be of little moment unless we can retain what we conquer, which . . . cannot be done in so large and populous a province as Virginia unless the inhabitants themselves are disposed to join us—which we cannot hope for there, as they are, I believe, almost universally hostile." Sir Henry's plan was to secure a post that would provide a respectable naval station at the entrance of the Chesapeake, commanding access to the bay. And back came Germain's enthusiastic response: "It is with the most unfeigned pleasure I obey His Majesty's commands in expressing to you *his royal approbation of the plan you have adopted* for prosecuting the war in the provinces south of the Delaware. . . ." And so it went between the two generals until the war's end, Clinton whining, Cornwallis complaining irritably, each convinced that he was right and that everything would have been fine had the other only listened to him.

It was late July before Cornwallis made the ultimate decision. Dutifully, he considered Old Point Comfort but determined with his engineers that it was unsuitable. Instead, he reluctantly chose York, about eleven miles from the mouth of the York River, and put his entire army to work digging trenches. The little town had sixty or seventy houses spread out along the main street and several cross streets, all on a high stony bluff that ran parallel to the river. Under the cliff were landings and various commercial establishments. From a distance, the most conspicuous landmarks were a church steeple and two imposing brick houses—both owned by people named Nelson.

In 1765 a Scottish officer, Lord Adam Gordon, had left the West

Indies and landed in Florida, where he began a sightseeing journey that was to take him all the way up the coast to Quebec. On his way he visited York, which he thought one of the pleasantest situations he ever saw. Located on the beautiful River York, he said, it "commands a full view of the river down towards the Bay of Chesapeake, and a pretty land view across to Gloucester town and country, which contains some of the best lowlands in the country." He admired the timber, saw great numbers of tulip trees not less than twenty feet in circumference and ninety feet tall, and noted the beauty of the local honeysuckle and how well European fruits, roots, and "garden stuff" did there. But within a single generation all that had changed, thanks largely to the British occupation.

Here the river was relatively narrow—less than a mile between the steep bluffs along the edge of the river and Gloucester, directly to the north, an arrow-shaped point that protruded into the York where it joined Chesapeake Bay. As Lafayette described the place, York was surrounded by "the river and a morass." The site chosen by Cornwallis was clearly vulnerable to an amphibious operation since it could be surrounded by an approaching army while naval supremacy kept it from being provisioned or relieved from the sea.

★   ★   ★

BEFORE THE CRUCIAL naval engagement between de Grasse and Graves took place, Cornwallis was leisurely fortifying his position at Yorktown,* knowing that Lafayette might try to coop him up on land, but confident that he could break through at any time or, failing that, the navy would extricate his army if the occasion warranted. On August 22 he wrote Clinton an assuasive letter, reporting that his engineer had finished a study of the grounds and had a plan for fortifying them which the earl had approved. Six weeks should be time

---

*Contemporaries called it York, but later it became known everywhere as Yorktown.

enough for the construction work, he told Clinton; after that he would be able to spare one or two thousand men if Sir Henry needed them in the offensive he was planning in the Chesapeake.

At the time, Clinton was corresponding with Admiral Graves, who had made the incredible request that if it was not necessary to keep his squadron together, he would like to send individual vessels on cruise. But Sir Henry tactfully warned him to be ready to meet the French if they appeared. Graves wrote in response that he was willing to put his ships at risk whenever Clinton "thought it advisable to risk the army," and, reassuring him further, "as early as it is possible to determine upon the day, the squadron will be fit to act. . . ." Meantime, a letter arrived from Admiral Hood, telling Clinton he was off Cape Henry and would look in on the Chesapeake to detect any sign of de Grasse's presence.

On August 27 Clinton was still fussing about the possibility that Washington might take action against New York, but he had concluded that the General was marching toward his old defensive post at Morristown, from which "he may detach to the southward." Clinton informed Cornwallis that he might as well retain the troops he had on hand, that Clinton would send him some recruits and convalescents as a temporary reinforcement since he figured that Washington's present move was a feint. Surely, de Grasse would "not approve any water movements till . . . the effects of the equinox are over," he conjectured, at which time Clinton planned to reinforce Cornwallis with all the troops he could spare—consistent, of course, "with the security of this important post."

Then came a letter headed "Yorktown, Virginia, August 31, 1781," which shattered the complacency in New York headquarters. A French ship of the line, two frigates, and the *Loyalist*—a prize taken by the French—lay near the mouth of the York River, and Cornwallis had received a report that between thirty and forty sail were within the capes, mostly ships of war and "some of them very large." Another report, written two days later, brought more bad news: "Comte de Grasse's fleet is within the Capes of the Chesapeake. Forty boats with troops went up James River yesterday, and four ships lie at the

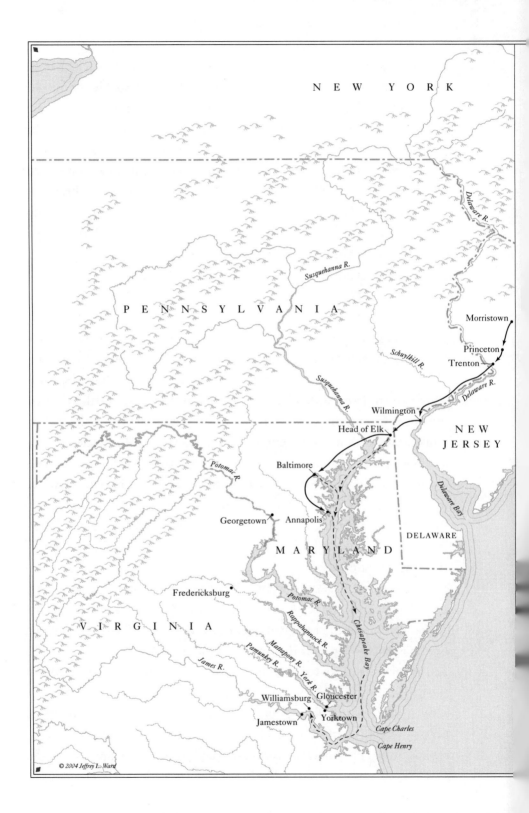

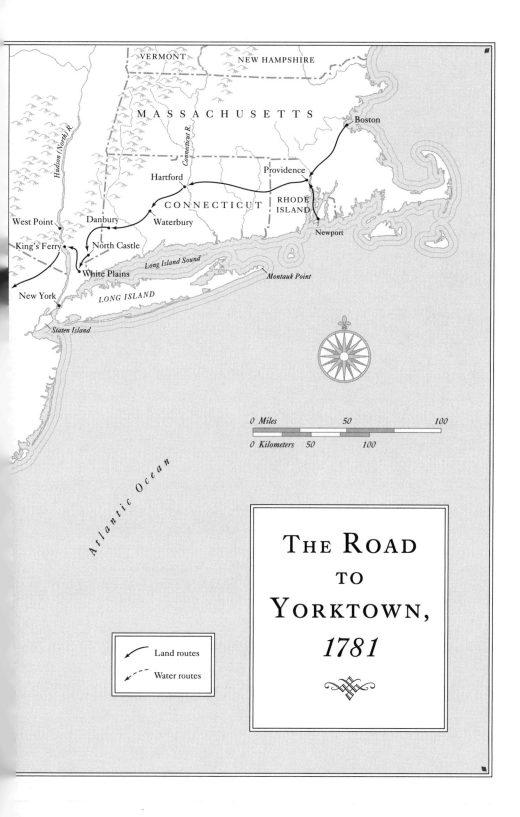

VERMONT NEW HAMPSHIRE

MASSACHUSETTS

Boston

Hudson (North) R.

Connecticut R.

Hartford Providence

CONNECTICUT RHODE ISLAND

West Point Danbury Waterbury

King's Ferry North Castle Newport

White Plains Long Island Sound

LONG ISLAND Montauk Point

New York

Staten Island

Atlantic Ocean

0 Miles 50 100

0 Kilometers 50 100

THE ROAD

TO

YORKTOWN,

1781

Land routes

Water routes

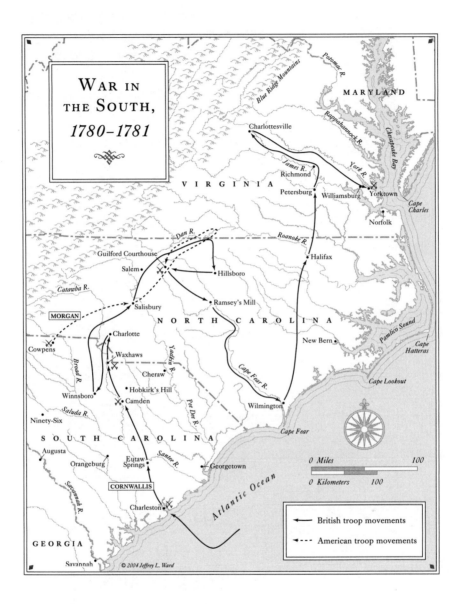

WAR IN THE SOUTH, 1780–1781

MARYLAND

Potomac R.

Rappahannock R.

Blue Ridge Mountains

Charlottesville

York R.

Chesapeake Bay

James R.

Richmond

Petersburg

Williamsburg

Yorktown

V I R G I N I A

Cape Charles

Norfolk

Dan R.

Roanoke R.

Halifax

Guilford Courthouse

Salem

Hillsboro

Pamlico Sound

Catawba R.

Salisbury

N O R T H   C A R O L I N A

Ramsey's Mill

MORGAN

Charlotte

Yadkin R.

New Bern

Cape Hatteras

Cowpens

Waxhaws

Broad R.

Cheraw

Cape Fear R.

Cape Lookout

Hobkirk's Hill

Pee Dee R.

Winnsboro

Camden

Wilmington

Ninety-Six

Saluda R.

Cape Fear

S O U T H   C A R O L I N A

Augusta

Orangeburg

Eutaw Springs

Santee R.

Georgetown

Savannah R.

CORNWALLIS

Charleston

Atlantic Ocean

GEORGIA

Savannah

© 2004 Jeffrey L. Ward

| 0 | Miles | | 100 |
| 0 | Kilometers | | 100 |

→ British troop movements

- - → American troop movements

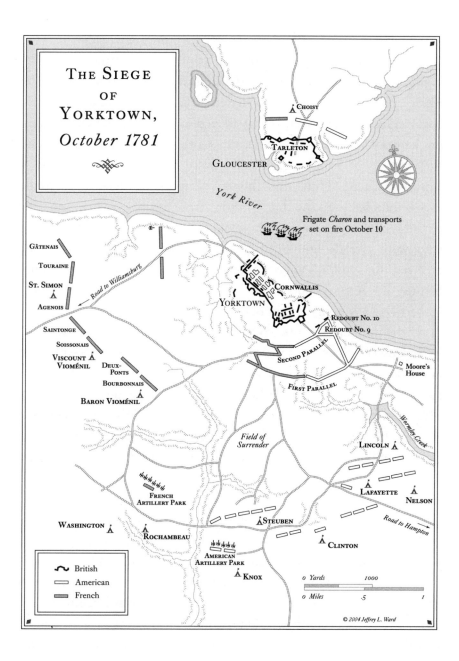

THE SIEGE
OF
YORKTOWN,
October 1781

CHOISY

TARLETON

GLOUCESTER

York River

Frigate *Charon* and transports
set on fire October 10

GÂTENAIS

TOURAINE

ST. SIMON

AGENOIS

Road to Williamsburg

YORKTOWN

CORNWALLIS

SAINTONGE

REDOUBT NO. 10
REDOUBT NO. 9

SOISSONAIS

VISCOUNT
VIOMÉNIL

DEUX-
PONTS

SECOND PARALLEL

BOURBONNAIS

Moore's
House

BARON VIOMÉNIL

FIRST PARALLEL

Wormley Creek

*Field of
Surrender*

LINCOLN

FRENCH
ARTILLERY PARK

LAFAYETTE

NELSON

WASHINGTON

ROCHAMBEAU

STEUBEN

Road to Hampton

AMERICAN
ARTILLERY PARK

CLINTON

KNOX

British
American
French

0 *Yards*   1000

0 *Miles*   ·5   1

© 2004 Jeffrey L. Ward

entrance to this river." On that very day Clinton had written a letter to Cornwallis that crossed one of the earl's in the mail, stating that Washington was moving an army "to the southward with an appearance of haste" and was letting it be known that he expected to cooperate with a considerable French fleet. If that proved to be the case, Clinton went on, he would "endeavor" to reinforce Cornwallis "by all means within the compass of my power, or make every possible diversion in Your Lordship's favor." How reassuring this temporizing message was to the earl is impossible to say, but Clinton wrote again, promising that he would relieve him as soon as possible with about four thousand men, who were already embarked on board transports. As soon as he received the admiral's approval, they would sail. And, to hearten him further, he said accounts from Europe indicated that Rear Admiral Robert Digby with a number of capital ships could be expected hourly.

At the moment the French fleet appeared on August 31, Cornwallis's avenue of escape was wide open. De Grasse had not disembarked any troops, and the army under Washington and Rochambeau was several weeks' march away (though Cornwallis was unaware of this). However, the British commander did nothing. His best chance of keeping his army intact would have been to attack Lafayette's weak force (a move urged on him by Tarleton), but at this moment he received Clinton's promise of relief and opted for inaction, while his soldiers continued working day and night on the outworks, with "every preparation made for a gallant defense," as one of them said.

By then most of the trees outside of town had been cut for use as chevaux-de-frise to block roads and other passages, and the stumps were left to hinder movement in the open land. Men were dying in the hospital; others were deserting, none of them in large numbers, but steadily, week by week. One would-be deserter, a man named Froelich, was caught and sentenced to run the gauntlet of three hundred men sixteen times, and again the next day, "only ten times," which left him pitifully cut and beaten and unable to walk. What troubled the troops most was the lack of anything decent to eat.

According to Johann Conrad Doehla, a soldier from Bayreuth, Germany, the provisions were terrible—"putrid ship's meat and wormy biscuits that have spoiled on the ships. Many of the men have taken sick here with dysentery or the bloody flux and with diarrhea. Also the foul fever is spreading, partly on account of the many hardships from which one has had little rest day or night, and partly on account of the awful food; but mostly, the nitre-bearing water is to blame for it."

By September 17 the earl knew the worst and could evaluate his chances. By then Barras had joined de Grasse, giving the French almost twice as many ships as Graves had, and Cornwallis was aware that Washington's army would soon arrive in the Chesapeake. Given a situation in which the possibility of rescue was virtually nil, he had only one option, which was to escape at any cost before the arrival of Washington's troops shut the trap. Once again, Banastre Tarleton perceived that attack was the army's sole hope of survival, but Major Alexander Ross, Cornwallis's aide, persuaded the earl that Clinton's promise of relief left him no choice but to hold his post. This was absurd, and Cornwallis had to know it; his obligation was to make the ultimate decision (as he had been doing regularly in the southern campaign), which could have meant the salvation of his army. Clinton, moreover, had no way of knowing the details or the extent of Cornwallis's plight—a very important one being the weakness of his fortifications. (The story was told that Tarleton's brother had jumped over the earthworks to demonstrate how inadequate they were, but true or not, Cornwallis as an experienced officer should have recognized their limitations.) In any event, he failed to act, and the window of opportunity slammed shut.

In New York, the approaching calamity was the topic of continual speculation and concern, with no acceptable solution in sight. Old General James Robertson, who was regarded by several associates to be in his dotage, suggested that nothing could be worse than failing to make an effort to rescue Cornwallis's army. "All the ills that may be foreseen are at most probabilities; they may not happen. But the destruction of the whole is certain if the army in Virginia be destroyed." We have only one chance, he insisted, and "we give up the game if we do not try to risk it. . . ."

While Clinton continued to jolly Cornwallis along, making hopeful noises, he was sending a contradictory message to Germain—"a very alarming report of our situation." He began by complaining in his usual fashion that he had not received the reinforcements he had requested and that this dire situation was the direct result of the government's failure to heed his warnings. But this was not a time for "vain lamentations." Things appeared to be "coming fast to a crisis." Nor was it a time for comparing the size of the two armies; he would exert himself to the utmost to relieve Lord Cornwallis with what he had, "inadequate" as it was.

As late as September 8, Cornwallis had no reason to think he would not be relieved and rescued. French troops—3,800 of them—had landed, Lafayette was at Williamsburg, and reportedly the allied armies would arrive soon. Nevertheless, the British were ready for them and had taken a very strong position just outside town, where the troops were working on the redoubts. Happily, "The army is not very sickly. Provisions for six weeks—I will be very careful of it," he wrote Clinton.

On September 9 Admiral Graves sent a real shocker to Sir Henry, who had written him the day before to remind him that the troops were loaded aboard transports "and ready for moving to the Chesapeake the instant I hear from you." The admiral, who was on his way to New York after his encounter with de Grasse off the Virginia capes, was sorry to inform the general that "the enemy have so great a naval force in the Chesapeake that they are absolute masters of its navigation." He had met them coming out of the bay, he said, and "had a pretty sharp brush with their van and part of their center." The French appeared to have suffered, he continued, but his fleet had taken much heavier damage. In this "ticklish state of things" the only hope of getting into the York River was by night, and even then it would be infinitely risky to send supplies by water. He closed by saying bravely that the fleet shall not be wanting, "for we must either stand or fall together." Five days later the admiral wrote to Lord Sandwich, first lord of the Admiralty, informing him candidly of Cornwallis's situation and adding, "We cannot succour him, nor venture to keep the sea any longer."

On that same day Clinton held a council of war. Those present were Generals Wilhelm von Knyphausen, James Robertson, Alexander Leslie, and John Campbell; Major Generals Thomas Stirling and James Paterson; and Brigadier Generals Samuel Birch and Benedict Arnold. The only naval officer present—in the absence of Graves and Hood—was Commodore Edmund Affleck. The question before them was occasioned by the letter from Graves: given his report that the enemy were "absolute masters" of the Chesapeake and had a superiority at sea, plus information from officers recently arrived from Cornwallis's post, indicating that the earl had an estimated eight thousand troops on hand and provisions for ten thousand until the end of October, what should they do? Since the garrison could evidently defend the post for at least three weeks, was it advisable to commit a reinforcement of five or six thousand men "to the hazards of the sea during our present inferiority and endeavor to relieve Lord Cornwallis at all costs"? Or should they await further accounts from Admiral Graves and see how Admiral Digby's squadron might affect their chances of success?

After what was apparently a good deal of harrumphing and "yes, buts" and "what ifs," it was unanimously resolved to "wait [for] more favorable accounts from Rear Admiral Graves or the arrival of Rear Admiral Digby." How these senior military officers could possibly imagine that Graves would give them a more favorable account is difficult to imagine, but since Digby had not been sighted and no one knew how many vessels he had with him, surely it would be safe to delay decision until he arrived. And so Clinton procrastinated, but when Digby arrived on September 24 he proved to have only three ships of the line, manifesting the terrible reality of Cornwallis's predicament. Sir Henry's reaction was to complain that "the Lords of the Admiralty could have furnished Mr. Digby with a larger force than three ships and have sent him to North America earlier in the season."

That was no help whatever to Lord Cornwallis; nor was the fact that mail was taking ten days and more to reach that gentleman, making it exceedingly difficult to make plans or determine what he was to do.

A week before Digby arrived in New York, Cornwallis had written to Clinton to say that de Grasse's fleet had returned to the Chesapeake after the engagement with Graves and that Washington and some of his troops were now at Williamsburg. "If I had no hopes of relief," the earl wrote, underlining a number of passages for emphasis, "I would rather risk an action than defend my half-finished works. But, as you say Admiral Digby is hourly expected and [you] promise every exertion to assist me, I do not think myself justifiable in putting the fate of the war on so desperate an attempt. My provisions will last at least six weeks from this day. I am of opinion that you can do me no effectual service but by coming directly to this place." That was on September 16. The next day he added a note to the letter, warning solemnly, "This place is in no state of defense. If you cannot relieve me very soon, you must be prepared to hear the worst." Sometime earlier Clinton had cautioned Germain that affairs were approaching a crisis. Now it was here.

On September 17 Clinton held another council of war with his general officers and read them Lord Cornwallis's letter dated the 8th, in which he had told his chief that he had provisions for six weeks. Unfortunately for the earl and his troops, the generals seemed to be oblivious to the passage of time and the fact that the Americans and French might be intensifying the earl's predicament, and once again they stalled for time, deciding that any attempt to "throw in supplies and reinforcements ought to be deferred until it could be undertaken with less danger than at present." Like chameleons seeking protective coloration, they turned to several loyalists who were familiar with the area and asked the Goodrich brothers and Hardin Burnley their opinion on "subsisting an army in Virginia without having the command of the waters of the Chesapeake." The gentlemen didn't think much of it. Their unanimous view was that "the difficulties would be great even to Mr. Washington, but almost insurmountable to an army of any considerable numbers who did not possess the good will of the inhabitants."

All of this led the generals to resolve that since an army could not act there alone without the cooperation of the fleet, it would be "highly improper to add considerably to the numbers already in Virginia" until such time as the presence of the fleet became practicable.

Lord Cornwallis was to be left dangling in the wind.

★　★　★

WASHINGTON AND ROCHAMBEAU wanted in the worst way to talk with de Grasse, and it was agreed that they would meet the admiral at his anchorage in Lynnhaven Bay, at the mouth of the Chesapeake. For their transportation, de Grasse sent an elegant little sailing vessel called the *Queen Charlotte*, which he had captured from the British—"[it will] bear you across as comfortably as it is possible to do in this kind of boat"—and they set off with Chastellux, Knox, the engineer Duportail, and their staffs on what proved to be a sixty-mile sail, half of it down the James River, half across open water. At first light the next morning they came in sight of more than thirty ships of the line—more, certainly, than the Americans had seen before—and at noon they were piped aboard the enormous *Ville de Paris* and "received with great ceremony and military naval parade and most cordial welcome," in Trumbull's words. "The Admiral is a remarkable man for size, appearance, and plainness of address."

The admiral was in fact taller and considerably heavier than George Washington, and the story goes that he stepped forward, embraced him, and said in a booming voice, "*Mon cher petit général!*" which provoked considerable laughter on the part of all those present—except Washington.

Another amusing incident occurred just as the Americans were boarding the admiral's flagship. An English brig, thinking the ships in the harbor were all British, sailed into the midst of the French vessels and was hailed in English by a man on board the *Ville de Paris* to anchor alongside her. The captain of the brig launched his gig and, with some other English officers and a Hessian, sailed over to call on the admiral. At the moment they arrived on deck on one side of the flagship, Washington and Rochambeau appeared on the other. As a Frenchman wrote, "They were much surprised to find themselves on board the flagship of M. de Grasse, having believed it to be that of Admiral Graves."

After the introductions and formalities, the allied officers sat down in the admiral's quarters, and Washington asked him a number of specific questions. The first two were the most important: Was the admiral bound by a definite date for the departure of the fleet? And if Saint-Simon's troops were obliged to leave ahead of the fleet, would the main naval force remain in the Chesapeake to cover operations against Cornwallis?

De Grasse replied that his instructions were to leave on October 15, but he would, on his own, stretch that until the end of the month. That gave Washington almost six weeks in which to force Cornwallis to surrender, and while he couldn't possibly know if that was long enough, it would have to suffice. As for Saint-Simon's troops, Washington could count on them until the warships departed.

Other questions followed. Did de Grasse have any men he could spare to strengthen the lines on either bank of the York? To which the admiral replied that he was willing to let Washington have eighteen hundred to two thousand men, as promised earlier, but he insisted that they be used only for a sudden attack. Could the admiral loan Washington any heavy cannon or powder? Yes, he could supply cannon, but little if any powder.

The end of the conference was followed by a formal dinner and a tour of the flagship, after which Washington and his party went aboard their barge. The sun was setting, the flagship fired a salute, and at that moment Washington and his party were treated to an extraordinary sight. In the red glow of the sunset, on every mast in the fleet, the crews of the ships in the harbor manned the yards and tops, each man with a musket in his hand, which was discharged in an incredible *feu de joie*, while puffs of smoke exploded from the sides of the vessels.

It had been a grand and satisfying affair, but Washington could not know that the six-hour visit would cost him almost four and a half days. For more than three of those days the little *Queen Charlotte* could make no progress whatever against the strong headwind sweeping down the river, and finally a frustrated Washington and Rochambeau went ashore and mounted horses for the trip back to Williamsburg.

Arriving there about noon on September 22, Washington learned that almost all his troops had come into camp, along with the first division of French soldiers. He was euphoric, writing that "Everything has hitherto succeeded to our wishes. Nothing could have been more fortunate than the cooperation of the several parts of this great expedition in point of time. . . . in a very few days, I hope, the enemy at York will be completely invested. . . ." The only item of interest he found on his return was a message to Rochambeau that the British admiral Robert Digby was expected in New York with only *three* ships of the line and a convoy he was escorting. After a council of war Closen was told to take a letter from Rochambeau to de Grasse notifying him of this, and the young man left at four the next morning.

By then Washington was accustomed to hearing rumors of all kinds, and he took little stock in this one since de Grasse had thirty-six ships of the line with which to oppose any British force.

But the admiral, on receiving the news, took an entirely different view of the matter. As Closen described the French reaction to the information about Digby, "these excitable gentlemen of the navy, who think only of cruises and battles and do not like to oblige or to cooperate with the land troops," were "alarmed and disquieted"—so alarmed in fact that de Grasse sent a reply back to Washington via Closen, announcing that since the enemy was now nearly equal to him in strength and it would be imprudent to remain in a position where he could not readily attack them, he would leave several frigates to block the James and two ships at the mouth of the York while he put to sea with the fleet. "I will sail with my forces towards New York," he said, "and I may possibly do more for the common cause than by remaining here as an idle spectator." Then, even more ominously, "it is possible that the issue of the combat may force us to leeward and deprive us of the power of returning. Under these circumstances what could you do? . . ." And finally, "I shall set sail as soon as the wind permits."

George Washington's reaction to this bombshell can be imagined. The decisions made at the recent conference had been so clear and straightforward that it was simply incredible to think that the French admiral could alter them arbitrarily and without warning, jeopardizing the entire campaign. After discussing the problem with Rochambeau, the General prepared a letter to de Grasse pleading with him to remain in the Chesapeake. Cornwallis's demise was certain; it was only a matter of time before he capitulated; and that surrender "must necessarily go a great way towards terminating the war and securing the invaluable objects of it to the allies." This letter was to be delivered to the admiral by Lafayette, on the theory that his social prestige would guarantee an attentive hearing.

Rochambeau also wrote a letter for Lafayette to carry: "The plan to go to New York, of which you ask our counsel, seems to us a matter of the greatest hazard" since the British would lose not a moment to rescue Cornwallis from his plight and "would be able in the night to pass without your seeing them. . . ."

Once again Washington had to wait on tenterhooks for a reply that could ruin the whole plan of operation. Taking every precaution now, he asked Rochambeau to send the Duc de Lauzun with three hundred infantrymen and his cavalry to Gloucester to beef up Weedon's twelve hundred Virginia militia, who were opposed by Banastre Tarleton. He also supervised the movement of cannon toward Yorktown and learned to his delight that French and Americans from the upper Chesapeake continued to land and join the growing camps at Williamsburg.

At long last the reply came from de Grasse on September 2 7, and a curious one it was. It seemed that even before the arrival of Lafayette a council of de Grasse's officers had disapproved of his decision to leave the bay. As the admiral put it, ". . . the plans I had suggested for getting underway, while the most brilliant and glorious, did not appear to fulfill the aims we had in view. Accordingly, it was decided that the major part of the fleet should proceed to anchor in York River. . . ." Poor Closen, who had already carried messages to and from de Grasse and was exhausted, having spent two nights on the water in open boats, now had to return with Lafayette to the admiral with yet another missive. "I did not fulfill my duties with very good grace," he wrote, "for the weather was devilish, the sea was rough, and I still had two hours of tossing in a bitch of an open launch, where I was pretty well soaked by the oarsmen." While the two arrived after de Grasse's decision to stay in the vicinity had already been made, Lafayette apparently persuaded the admiral to leave the York River, where his actions were restricted, and return to his original anchorage near Cape Henry. They also discussed the possibility that de Grasse might attack Charleston on his way back to the West Indies.

★   ★   ★

AT EIGHT O'CLOCK in the morning on September 28—a day when news of Nathanael Greene's battle with the British at Eutaw Springs* was received—Washington, with Rochambeau and the two allied armies, began a brief, twelve-mile journey. The General had been dreaming about this day for a year and more—the day that would

---

*Neither side won a victory. Greene lost about 500 men, killed or wounded; Alexander Stewart, leading the British, lost 435 killed or wounded and another 480 captured. Greene had to withdraw; Stewart was forced to return to Charleston.

finally bring a major victory over a British army. Leaving about eight hundred men in the rear, they headed for Yorktown, where Cornwallis and his troops were entrenched. Short as the distance was, the troops suffered terribly from the oppressive heat that was "incomparably worse than anything we had previously endured" and the burning sand. All the officers, as well as the infantrymen, were obliged to walk because their horses had not yet arrived, so they were as tormented as the foot soldiers. Clermont-Crèvecoeur said two men fell at his feet and died on the spot. Astonishingly, he said, the roads that the British should have defended foot by foot were uncontested.

About five miles down the road the armies split, the French taking a fork in the road that led to the left, the Americans to the right. They marched across beautiful, fertile country that lay between Williamsburg and Yorktown, which had been made a desert by the war. Houses were silent and empty, with no sign of life; doors flapping, windows broken, fields lying fallow, and grass waist-high in the roads. To their surprise, it was not until the British fortifications came into view that the enemy showed themselves, with a troop of dragoons parading in the distance the only sign of activity. Several allied guns fired a few shots, and the cavalry disappeared behind the outworks.

Off to the left Baron de Vioménil led the advance of the French with his grenadiers and chasseurs, taking advantage of the woods for cover. With the approach of night Washington's men set up camp in forested land about a mile from the enemy's left, and the General and his staff bivouacked under the trees. This was on the near side of Jones's Run, on level ground at the edge of an old field, with a spring just down the hill to the west. Rochambeau's tents were pitched about five hundred yards from this pleasant spot. In front of them was Great Run, and the next morning, despite some desultory cannonades from two British outposts, the troops crossed it and began digging.

With a huge French fleet anchored in Chesapeake Bay, blocking Cornwallis from escaping by sea, and on land a vastly superior allied army confronting him, the siege of Yorktown had begun.

9

I PROPOSE A CESSATION
OF HOSTILITIES

One of Washington's first moves was to seal off the British outpost at
Gloucester by sending Lauzun's cavalry and infantry there to reinforce the twelve-hundred-man outfit led by George Weedon, a
brigadier who was a former Fredericksburg tavern keeper known to
his clientele as "Joe Gourd." The Duc de Lauzun described Weedon
as "a rather good commander, but hating war that he had never
wanted to wage, and above all, mortally afraid of gun shots." That was
unfair. Lauzun may not have known it, but after actively "blowing the
seeds of sedition" in the early 1770s, Weedon had served in Washington's New York and New Jersey campaigns in 1776, became acting
adjutant general of the army in 1777, and fought at Brandywine and
Germantown before asking to be put on the inactive list. Then he
returned to organize military resistance in Virginia and serve in the
Yorktown campaign.

The first fighting of the siege occurred in Gloucester. What faced
Weedon when he got there was a daunting prospect: the village, fortified by a line of entrenchments with four redoubts and three batteries, mounting nineteen guns, suddenly erupted in a shattering display

of firepower. That was too much for the American force, and Wee-don's boys turned tail and headed for the rear. As they did, the Duc de Lauzun and his legion arrived on Gloucester plain and met some Virginia dragoons riding for their lives, saying Tarleton was after them. Lauzun rode ahead and "saw a very pretty woman at the door of a little farmhouse on the high road," who told him that Colonel Tarleton had left her house only a moment before, after saying he was eager to shake hands with the duke. The Frenchman informed her he had come on purpose to gratify Tarleton, and rode on. Not more than a hundred paces from the house he heard pistol shots, galloped forward, and saw the English cavalry, about three times his own num-ber, which he charged without halting. Tarleton, who had about six hundred men, including four hundred cavalry, caught sight of the French officer and rode toward him with pistol raised. As they were about to fight mano a mano between the troops, one of the English cavalry horses was hit by a spear thrown by a rider in Lauzun's regi-ment and, plunging, overthrew Tarleton's horse and the colonel him-self. The duke put spurs to his horse, hoping to capture his foe, but Tarleton's men were quicker and covered their leader's retreat. Lauzun pushed his hussars forward, leaving his infantry in the rear, but as soon as they came within musket shot of the enemy the hussars retired to right and left, leaving the infantry a clear field of fire, to which Tarleton's men replied. The English charged twice without breaking the French line; then Lauzun countercharged several times with great success, wounding Tarleton, overthrew some of the enemy cavalry, and drove them back to the Gloucester entrenchments before retiring on orders from the Marquis de Choisy.* According to Lauzun, Tarleton lost an officer, some fifty men, and quite a number of his men were taken prisoner.

What he did not report, which a fellow officer said was infinitely

---

*Choisy outranked Lauzun and Weedon and was directly responsible to Rochambeau. No love was lost between him and Lauzun, who said Choisy was "a good and brave man, ridiculously violent, constantly in a passion, making scenes with everybody, and always without reason."

to his credit and revealed his bravery, was that during the skirmish Lauzun saw one of his hussars assailed by three of Tarleton's cavalry, rushed to the badly wounded man's defense, and managed to rescue him.

★ ★ ★

NOW THAT THE allies had control of the Yorktown area, they could see that it was no easy place to defend. Certainly, Cornwallis had never contemplated the possibility of a siege. In fact, he was to tell Clinton later, "Nothing but the hopes of relief would have induced me to attempt its defense." Even so, to make the attackers' progress as difficult as possible, he had cleared the approach to the town of all vegetation. One disgusted New Englander grumbled that in this part of the country "a rise of five yards is called a hill," and the absolutely flat, sandy plain was so swept by English cannon that it was worth a man's life to walk there in daylight.

The defenders had surrounded the town with a line of earthworks that connected ten redoubts. Two covered the British right, guarding the river road to Williamsburg, three were on the land side of the town, three more—looking down the river—defended the left, and the remaining two, known as Number 9 and Number 10, were freestanding beyond the defensive line on the left. Finally, one protruding, arrow-shaped redoubt known as the Horn Work was at the southeast corner of town, commanding the road to Hampton. Along the defensive perimeter sixty-five cannon had been mounted—none of them larger than eighteen-pounders.

The terrain on Cornwallis's left favored an attacker, so the earl had built a strong perimeter position about half a mile beyond his interior defenses. He was also favored by a ravine that extended from the river almost halfway around the inner works, and this extended to Wormley Creek south of town, adding a natural barrier to his lines. Rising ground covered with tall, handsome pines lay between the road to Williamsburg and another leading to Hampton, and this was known as Penny's Hill, or the Pigeon Quarter, where the engineers had laid out three redoubts. Trees were felled, flèches thrown up, and batteries constructed at the points deemed most vulnerable. One of these strong points, known as the Fusiliers' Redoubt, garrisoned by some of the Royal Welsh Fusiliers and marines under Captain Apthorpe, was a star-shaped affair on the riverfront close to the Williamsburg road, and it was backed up by guns of the frigate *Guadaloupe*, moored in the river.

By the time his defenses were completed, Cornwallis's letters to Clinton and Germain revealed a good deal of bravado. The allies no sooner arrived on the scene than the earl was writing, "I have ventured these last two days to look [at] General Washington's whole force in the position outside my works, & I have the pleasure to assure Your Excellency that there was but one wish throughout the whole Army, which was, that the Enemy would advance." His attitude even extended to telling his own troops that the enemy had fewer men than the British, that they had no siege artillery, that the French would leave before long.

He could also take heart that the men inside his lines included the elite of George III's expeditionary force in America—nearly 7,500 officers and men, including two Anspach battalions and a Hessian regiment, all veterans—plus 800 or 900 marines from the fleet. The only general present besides Cornwallis was Brigadier General Charles O'Hara, in addition to two colonels, twelve lieutenant colonels, and twelve majors—a sure sign that this army had been decimated by harsh campaigning and combat.

Confronting the British and Germans were about 16,000 Americans and French soldiers, plus some 800 of de Grasse's marines. Among those Americans was a surprising number of Negroes, whose presence reflected the desperate manpower situation. In the early days of the war, blacks were deliberately excluded from service—"lest," one Carolinian warned, "our slaves when armed might become our masters." But by January of 1776, having seen the British raising Negro companies, George Washington recommended that free blacks be enlisted. As the war wore on and the shortage of troops became critical, more talk was heard about the need to use slaves as Continental soldiers, and Rhode Island, which was kept so busy defending itself that it couldn't possibly meet the quota set for it by Congress, came up with the idea of permitting slaves to enlist, with the promise that they would be freed and entitled to the same benefits as white soldiers for service until the war was over.

In the summer of 1778 Colonel Christopher Greene took charge of the black battalion, which eventually numbered 226 officers and enlisted men and served heroically in the Battle of Rhode Island. In May 1781 Colonel Greene was killed in action and replaced by Lieutenant Colonel Jeremiah Olney, who led his men until the end of the war, fighting with distinction at Red Bank, Yorktown, and Fort Oswego. (To Olney's profound regret, the Negroes never received the bounties given to whites or the compensation the latter got for depreciated currency.)

★　★　★

WASHINGTON, OF COURSE, was the commander in chief of the entire allied force, but he also issued daily commands to the American wing; Benjamin Lincoln, who was next in rank, took his turn on duty with other division commanders. Henry Knox, Washington's artillery chief since 1775, was in charge of that arm, Stephen Moylan had the cavalry, and the division commanders were Lafayette, Lincoln, and Steuben, with General Thomas Nelson, the governor of Virginia, in charge of the three-thousand-man militia force—many of whom had little or no training or prior experience. The Comte de Rochambeau commanded the French, and under him were four so-called *maréchaux de camp*: Major Generals Saint-Simon, Baron Vioménil, Comte de Vioménil, and Chastellux.

The British had suffered more than thirty men wounded on September 29, the first day of serious fighting, and the next morning the Americans were surprised to discover that the enemy pickets had quietly abandoned their advanced posts during the night and sneaked back to the defensive lines around Yorktown. This set off a lively discussion among French and American officers. (Anthony Wayne pronounced the movement "not only unmilitary, but an indication of a confused precipitation" and couldn't understand why Cornwallis had done it.) General Clinton later criticized it severely, finding it extraordinary that the earl had quit "such works in such a position without a conflict." Sir Henry, of course, had heard from several officers who had seen the Yorktown defenses that "his Lordship might defend that position twenty-one days, [in] open trenches, against 20,000 men and a proportionable artillery." But then Clinton was not there, and he had assured Cornwallis that reinforcements would sail within a few days, prompting the latter to say he would "retire this night within the works, and have no doubts, if relief comes in time, York and Gloucester will be both in the possession of his Majesty's troops." In fact, the British had withdrawn for fear that their outer works were too far from their supporting redoubts; but while it shortened their front, it also gave the allies an unexpected advantage and all but guaranteed that the unfortunate town and its inhabitants would be devastated by saturation bombing.

★ ★ ★

ON OCTOBER 1 HENRY Dearborn was one of the men taking over works the British had abandoned. He and his colonel, Alexander Scammell, had been in this fight since 1775, and on this particular morning Scammell was officer of the day and led a reconnoitering party at dawn to inspect the deserted works. Advancing close to the British position, they were attacked by some of Tarleton's mounted dragoons and taken prisoner by three of them. As two of the troopers were taking Scammell within their lines, Dearborn wrote, "one of the horsemen came up in his rear, put his pistol near his back & shot him. The ball enter'd between his hip bone & his ribs & lodg'd in him. he was carried into Town, & the next day came out on Parole. His wound appeers dangrous." In fact, the wound was mortal, and he died on October 6, universally mourned by his comrades. His death, Henry Lee said, "was the severest blow experienced by the army throughout the siege; not an officer in our army surpassed in personal worth and professional ability this experienced soldier."

Scammell was one of the genuine heroes of the Continental Army. He had served from the very beginning of the war, having hurried to Boston immediately after Lexington and Concord, participated in the siege of Boston, in Canada, and in the two battles at Saratoga, where he was wounded. When Nathanael Greene gave up the job of quartermaster general, Scammell took over that important post and recently had marched from Dobbs Ferry to Yorktown at the head of the elite light infantry in order to take an active part in the operation against Cornwallis.

As Henry Dearborn wrote to a friend in New Hampshire, "our good friend Colo. Scammel is no more," and after telling what had happened, added that "No officer of Colo. Scammell's rank that has been killed or died in the Army has been more, if so *much*, lamented by all ranks as he is." Dearborn knew what the death meant to his state: "New Hampshire has met with one more cappital loss. . . . universally lamented by all who knew him, the loss of so great & good an officer must be very severely felt in the Army at large; but in the New Hampshire line, in perticular."

Although in the long run the British evacuation of their forward posts made little difference other than shortening the time needed to subdue Cornwallis, Washington was understandably delighted. Writing to the president of Congress, he observed that the British withdrawal from their outer works meant that "we are in possession of very advantageous grounds. . . ." That morning a party of Saint-Simon's command drove in the pickets in front of the Fusilier redoubt and in a brief skirmish one man was killed and several wounded, but the result was a far better position for the French. In the afternoon French chasseurs and grenadiers occupied the two redoubts at Pigeon Quarter while the American light infantry began building a new redoubt not far from the existing one flanking the Hampton Road.

An observer may have wondered why so little activity was visible in the allied sectors, but the problem the allied work details faced was digging trenches to open a path from the infantry as well as manhandling artillery into position. The first parallel, for example, was ten feet wide, four feet deep, and two miles long—a major excavation project that afforded protection as well as access.

Few of the Americans could have known it, but they were following a ritual for sieges laid down by the French marshal Sébastien Le Prestre de Vauban three-quarters of a century earlier, under Louis XIV. It was all scrupulously prescribed: investiture, circumvallation, countervallation, bombardment, and the digging of a series of parallel encircling trenches "with drums beating and flags flying." In most circumstances the first parallel was dug six hundred yards from the besieged works, beyond the range of grape, canister, and small arms. Dirt from the excavation was thrown onto fascines in front of the parallels, forming parapets, while battery locations were dug out and connected to the parallels by other trenches. Saps, or smaller trenches, were dug in zigzag paths toward the fortress, while gabions were filled and covered on the side facing the enemy. As Joseph Plumb Martin described them, fascines were "bundles of brush bound snugly together, cut off straight at each end; they are of different lengths, from twelve to five feet." Gabions were made by "setting sticks in the ground in a circle, about two feet or more in diameter; they are interwoven with small brush in the form of a basket; they are then laid by for use, which is in entrenching. Three or more rows of them are set down together. . . . the trench is then dug behind and the dirt thrown into them, which, when full, together with the trench, forms a complete breastwork." (Martin, acquainting his readers with the French tongue, said the two words were pronounced *fasheens* and *gab-beens*.)

At three hundred yards a second parallel was dug, and, if necessary, a third was excavated close enough so that attackers could breach the fortress walls for an assault by infantry. The engineers laid out the first parallels—long trenches that began beyond the range of British guns and angled ever closer to their lines. Large openings were sited at intervals in each trench to accommodate cannon. All this digging, of course, had to be done at night, out of sight of the enemy, after which the guns had to be carried or dragged to their assigned positions. Beginning on October 1 the British artillery was firing steadily every day—one American counted a total of 351 rounds between sunrise and sunset—and they continued at night, not only from the Yorktown batteries but also from ships in the bay. Soon the pace picked up: fifteen to twenty minutes between shots at first, then at five-minute intervals, then one or two.

On the night of October 3 four men of the Pennsylvania line were killed by a single cannonball; the dead included one of the finest men in the army, according to James Duncan. He also observed a militia-man, possessed of more bravery than prudence, who stood constantly on the parapet and "damned his soul if he would dodge for the buggers." When he took to brandishing his spade at every ball that was fired, Duncan despaired for the man's life, and sure enough "a ball came and put an end to his capers." By then the wiser new recruits had learned from veterans to keep their heads down on these brilliant starlit nights.

Preparation of the parallels was no simple matter. Twelve hundred Pennsylvania and Maryland militia were detailed to collect wicker material in the woods for making six hundred gabions. Stakes were cut—six thousand of them—and two thousand round bundles of sticks were bound together for fascines, as were six hundred *saucissons*—long, sausage-shaped pipes filled with gunpowder.

Meanwhile a complex list of regulations was issued, covering the system that was to be observed when the trenches were opened. A general from Georgia named Elbert was placed in charge of all the materials to be used and instructed to keep an account of them. Fatigue parties were to be logged in and out and instructed to be absolutely silent, with no straggling. Officers were to seek all the "avenues, places of arms, and advantageous angles" for the disposition of troops in an attack. Sentries, posted at intervals throughout, protected by sandbags, were to sound the alarm if troops from the town attacked. In case of skirmishing, fatigue parties were to retire and give way to the troops under arms, and when the enemy was repulsed they were not to be pursued. All this and more was set down, as were instructions for the care of the troops—straw, good bread, and a gill of rum per man daily—plus discipline.* Because of the threat of smallpox, soldiers were forbidden to have any communication with houses or inhabitants in the neighborhood. And finally, since several men had been foolish enough to desert to the enemy, the troops were warned that anyone found within enemy lines would be instantly hanged.

Chaplain Evans observed that the soldiers "vie with one another in the performance of duty and the love of danger," but Anthony Wayne was less sanguine. The reduction of Cornwallis's army was going to require time and much bloodshed, he predicted, for it was absurd to think that Cornwallis would tacitly surrender seven thousand troops without "many a severe sortie." His political and military reputations were at stake, and "his manoeuvre into Virginia was a child of his own creation, which he will attempt to nourish at every risk and consequence."

On October 4 two deserters came into camp and reported that Cornwallis's army was very sickly—two thousand men were in the hospital, they estimated—while the other troops had scarcely enough ground to live on, the horses were desperately short of forage, and their shipping was "in a very naked state." They also observed that the enemy soldiers lay on their arms every night, expecting a general attack. That night, after some two thousand marines from de Grasse's fleet landed on the Gloucester side, the cannonading from the British was heavier than usual and incessant throughout the night, killing an officer and several soldiers over on the left. A lieutenant colonel in Brigadier

---

*Yorktown was the first and only siege conducted by the Continental Army during the entire war. It was also the last of its kind in history.

Robert Lawson's Virginia militia brigade, St. George Tucker, went into graphic detail about many of the casualties: one man mortally wounded "by a Cannon Ball which carried off part of his Hips"; a major in the Deux-Ponts regiment whose arm was shot off as he entered the trenches; another unfortunate who died without a mark on him—he was sleeping with his head on a knapsack, which was blown out from under him by a cannonball. In the morning the barrage continued.

As early as October 2 allied observers detected unmistakable signs that Cornwallis could not hold out for long. Tucker was peering through a spyglass and noted some seventy to a hundred dead horses floating in the water beyond the town. Clearly, the British lacked forage for these animals and had been forced to shoot them. The next day nearly four hundred dead horses could be seen floating in the river or lying on the shore.

★ ★ ★

IN THEIR OFF-DUTY hours soldiers wrote to their wives or other family members, giving them the news, beseeching them for letters from home, and many kept journals as well, recording the day's events as best they could. One of the best journals was kept by Tucker, who decided to keep a record of the siege since "the Close of the present Campaign will probably be more important than any other since the commencement of the American war."

St. George Tucker, twenty-nine years old, was a native of Bermuda who had come to Virginia to study at the College of William and Mary, and eventually made his home in Williamsburg, where he established a law practice and, through friendship with the Nelson family of Yorktown, gained a firsthand knowledge of the town and its environs, which gave his meticulous journal an accuracy few others had.

On a dark rainy night all the miners and sappers were out laying laths of pine end to end in the trenches when they were told to remain where they were without moving. A few moments later a man wearing a surtout appeared and asked if they had seen the engineers. He asked what troops they were, chatted with them for a few minutes, and then, after telling them if they were captured to disclose nothing about their outfit to the enemy, disappeared in the darkness. The men knew better than to reveal that information, of course, knowing that sappers and miners were entitled to no quarter by the laws of warfare. Sometime later the engineers returned in company with the stranger, whom they addressed as "Your Excellency." That was the first inkling the sappers had that their visitor had been the commander in chief.

At another time Washington was reconnoitering not far from the British lines and drew the fire of one cannon. The ball buried itself in the earth, and some sand was sprinkled over the head of Chaplain Evans, who took off his hat, looked at it, and said, "See here, general!" To which the commander in chief replied, "Mr. Evans, you had better carry that [ball] home and show it to your wife and children."

Alexander Hamilton was familiar with Vauban's protocol for a siege, and he was a stickler for following the rules. On October 7 James Duncan of the Pennsylvania line wrote that the trenches were to be "enlivened" with colors flying and drums beating, and his division of light infantry was assigned to carry out this order. Colonel Hamilton gave instructions on exactly how it must be done. First the colors were planted on the parapet accompanied by a motto: *Manus haec inimica tyrannis.* Then, Duncan said, they executed an extraordinary maneuver: mounting the bank and confronting the enemy, they went through the entire manual of arms. What the British may have thought of this is not recorded, but they ceased firing, probably— Duncan thought—because of their astonishment at the American conduct. He esteemed Colonel Hamilton as one of the first officers in the army, but "must beg leave in this instance to think he wantonly exposed the lives of his men."

★ ★ ★

ON AUGUST I A twenty-two-year-old German youth named Stephen Popp had arrived in Yorktown with other hired troops who joined the British. A day later Popp wrote, "there are reports that we are in a very bad situation." He kept a diary and began to fill its pages with distressing notes to the effect that they were working day and night strengthening the lines and had little time to eat the food that was becoming scarcer all the time. As late as the morning of October 9 he kept wondering why the enemies—the French and Americans—did not fire back at the cannonading by the British.

The reason, of course, was that the allies were holding back until all their guns were in place; if they fired from each battery once it was completed, the enemy would concentrate on that one and destroy it. According to Joseph Plumb Martin, who was in the trenches, "All were upon the tiptoe of expectation and impatience to see the signal given to open the whole line of batteries, which was to be the hoisting of the American flag in the ten-gun battery. About noon the much-wished-for signal went up," and Martin felt a secret pride swell in his heart when he saw the Continental flag run up over the battery on the American right, and the white fleur-de-lis of the French hoisted over their batteries. To Martin, "It appeared like an omen of success to our enterprise and so it proved in reality."

An American officer exclaimed, "Happy day!" when "Forty-one mouths of fire were suddenly unmasked." Colonel Philip van Cortlandt of the 2nd New York regiment recalled that when the first gun was fired he could distinctly hear the cannonball pass through the town: "I could hear the ball strike from house to house, and I was afterward informed that it went through the one where many of the officers were at dinner, and over the tables, discomposing the dishes, and either killed or wounded the one at the head of the table."

Washington himself had put the match to the gun that fired the first shot, and as the firing continued into the night the shells from the works of both armies passed high in the air and descended in a curve, each with a long train of fire. It was a spectacular sight, but not many of the American or French soldiers had a chance to watch it since they were busy digging.

Early the next morning the French Grand Battery opened with eighteen- and twenty-four-pounders and mortars, and Stephen Popp said the defenders could find no refuge in or out of the town. Residents fled to the waterfront and hid in hastily built shelters on the sand cliffs, but some eighty of them were killed and others wounded—many with arms or legs severed—while their houses were destroyed. In all that day some thirty-six hundred shots were fired by the cannon, inflicting heavy damage on ships in the harbor, killing a great many sailors as well as soldiers, after which a number of others deserted. A British officer reported that the allied cannonade was so intense that his men could scarcely fire a gun of their own since "fascines, stockade platforms, and earth, with guns and gun-carriages [were] all pounded together in a mass."

During the day the Nelson house on the edge of town was severely damaged, and when Cornwallis decided to move to safer haven, he told old Thomas Nelson, formerly secretary of the Virginia council and the uncle of the state's governor, that he could leave town under a flag of truce if he chose to do so. Nelson did and the next day talked with St. George Tucker, the young Virginian, noting that the allied "bombardment produced great effects in annoying the enemy and destroying their works." On the first night of the artillery barrage two officers were killed and another wounded, Lord Chewton's cane was knocked out of his hand by a cannonball, and Cornwallis was said to have had a sort of grotto built for him at the foot of a garden "where he lives underground." It was Thomas Nelson's opinion, Tucker said, that "the British are a good deal dispirited, although he says they affect to say they have no apprehension of the garrison's falling." Finally, the allies had fifty-two big guns firing in what one man called "aweful music."

Huge Henry Knox had acquired his knowledge of artillery from what he read in his Boston bookstore before the war, and this extraordinary display of firepower must have reminded him of his first triumph, six years earlier, when he journeyed to Fort Ticonderoga, collected the cannons there, and brought them by oxen across the mountains—"from which we might almost have seen all the King-doms of the earth"—to Dorchester Heights overlooking Boston. Once Knox's guns commanded the British fleet anchorage, the ship channels, and Boston itself, General Sir William Howe's only option was to evacuate the city, giving the first great victory of the war to the Americans.

What Knox had done in the Yorktown campaign was appreciated by Chastellux, who wrote, "One cannot too much admire the intelligence and activity with which [Knox] collected from all quarters, transported, disembarked and conveyed to the batteries the train destined for the siege, and which consisted of more than thirty pieces of cannon and mortars of a large bore: this artillery was extremely well served, General Knox . . . scarcely ever quitted the batteries. . . ."

By October 11 the parallel directed at Cornwallis's works was within 360 yards of the most advanced enemy post, and at dusk Steuben's men entered the zigzag trench and began digging the second parallel. The entire night, a man said, "was an immense roar of bursting shell," and they were glad of the chance to burrow into the soft earth, knowing that the opening of this new parallel was the most hazardous moment of a siege since it was almost certain to draw the enemy out to prevent it. Throughout the night guards stood watch, muskets at the ready, with orders not to sit or lie down, and they were at risk not only from the enemy but from their own gunners in the first parallel, who often cut their fuses too short. Morning dawned, and not a man had been killed.

But that was on the allied side. Johann Doehla wrote that ". . . the bombs and canon balls hit many inhabitants and negroes of the city, and marines, sailors, and soldiers. One saw men lying nearly everywhere who were mortally wounded and whose heads, arms, and legs had been shot off." Someone counted more than 3,600 shots from the cannons during a twenty-four-hour period, some of them landing across the river in Gloucester, wounding soldiers on the beach. Marines and sailors from a number of ships were ordered to serve in the trenches, where they may actually have been safer, since the night's bombardment cost the British several vessels in the harbor— the forty-four-gun *Charon* was hit by a red-hot shell and caught fire, and two or three smaller vessels were consumed by flames that roared through the rigging and presented what Surgeon James Thacher described as "one of the most sublime and magnificent spectacles which can be imagined."

On Sunday the 14th all the American batteries concentrated on the British strongholds in the sector opposite them—notably the Number 9 and Number 10 redoubts that lay behind a moat and a tangle of abatis, and bristled with the angled, sharp-pointed stakes known as fraise work. Early in the evening as the American light infantry prepared to assault Number 10, Joseph Plumb Martin observed that the two brilliant planets, Jupiter and Venus, were close in the western hemisphere, and every time he looked at them he was ready to leap to his feet, thinking they were the signal to attack. At the same time the French under Guillaume, Comte de Deux-Ponts, waited for darkness to fall and the same signal, when he would advance against Number 9 with four hundred of his own men plus the Gâtinais regiment, many of them with long storming pikes. The count said a fond farewell to his brother, the baron, and, when he saw the three shells rise into the air in quick succession, silently advanced.

After walking about 125 paces, the French were discovered: a Hessian soldier called out, "Werda?" and when they did not reply, the enemy opened fire. The French kept moving up, and when they reached the abatis, about twenty-five paces from the redoubt, they were caught in a hail of bullets* and took a number of casualties because only a few could emerge from the trench at one time. After firing again, the British charged with bayonets leveled, but the French held. Enough of them had reached the redoubt by then that they outnumbered the enemy defenders, who were massed behind a

---

*The term *bullet* was used as early as the fifteenth century.

line of barrels on which the French directed an intense fire. Deux-Ponts was about to give the order to charge when the British unexpectedly laid down their arms; he shouted, "Vive le Roi!" which all the troops in the area repeated. The count later commented, "I never saw a sight more beautiful or more majestic. I did not stop to look at it. I had to give attention to the wounded and directions to be observed towards the prisoners." Baron de Vioménil came to give him orders, warning that it would be important to the enemy to retake this work. "An active enemy would not have failed," he observed, but no such attempt was made by the British—quite possibly because they thought the allies had three thousand men in this attack.

The allied pioneers—sappers and miners—were having the devil's own time in this general assault. Joseph Martin arrived at the trenches a little before sunset and knew they were in for a fight when he saw officers fixing bayonets to the end of long staves. Then he and his mates were handed axes and told to proceed in advance of the troops to cut a passage through the abatis, which were made of the tops of trees with the small branches cut on a slant, making them as sharp as spikes. Then the trees were laid at a short distance from the trench or ditch, pointing outward with the butt fastened to the ground so they couldn't be moved by those approaching them. As Martin said, "It is almost impossible to get through them," but "Through these we were to cut a passage before we or the other assailants could enter."

On both fronts it had come down to hand-to-hand fighting, with the pioneers ignoring enemy fire and slashing anyone who resisted them with axes in order to open holes in the defenses. In the French lines, where the Deux-Ponts and Gâtinais regiments were engaged, the latter were preparing to attack when General Rochambeau spoke to them. These men were from Auvergne and, having had their own regiment, were not happy about fighting under another name. The general addressed them, saying, "*Mes enfants*, I hope you have not forgotten that we have served together in that brave regiment of

Auvergne *Sans tache*,* an honorable name that it has deserved ever since its creation." They answered that if he would restore their name to them, they would fight to the last man; as it turned out, "They kept their word, charged like lions, and lost one-third of their number."[†] Evidently the reason the French had far more casualties than the Americans was that when the latter reached the abatis they removed sections of it with their own hands and then leaped over the rest, whereas the French waited, under intense fire, for their pioneers to clear away the obstruction.

In this firefight the French lost forty-six men killed and sixty-two wounded, including six officers. Among the latter was a captain named de Sireuil, whose leg was shot off and who died a year later. Two weeks earlier another French officer, the Chevalier de La Loge, a charming, witty, twenty-five-year-old poet, had had a leg shot off and died three days later. In those days all wounds tended to be serious, and the serious ones were almost always fatal since medical treatment was so primitive and the chance of infection so great.

★   ★   ★

ON THE MORNING of October 16 a hundred French workmen were employed in repairing the batteries, and in the predawn light around 5 A.M. some 350 British, led by Lieutenant Colonel Robert Abercrombie, made a sortie with the light infantry and guards, and massacred the picket of the Agénois regiment. After taking the captain prisoner, the British broke into a trench where some Soissonnais put up only token resistance before abandoning the post, and Abercrombie's men took possession of a trench where the allied line was weak. From here they ran on to an undefended battery, spiked the cannon with their bayonets, killed four or five men, and proceeded to

---

*Literally, without a blemish, or stain.
[†]They kept their word, and so did Rochambeau. Two years later a royal ordinance was read to the regiment, stating that "This regiment . . . known by the name of Gâtinais, has resumed that of Auvergne by Ordinance of 11 July 1782."

the junction between the first and second parallels, where they discovered a battery commanded by Captain Savage of the Americans and halted. "What troops?" they called out, and when Savage replied, "French," the British commander said, "Push on, my brave boys, and skin the buggers."

The Comte de Noailles, who was nearby with a covering party, heard this and ordered his grenadiers to charge with the bayonet, which they did, shouting, "Vive le Roi!" Recounting this story, Colonel Richard Butler of the Pennsylvanians said, "to use the British phrase, [they] skivered eight of the Guards and Infantry and took twelve prisoners and drove them quite off." The allied loss was trifling, he added, but he admired the way the British had executed the sortie with "secrecy and spirit."

It was discovered later that Chastellux had been warned by a deserter the day before that the British were planning a sortie at daybreak and had even been told where the attack would come. But as Verger wrote, "the General had paid no attention to the warning and in consequence had made no dispositions." Clermont-Crèvecoeur dismissed the whole episode: "it was of no significance, since [the British] could have done better. They were nearly all drunk," he added, "and by the way they maneuvered they would have had great difficulty surprising a trench where the men were on the alert." But he had to admit that a lot of damage could have resulted had they "done better": "We must confess that we hardly dreamed of being attacked that night. The time was propitious, for the night was very dark." And—what he did not add—the French were very lucky.

At the same time the Comte de Deux-Ponts's outfit was engaged, Colonel Alexander Hamilton was attacking Number 10, but with quicker success. The Americans, preceded by Martin and the other sappers and miners, led the way, and the infantrymen followed, advancing beyond the trenches and lying down on the ground to wait for the signal to attack. They did not have long to wait. Their watchword was "Rochambeau," which, when pronounced quickly, sounded to the Americans like "Rush on, boys."

They were ready when the three shells lit up the sky, leaped to their feet, and moved immediately toward the redoubt. Although it was dark, Joseph Martin could make out that a lot of his buddies were falling to the ground and disappearing, and discovered as he neared the abatis that the area was pockmarked with huge holes—big enough to bury an ox in, he said. This was the place where many of their own large shells had landed, and the running men, their eyes fixed on what was ahead, were falling into them. "I thought the British were killing us off at a great rate," he said, but "At length, one of the holes happening to pick me up, I found out the mystery of our huge slaughter."

As quickly as the firing began, the men up ahead cried out, "The fort's our own! Rush on, boys!" and the pioneers immediately cleared a passage for the infantry, who swarmed over the abatis. The officers ordered the miners not to enter the fort, but there was no stopping them. Martin couldn't get through the entrance they had made, it was so crowded, but he found a place where cannon fire had blasted away some of the abatis, squeezed through, and as he was doing so a fellow at his side was hit in the head with a musket ball and fell under his feet, crying out piteously. The enemy was also throwing hand grenades; they were so thick, Martin said, that he thought they were burning cartridge paper, but he was soon "undeceived by their cracking." As he mounted the breastwork he recognized an old friend in the light of the enemy's musket fire, it was so vivid. "The fort," he said, "was taken and all quiet in a very short time."

Later that night the skies clouded over and it began to rain, a steady downpour that turned the trenches into a morass of mud, making the digging miserable for the fatigue parties, whose job it was to connect the captured redoubts to the second parallel and bring up howitzers to within three hundred yards of the enemy's works. Henry Knox had a lot of faith in these weapons. At New Windsor this past summer he had his gunners practice ricocheting shells with them until one of his captains said they could drop them "just over the enemy's parapet, destroying them where they thought themselves most secure."

★ ★ ★

EARLY THE NEXT morning, Lord Cornwallis came out to observe the allies' work and returned to his quarters to write Clinton, from whom he had learned only a few days earlier about a rescue fleet that would be sent from New York. Sir Henry had sent Major Charles Cochrane, who arrived by whaleboat on October 10, with bad news for Cornwallis, the nub of which was that no rescue effort would be made in the immediate future.* (Admiral Graves—a reluctant fighting man if ever there was one—had led Clinton to believe that his fleet would be ready to leave New York by October 5. Now—incredibly— he told the general on October 17 that the "show of signals and top- sails" that Clinton witnessed was nothing more than "spurs to push forward the lazy and supine. And I am sorry to find that difficulties go on increasing and . . . nothing can turn the current but being actually at sea.") In other words, the commanders of the admiral's warships were too lazy to move and he was unable to persuade them to get under way, so there was no telling when the fleet would attempt to rescue Lord Cornwallis and his army.

Almost a week earlier, Cornwallis had written to New York reporting that Cochrane had arrived, adding that "nothing but a direct move to York River—which includes a successful naval action—*can save me.*" Suddenly, the bravado was gone. Enemy paral- lels were drawing closer all the time, the earl said; they had con- structed batteries with great regularity and caution; and have been firing "without intermission with about forty pieces of cannon (mostly heavy) and sixteen mortars from eight to sixteen inches." He

---

*Cochrane, as a lark, asked to fire a gun from behind the parapet in the horn work and, Captain Samuel Graham wrote, was "anxious to see its effect, looked over to observe it, when his head was carried off by a cannon ball."

had lost about seventy men in recent days, and his works were substantially damaged. In conclusion, he stated, "we cannot hope to
make a long resistance." And then he added a postscript: "Since the
above was written we have lost thirty men." On October 12 he
penned another addendum: "We continue to lose men very fast."
Standing beneath the bluff leading down to the York River, he peered
anxiously in the direction of Chesapeake Bay, hoping against hope
that he would see the topsails of a British fleet, bringing the relief
promised by Clinton.

On October 15, the morning after seeing the allies' progress toward
his works, he wrote again to his chief, using a cipher: "My situation
now becomes very critical. We dare not show a gun to their old batteries, and I expect that their new ones will open tomorrow morning.
Experience has shown that our fresh earthen works do not resist their
powerful artillery, so that we shall soon be exposed to an assault in
ruined works, in a bad position, and with weakened numbers. The
safety of the place is, therefore, so precarious that I cannot recommend
that the fleet and army should run great risk in endeavoring to save us."

The bombardment continued unabated, but despite the danger
the allies stood around watching the results until Washington
ordered the field cleared of spectators. Over in the captured redoubt
Number 10 Alexander Hamilton was arguing with General Henry
Knox, the army's chief of artillery. A general order had been issued
that when a shell was seen, the troops might shout, "A shell!" but they
were forbidden to cry out "A shot" when a shot was seen, the reason
being that the explosion of a shell after it hit the ground could be
avoided, while warning of a cannonball would serve little purpose.
Hamilton considered it unsoldierlike to halloo "A shell!" while Knox
disagreed, saying that the commander in chief had given the order so
as to protect the lives of the men.

Suddenly, two shells landed in the redoubt—*spat! spat!*—and from
all sides the shout went up, "a shell!" and both men dove for cover
behind the blinds in the trench. To protect himself, Hamilton, who
was the smaller of the two, got behind Knox, who was very large, but

Knox shrugged him off, rolled over, and unintentionally threw Hamilton in the direction of the shells. The latter quickly jumped back to safety, the shells burst and scattered their deadly missiles in all directions, and Knox, brushing himself off, asked, "Now, Mr. Hamilton, what do you think about crying 'shell'? But let me tell you not to make a breastwork of me again!"

★   ★   ★

ON THE NIGHT of October 16 Cornwallis sent Lord Chewton to direct Tarleton to concentrate his troops at Gloucester, prepare the artillery to accompany the British troops in an attack against Brigadier Choisy before daybreak, and have horses and wagons ready to retreat north through the countryside. Behind this decision was the calamitous pounding of Yorktown by allied guns, which had shredded abatis, destroyed large sections of the British works, and dismounted many of their cannon, in addition to which they had almost exhausted their supply of shells.

Banastre Tarleton concurred. A retreat by way of Gloucester "was the only expedient that now presented itself to avert the mortification of a surrender. . . . Though this plan appeared less practicable than when first proposed, and was adopted at this crisis as a last resort, it yet afforded some hopes of success." He sent a number of soldiers and sailors with boats to assist in the retreat, and before eleven o'clock the light infantry, most of the Guards brigade, and the 23rd Regiment, constituting the first wave of evacuees, shoved off for Gloucester. Most of the small craft had been damaged during the siege, but even so, Tarleton figured they could embark all the troops in three trips.

Cornwallis planned to accompany the second group himself, but before doing so he had to finish writing a letter to General Washington, "calculated to excite the humanity of that officer towards the sick, the wounded, and the detachment that would be left to capitulate." The first division arrived in Gloucester before midnight, and part of the second had embarked when a rain squall came up. "At this critical moment," the earl wrote, "the weather, from being moderate and calm, changed to a most violent storm of wind and rain and drove all the boats, some of which had troops on board, down the river. It was soon evident that the intended passage was impracticable. . . ." At least one American soldier feared there might be an evil omen in the sudden, unexpected chill at midnight, the fury of the wind and rain down the York; it was "almost as severe a storm as I ever remember to have seen," he wrote.

Not until two in the morning did the storm begin to moderate, and orders then came to Gloucester for all the corps that had landed there to return to Yorktown. Since the boats were all on the York-town side, it took a long time to row them to Gloucester, and soon after daybreak they were under way to Cornwallis's headquarters, but now under fire of the allied batteries.

"Thus expired the last hope of the British army," Tarleton concluded.

★ ★ ★

THE CANNONADE THAT began at daybreak was more devastating by far than anything before, and the Hessian soldier Johann Doehla thought it would never end. The enemy, he wrote, "fired from all redoubts without stopping. . . . One saw nothing but bombs and balls raining on our whole line." The sick and wounded had been sent to Gloucester on the supposition that those who were mobile would accompany the army when it moved out from that point, for it was clear to all that "we could not hold out much longer in [Yorktown] if we did not get help soon." The worst news was that the English light infantry returning from Gloucester reported that "it would be impossible to break through there . . . nothing at all can pass in and out any more. Also, this morning right after reveille General Cornwallis came into the horn work and observed the enemy and his works. As soon as he had gone back to his quarters, he immediately sent a flag of truce with a white standard over to the enemy."

Cornwallis had seen enough. Informing Clinton of his decision, he wrote, "Under all these circumstances, I thought it would have been wanton and inhuman to the last degree to sacrifice the lives of this small body of gallant soldiers, who had ever behaved with such fidelity and courage, by exposing them to an assault, which from the numbers and precautions of the enemy could not fail to succeed. I therefore proposed to capitulate."

Cornwallis had no way of knowing this, of course, but the long-promised rescue mission finally did sail from New York with General Clinton and some six thousand troops on board on the very day of that capitulation, only to turn around and return to Manhattan when they found the French fleet in control of the Chesapeake.*

★ ★ ★

THE PENNSYLVANIA LIEUTENANT Ebenezer Denny was exhausted after a long sleepless night and was eagerly awaiting his relief. Before his replacement arrived, he said, "I had the pleasure of seeing a drummer mount the enemy's parapet and beat a parley, and immediately an officer, holding up a white handkerchief, made his appearance outside their works. Our batteries ceased." An officer from the American lines ran to meet the British officer and tied the handkerchief over his eyes. The drummer was sent back, and the British officer was conducted to a house in the rear of the American lines. "Firing ceased totally," Denny wrote, and the thought ran through his head when he heard that drummer boy, that "I never heard a drum equal to it—the most delightful music to us all."

The drummer was fortunate that he had been so visible. "Had we not seen [him] in his red coat when he first mounted," an American officer said, "he might have beat away till doomsday," because the

---

*Alexander Anderson, a naval surgeon aboard one of the ships in the fleet, wrote to his wife, ". . . it is everyones Oppinion here, that America is lost to Great Brittain and must Obtain its Independance."

noise from the cannons simply drowned out the sound of a single drum.

The British officer carrying the flag from Cornwallis bore a message to General Washington, but the commander in chief was at his headquarters behind the lines, writing to the president of the College of William and Mary about the possibility of using some of the buildings there, and addressing Admiral de Grasse on the subject of pilots for the river passage. A man on horseback pulled up before the General's tent, bringing a letter the blindfolded British officer had handed him. Washington broke the seal and opened the sheet of paper.

> Sir, I propose a cessation of hostilities for twenty-four hours,
> and that two officers may be appointed by each side, to meet at
> Mr. Moore's house, to settle terms for the surrender of the posts
> at York and Gloucester.
> I have the honour to be, &c
>
> Cornwallis

10

THE HAND OF HEAVEN DISPLAYED

October 17 was a day Henry Dearborn would never forget, and the first entry in his journal on that day in 1781 explained why: "four years this day since Gen¹ Burgoyne & his Army surrendered to the American Armies at Sarratoga." Dearborn had soldiered in the campaign that brought the French into this war on the side of the Americans, and on the day of that victory he had recorded his feelings: "this Day the Great Mʳ Burguoyn with his whole Army Surrendered themselves as Prisoners of war with all their Publick Stores, & after Grounding their armes, march'd off for New England, the greatest Conquest Ever known."

In those four years just past he had learned how to spell Burgoyne's name and his comments on the British surrender were now more temperate, but it is clear that he recognized the enormous significance of the victory at Yorktown—the second time an entire British army had been captured—because he carefully recorded in the journal all fourteen Articles of Capitulation.

On October 17, after the British experienced "the heaviest fire yet poured on them" and the blindfolded emissary was taken to

Washington's quarters to deliver Cornwallis's short note, the American commander responded at 2 P.M.: "I wish previously to the Meeting of Commissioners, that Your Lordship's proposals in writing, may be sent to the American Lines, for which Purpose, a Suspension of Hostilities during two Hours from the Delivery of this Letter will be granted."

Cornwallis sent his reply at 4:30 P.M., and although his suggested terms were not acceptable to Washington, the American permitted hostilities to be suspended until the signing of the capitulation agreement—this, despite the possibility that the enemy "might wreck or burn equipment before such acts were forbidden." To reach final terms, two commissioners from each side were to meet the following afternoon at the Moore house, about half a mile downriver from Yorktown.

The October night was chilly, and St. George Tucker wrote in his diary, "A solemn stillness prevailed. The night was remarkably clear, and the sky decorated with ten thousand stars. Numberless meteors gleaming through the atmosphere," unlike the previous night, when the bombs had provided the fireworks, but with a trail of horror. With the sun's first light the eerie shrill of bagpipes came from the British lines—a salute to the allies that was answered by the French band of the Deux-Ponts regiment. And as the sun rose, Tucker added, "one of the most striking pictures of war was displayed. . . . From the Point of Rock battery on one side our lines completely manned and our works crowded with soldiers were exhibited to view. Opposite these at the distance of two hundred yards, you were presented with a sight of the British works, their parapets crowded with officers looking at those who were assembled at the top of our works."

Beyond the red-coated figures on the parapets the Americans and French could see something of the destruction they had inflicted on the village: a number of houses in total ruin, others damaged beyond a likelihood of repair, the Thomas Nelson home with one corner broken off and large holes through the roof and walls, shattered masonry everywhere, and beyond—on the beach—hundreds of people moving around aimlessly, staring at the charred hulks leaning crazily in the shallows, ghostly masts and topgallants rising above the water in the deep channel beyond.

Cornwallis, in his underground quarters, received early that morning a flag with a message from General Washington, stating the terms for capitulation, and they were on the whole tough, though no more so than the British commander could have expected, as well as generous; but one sentence, and one only, filled the British commander with dismay. It read: "The same honors will be granted to the Surrendering Army as were granted to the Garrison of Charleston."

This was an allusion, of course, to the defeat of Benjamin Lincoln's army in 1780, when Charleston fell in the largest single American loss of the Revolutionary War—about five thousand men. Lincoln had requested that he be allowed to surrender his army with the customary honors of war, to which Clinton had replied, "The alterations you propose [to the British terms] are all utterly inadmissible." Now, in normal circumstances, when an army had fought bravely and well before surrendering, the vanquished soldiers were accorded the honors of war, which meant that they marched from their works with flags flying, drums beating, and their band playing a tune of the conqueror, as if to demonstrate that the beaten men were equal in bravery to the victors. But Clinton flatly refused Lincoln's request, stipulating that "The drummers are not to beat a British march or colors to be uncased." Washington had not forgotten this humiliation of Lincoln or the slur cast on his troops.

That afternoon the British commissioners, Colonel Thomas Dundas and Major Alexander Ross, Cornwallis's aide, walked up the bluff from the river's edge to the house where the allied representatives, Colonel John Laurens (who had been with Lincoln at Charleston) and Comte de Noailles, Lafayette's brother-in-law, were waiting for them. When the articles of capitulation were laid before the British, Ross immediately focused on the one denying them the honors of war, saying it was harsh. Laurens agreed. Why, then, was it included? Ross inquired.

Laurens replied that he had been present at Charleston, where General Lincoln's army had fought bravely in open trenches for six weeks only to be denied the honors of war and be humiliated by having to march out with colors cased and drums not beating a German or British march.

"But my Lord Cornwallis did not command at Charleston," Ross replied.

"It is not the individual that is here considered," Laurens told him. "It is the nation. This remains an article, or I refuse to be a commissioner."

Long into the night the negotiations continued, and early the next morning Washington carefully reviewed the terms, scratching out a few of them while letting most stand. He had the final version copied and sent it to Cornwallis with a note saying he expected to have it signed at eleven o'clock so that the garrison would march out at two o'clock that afternoon.

About eleven o'clock on the morning of October 19, a group of allied officers met in the captured British redoubt nearest the river for the signing of the historic document. The text of the articles had been delivered from the British lines and bore the signatures of Cornwallis and Thomas Symonds, the senior naval officer present. To this, Washington had a short paragraph added: "Done in the trenches before Yorktown, in Virginia, October 19, 1781," below which he wrote, "G. Washington." Then the French commander signed, "Le Comte de Rochambeau," and his naval colleague added, "Le Comte de Barras En mon nom & celui du Comte de Grasse."*

Pennsylvania's Lieutenant Ebenezer Denny wrote, "All is quiet. Articles of capitulation signed." He reported that detachments of French and Americans moved immediately into the shattered village

---

*"The Count de Barras in my own name and that of the Count de Grasse." The latter, unfortunately, was sick and unable to attend the signing, so Barras substituted for him.

of Yorktown and took possession of the British forts, on one of which Baron Steuben planted the American flag. What they found within this "rather small and ugly" town—as the Comte de Clermont-Crèvecoeur described it—was almost total destruction. "There was only one pretty house and that was not spared by the bombs and shells and is now beyond repair." It belonged to Governor Nelson, who had visited the French batteries at the height of the siege and told the gunners, "True, it is my house; but, my friends, it is full of English. Do not spare it." (He also had two farms in the vicinity, which had been completely burned, pillaged, or plundered.) The governor, who had served with uncommon bravery as leader of the Virginia militia, whom he paid with his own money by mortgaging his property because the state had no funds to spare, then had the allied troops camp on his cropland while their artillery destroyed his house and outbuildings. When the artillery lacked means of transportation, he provided his own and his farmers' horses and then requisitioned animals from the state.*

Nelson's reward for all this was to be financially ruined and summoned to appear before the legislative assembly to answer charges from citizens that he had behaved arbitrarily. He resigned as governor in order to defend himself and was acquitted with praise; however, he did not resume his duties as governor but left them to Benjamin Harrison, who had taken over in his absence.

The magazines were filled with every kind of dry stores, according to Clermont-Crèvecoeur, but the French were forbidden to enter the town for four or five days, by which time the Americans had plundered everything in sight. Although no clothing of any sort remained, the French officers did find 140 iron cannon and 74 brass weapons, 22 flags, 69 bombs, more than 7,000 small arms, and 122 bullets of every caliber. Baron Closen viewed the scene and reported, "I will never forget how frightful and disturbing was the appearance of the city of York, from the fortifications on the crest to the strand below. One

---

*He was said to have had seven hundred slaves before and now had eighty or one hundred.

could not take three steps without running into some great holes made by bombs, some splinters, some balls, some half-covered trenches, with scattered white or negro arms or legs, some bits of uniforms. Most of the houses [were] riddled by cannon fire," he added, and few of them had windowpanes. What struck him hardest was the deep concern of the few inhabitants; they feared that what little remained to them would be pillaged by the American troops, who "(they falsely said) excelled in such ventures!"

Another discovery that astonished the allies was the number of slaves the British had requisitioned as servants and laborers during their campaigns in the South. Clermont-Crèvecoeur commented on how many sick were in both armies, blaming it on excessive fatigue, bad food and water, and shortages of all kinds. "Many officers also paid their toll in the form of serious illnesses. We lost many from the bloody flux." He added that the Negroes had spread the plague. "These miserable creatures could be found in every corner, either dead or dying. No one took the trouble to bury them, so you can imagine the infection this must have engendered. Still, a large number of them survived." Most were reclaimed by the local inhabitants, but "Negroes without masters found new ones among the French, and we garnered a veritable harvest of domestics. Those among us who had no servant were happy to find one so cheap."

Faithfully continuing his journal, Johann Doehla made a meticulous list of the officers and soldiers surrendered, the artillery, munitions, and ships captured, and the names of officers who went into captivity with their men as well as those who went on parole to New York. Among the latter was "Second Lieutenant Popp, who was named an officer from a Corporal in Yorktown on October 16." Clearly, Popp had done something worthy of a battlefield promotion.

When the losses of troops were tallied, the siege had cost the British a total of between 8,000 and 9,000: 556 of them killed or wounded, plus 5,051 prisoners at Yorktown and Gloucester, and more than 2,000 sick. (To that number, Doehla added 85 deserters, most of them Hessians.) The total also included 1,228 seamen and officers from the navy. The French had lost 389, of which 98 soldiers and officers had been killed, the rest wounded. Americans had the fewest casualties: 10 officers and 289 soldiers killed or wounded. The British total did not include Tories, many of whom remained in the town and would need protection from angry patriots. Fortunately for them, Cornwallis had come up with an imaginative solution to save them from vindictive Americans.

Writing to Washington on the 18th, the earl said he wanted the sloop of war *Bonetta* to be left entirely at his disposal, from the moment the capitulation document was signed, to receive one of his aides-de-camp who would carry dispatches to Sir Henry Clinton. Other passengers were to include as many soldiers as he saw fit to send, and fifty members of the sloop's crew. The ship was to be permitted "to sail without examination, when my dispatches are ready," with the understanding that she would be brought back and delivered to Washington, that she would not carry any officer without the American commander's consent, and that "no person may be punished or molested for having joined the British troops." The phrase "without examination" was an escape hatch for Tories, as Washington probably realized, but he could afford to look the other way, for they were subject not to military authority but to civilian and if there was anything the General did not need just then it was another problem. As for the indefinite number of soldiers to be taken, this hid any American deserters the British might have who would, if captured in enemy service, have to be hanged.

The terms of the surrender were long and rather complicated, but they were neatly summarized by Surgeon James Thacher, who, like so many of the Continentals, had been part of this war ever since 1775, serving most recently in the elite corps of Colonel Alexander Scammell. "The captive troops are to march out with shouldered arms, colors cased and drums beating a British or German march, and to ground their arms at a place assigned for the purpose." Officers were allowed to keep their sidearms and personal property; the generals and other high-ranking officers could go on parole to England or

New York; marines and seamen of the king's ships were to be prisoners of war to the French navy, land forces to the United States. All military and artillery stores were to be delivered up unimpaired. "The royal prisoners to be sent into the interior of Virginia, Maryland and Pennsylvania in regiments, to have rations allowed them equal to the American soldiers (which must have been cold comfort to the prisoners), and to have their officers near them."

★ ★ ★

ON OCTOBER 19, 1781, the day "when the pride of Britain was to be humbled in a greater Degree than it had ever been before, unless at the Surrender of Burgoyne," in St. George Tucker's words, the allied armies marched out about noon and lined up, two ranks deep, on both sides of the Hampton road from Yorktown—Americans on the right side, French on the left. It was a glorious, warm autumn day, sunny and bright, with the leaves on the trees just beginning to turn. These double ranks of uniformed men stretched for more than a mile, and at the end farthest from Yorktown were the commanders of the two forces and their ranking officers, all on horseback. The French troops were brilliantly turned out, their white uniforms trim and spotless, their legs encased in clean white gaiters. Facing them from across the road the men of the United States Army were mostly in dun-colored hunting shirts or grimy white uniforms, looking for all the world like irregulars, not professional soldiers like the French.

A surprising number of these Americans had six years of punishing, bloody warfare behind them; six years of hardship and suffering, hunger and tedium, no pay, and unparalleled neglect by their government and fellow Americans, all of whom would be only too glad to share in the benefits of victory if it came, but were too occupied or unconcerned to risk their lives or security for freedom. Some of these men standing in line under the hot Virginia sun were survivors of the fights at Concord and Bunker Hill, had suffered bitter defeat with Arnold and Montgomery before Quebec, had been part of the humiliating loss of New York and the retreat across New Jersey, and endured the killing winters of Morristown and Valley Forge. They had experienced the glorious and all too rare victories of Trenton and Princeton and Saratoga, the disappointments of Germantown and Brandywine, the staggering losses of Charleston and Camden, the triumphs of Kings Mountain, Cowpens, and a hundred little crossroad hamlets from Montreal and Quebec to South Carolina and Georgia. Yet somehow they had endured to participate in and savor this glorious moment. Few, if any, of them could have understood the magnitude of what they had achieved, which was not only to ensure the independence of the United States but, eventually, to change the history of the world.

★　★　★

NATHANAEL GREENE HAD described his own situation humorously but accurately in a letter to his friend Henry Knox: "We have been beating the bush and the General has come to catch the bird." The General had indeed caught the bird, with a lot of help from men like Greene and Moultrie, Marion and Pickens, France's army and navy, the unknown and unnamed militiamen from the thirteen former colonies, and everyone collecting on the fields outside Yorktown—including a prodigious "concourse of spectators" from the surrounding countryside—who wanted to see that bird in the person of the commander of the British army. "Every eye was prepared to gaze on Lord Cornwallis, the object of peculiar interest and solicitude," Thacher wrote, "but he disappointed our anxious expectations . . . [and] made General O'Hara his substitute as the leader of his army. This officer was followed by the conquered troops in a slow and solemn step, with shouldered arms, colors cased and drums beating a British march." (It was a slow, melancholy air, almost certainly "The World Turn'd Upside Down," which was a popular tune to which innumerable songs and ballads had been set.)

Cornwallis had signed the document affirming his surrender and denying his army the honors of war, but he could not stand the thought of being present at "the humiliating scene" and decided to pretend that he was ill.

One of the waiting French officers was pleased to see the smiles of pride on all the generals' faces, and Surgeon Thacher said, "every countenance beamed with satisfaction and joy." As well they might. While they waited, the French regimental bands came nearer, playing jubilant music that was accompanied with the timbrel, an ancient percussion instrument similar to a tambourine—"a delightful novelty [which] produced . . . a most enchanting effect." For a while they kept playing, the French "magnificently," the Americans "moderately well."

At two o'clock, it was possible to hear the distant sound of fifes and drums coming from Yorktown, and the waiting armies that had finally shattered the powerful British force were suddenly silent. As the scarlet ranks came closer, the music was louder and the "strain of melancholy" more pronounced; Ebenezer Denny thought the "drums beat as if they did not care how."

The scene captured so accurately on canvas in 1785 by Louis-Nicolas van Blarenberghe, whose work was based on eyewitness accounts and sketches (some by Louis-Alexandre Berthier), has the defeated army, colors cased, marching out of Yorktown between the American and French forces, and heading to the field where they lay down their arms. The artist, who was one of several battle painters attached to the French war department, had been working for years on a series of depictions of battles fought during the reign of Louis XV. When he was commissioned to do two paintings of the recent victory in America for Louis XVI's collection in the royal palace at Versailles, he set aside his other project and began work on the *Siege*, showing allied troops marching toward Yorktown, and another painting of *The Surrender.* Later, Rochambeau requested that the artist make copies for him, and they were hung at his château.*

---

*The paintings remain today at the same locations; Louis XVI's set is at the former royal palace in Versailles, Rochambeau's at the Château de Rochambeau.

Leading the approaching ranks of British troops was Charles O'Hara, a red-faced, fast-talking Irishman with gleaming white teeth. He was a natural son of the second Lord Trawley, colonel of the Coldstream Guards, and had entered his father's regiment at the age of sixteen as "lieutenant and captain." After service in Europe and Africa, he came to America in 1778 and was posted to New York under Clinton, who said later, "I soon found he was the last man I should have sent with a detached corps—plans upon plans for defense; never easy satisfied, or safe; a great, nay plausible, talker."

Sent south to join Cornwallis, he showed himself to be an aggressive commander in the race to the Dan and performed heroically at Guilford, where he was twice wounded leading the attack that broke through Greene's defenses. Now he had been given the heartbreaking task of surrendering Cornwallis's army, and as he rode toward the waiting French and American officers the first man to greet him was a Frenchman, the Comte Mathieu Dumas, Rochambeau's adjutant general, who had been deputized to direct the garrison troops.

O'Hara asked Dumas where General Rochambeau was and was told, "On our left, at the head of the French line." As the Englishman spurred his horse forward, Dumas realized that he was going to present his sword to the French general, and galloped quickly between the two just as Rochambeau signaled, pointing to General Washington.

"You are mistaken," Dumas told O'Hara. "The commander-in-chief of our army is on the right."

Understandably flustered, O'Hara turned and rode over to Washington, explained that Earl Cornwallis was indisposed, and offered his sword to the commander in chief, who declined to receive it, indicating that O'Hara should present it to Benjamin Lincoln, his second in command. Lincoln held it for a symbolic moment and, returning it to O'Hara, pointed to the field just beyond them, which was encircled by Lauzun's legion, hussars and lancers with sabers drawn and spears raised. That was where the British and German troops were to lay down their muskets.

As the redcoats passed between the two lines, they were sullen and angry, as Closen observed, showing "the greatest scorn for the Americans, who, to tell the truth, were eclipsed by our army in splendor of appearance and dress, for most of these unfortunate persons were clad in small jackets of white cloth, dirty and ragged, and a number of them were almost barefoot." Comparing the British with the German troops that were with them, Closen said the former seemed to be more tired and less heroic than the Anspach or Hessian regiments. The latter "made a more military appearance," a New Jersey officer observed, "and the conduct of their officers was far more becoming men of fortitude," while "the British officers in general behaved like boys who had been whipped at school. Some bit their lips; some pouted; others cried. Their round, broad-brimmed hats were well-adapted to the occasion, hiding those faces they were ashamed to show."

Johann Doehla said he and the other Germans were awed by the sight of "the great multitude which had besieged us," and saw at once that "they could have devoured us, who were only a corporal's guard compared with them." He was especially impressed by the French, whose bands made splendid music, and whose troops "were good looking, tall, well-washed men."

As far as their arms and uniforms were concerned, the British troops had a parade-ground look about them, since every soldier had been given a new suit of clothes, but in their line of march onlookers observed disorderly and unsoldierly conduct, their step irregular, and their ranks frequently broken. A Pennsylvania soldier noted, "The British prisoners appeared much in liquor."

The moment of truth came when the redcoats and Germans reached the field where they were to lay down their arms and could no longer conceal their mortification. Platoon officers could hardly bring themselves to order "Ground arms!" and did so in a very "unofficer-like manner." A number of soldiers threw down their weapons violently, hoping to make them useless—an irregularity stopped by an order from General Lincoln. After grounding their weapons, the captives were conducted back to Yorktown and guarded by allied troops until they could be sent off on the long march to captivity.

Captain Samuel Graham of the Highland regiment recalled how "the scene made a deep impression at the moment, for the mortification and unfeigned sorrow of the soldiers will never fade from my memory. Some cursed, some went so far as to shed tears, while one man, a corporal, who stood near me, embraced his firelock and then threw it on the ground, exclaiming, 'May you never get so good a master again!'" Colonel von Seybothen, the commander of an Anspach battalion, shouted the command "Ground muskets!" with tears running down his cheeks, and Lieutenant Colonel Robert Abercrombie of the British light infantry pulled his hat down over his eyes and bit the hilt of his sword in frustration. To do the Americans justice, Graham said, they behaved through all this with delicacy and forbearance, while the French were "profuse in their protestations of sympathy." He visited the French lines after their parade had been dismissed and was overwhelmed with their civility.

Doehla said the Germans tramped back to Yorktown in silence, and "all spirit and courage which at other times animated the soldiers had slipped from us, especially inasmuch as the Americans greatly jeered at us like conquerors as we marched back through the armies." The French, on the other hand, conducted themselves very well toward them, and when they were back in their own lines surrounded them to prevent the American militia from stealing and plundering.

That night, speaking of his comrades, an American colonel said, "I noticed that the officers and soldiers could scarcely talk for laughing, and they could scarcely walk for jumping and dancing and singing as they went about."

James Thacher was still fuming over Cornwallis's refusal to appear for the surrender. He was not surprised that the British officer corps was humbled, since they had always held an exalted opinion of their own military prowess and "affected to view the Americans as a contemptible, undisciplined rabble." But he thought a "great commander" was above such pettiness and should not shrink from the inevitable misfortunes of war. Lord Cornwallis, after all, had often appeared in triumph at the head of his army, which was said to adore him, so he ought to participate manfully in their misfortunes, however humiliating, "but it is said he gives himself up entirely to vexation and despair."

Washington gave a dinner that night for the general officers of all three armies. When Cornwallis still claimed indisposition, O'Hara led the British contingent and, to the relief of everyone, was sociable and completely at ease, without the slightest sign of resentment or the air of a captive. As the evening wore on, the Americans became increasingly annoyed at the easy camaraderie of the French and British. It was quite apparent that the French nobles and the English upper-class officers felt more comfortable with men they regarded as their social equals than with the Americans. After all, Benjamin Lincoln was a former farmer, son of a maltster; Henry Knox was a bookseller; Anthony Wayne a tanner.

Even the French were amazed at the "sang froid and gaiety" of O'Hara and his fellow officers, and the Comte de Clermont-Crèvecoeur put his finger on the root of the problem:

> The English and French got on famously with one another. When the Americans expressed their displeasure on this subject, we replied that good upbringing and courtesy bind men together and that, since we had reason to believe that the Americans did not like us, they should not be surprised at our preference [for the English]. Actually you never saw a French officer with an American. Although we were on good enough terms, we did not live together. This was, I believe, most fortunate for us. Their character being so different from ours, we should inevitably have quarreled.

Men like these foreign officers made it seem a gentlemanly war. It turned out that Cornwallis had no money with which to pay his troops, so the French advanced him 100,000 écus for that purpose. As Rochambeau wrote to Sir Henry Clinton, "When Lord Cornwallis and his army left York, he informed me of his need for money, and I shared with the greatest pleasure the few funds that we then had in our military chest. I placed but a single condition on the reimbursement, which was that it be made to us by the [English] chest in New York. . . ." The earl not only repaid the loan after arriving in Manhattan but sent with the funds one hundred bottles of porter as an expression of his appreciation.

★　★　★

ON SATURDAY, OCTOBER 20, 1781, General Cornwallis wrote a long letter to his superior officer, Sir Henry Clinton, whom he despised. "I have the mortification," he began, "to inform Your Excellency that I have been forced to give up the posts of York and Gloucester and to surrender the troops under my command by capitulation, on the 19th instant, as prisoners of war to the combined forces of America and France." His reason for doing so, as the letter made abundantly clear, was largely the lack of support from Clinton and the navy, and their failure to come to his relief, as promised.

He had never seen Yorktown in a favorable light, he added, and "nothing but the hopes of relief would have induced me to attempt its defense." In his letters, Clinton had assured him repeatedly that "every possible means would be tried by the navy and army to relieve us," and when he was told that relief would sail about October 5 he resolved to resist the enemy until help arrived. But the promised help had not arrived.

For their courage, firmness, and patience, his men deserved the highest praise, but the situation in which they found themselves had made a successful defense impossible. Then he paid tribute to the victors, especially the French—whose sensitivity to the British situation and generosity "has really gone beyond what I can possibly describe"—and should be a model for British officers if ever they found themselves in the same position.

The letter was the beginning of a bitter feud between Cornwallis and Clinton that would continue for years, and when Sir Henry received it he wrote at once to Lord George Germain, covering his own flanks by informing him that not only was the navy to blame, but Germain as well, for encouraging him to expect that the fleet in American waters would be augmented in time and numbers sufficient to neutralize the French.

★ ★ ★

DURING THE SIEGE, Joseph Martin and others saw in the woods "herds of Negroes" whom Lord Cornwallis had lured from their owners by promising them freedom and then turned loose "with no other recompense for their confidence in his humanity than the smallpox for their bounty and starvation and death for their wages. They might be seen scattered about in every direction, dead and dying, with pieces of ears of burnt Indian corn in the hands and mouths, even of those that were dead." When the siege ended, many owners of these unfortunate people came to the American camp and searched for them, offering a guinea a head for each one. A Colonel Banister, who had lost eighty-two of his slaves, said he did not blame them for leaving him, that the blame was Cornwallis's, and when he found them he said they were free to go with him or stay where they were. "Had the poor souls received a reprieve at the gallows they could not have been more overjoyed," Martin wrote. (For locating several slaves for their owners, Martin was rewarded with twelve hundred paper dollars. It cost him the entire sum for a single pint of rum.)

On one occasion, at least, the British had made use of the slaves they found as instruments of germ warfare, as suggested in a letter from General Alexander Leslie to Cornwallis: "About 700 Negroes are come down the River [with] the Small Pox. I shall distribute them about the Rebell Plantations."

One man who had seized many of those slaves was Banastre Tarleton, and he was pointedly not invited to any of the festivities held in American quarters. When he surrendered at Gloucester, Tarleton feared he would be harshly used, but that had not happened, and now his aggressive nature was evident when he asked Lafayette if the neglect was deliberate or accidental. The Frenchman suggested he talk with Colonel John Laurens, one of Washington's aides and a South Carolinian. Laurens had been wounded twice, captured at Charleston and exchanged, and had led a bayonet charge on the British redoubts at Yorktown, and he was in no mood to indulge "Butcher" Tarleton.

When Tarleton inquired if the slights had occurred by chance, Laurens replied, "No, Colonel Tarleton, no accident at all; intentional, I can assure you, and meant as a reproof for certain cruelties practiced by the troops under your command in the campaigns in the Carolinas."

This ostracism was disgracing him in front of the British junior officers and in the eyes of all three armies, Tarleton protested, and Laurens should recognize that severities were part of war. Laurens looked at him and said quietly that a soldier's duty can be discharged in different ways, and where mercy is shown it makes the duty more acceptable to friends and foes alike.

Tarleton was in for more ignominy. Like other British officers, he had been permitted to keep his sword and his horse, but the animal he had was taken from a plantation in Virginia and the owner was determined to get it back. Out of nowhere the plantation's overseer suddenly appeared one day when Tarleton and a servant were riding down the road. The Virginian stepped in front of the British officer and said, "Good morning, Colonel Tarleton. This is my horse. Dismount." When the cavalryman hesitated, the overseer raised a lethal-looking stick, and a witness told what happened next: the Englishman "jumped off quicker than I ever saw a man in my life." Another American who saw the overseer ride off on the horse said, "Oh! How we did laugh to think how the mighty man who had caused so much terror and alarm in Virginia had been made to jump off the wrong side of his horse so quickly, with nothing but a sweet gum stick and a chunky little man beside him, while he . . . had a fine sword by his side."

★　★　★

IN THE WAKE of their triumph, both Washington and Rochambeau were desperately eager to get official word of the victory to their governments at the earliest possible moment. Rumor and hearsay would travel faster than their messengers, so it was extremely important that the official account arrive promptly.

Rochambeau wrote a dispatch to Philippe-Henri, Marquis de Ségur, the minister of war, who would present the news to the court at Versailles, and entrusted the letter to the Duc de Lauzun, who sailed on the frigate *Surveillante* on October 24. Two days later the frigate *Andromaque* slipped out of the harbor with the Comte de Deux-Ponts aboard, carrying duplicate dispatches in case the original was lost, along with a *mémoire pour les grâces*—a memorandum suggesting rewards and promotions and a note regarding Lauzun and Deux-Ponts. "They are the two officers of rank who have most distinguished themselves," it read. On the way to France, both messengers narrowly escaped capture by British warships and arrived in near-record time. Reporting on his audience with the monarch, Lauzun said, "My news caused the King great joy. I found the Queen with him; upon his questioning me, I told him I intended to return to America, and he asked me to assure the Army that it would be treated handsomely—better than any other army ever had been."

Louis XVI and Vergennes sent messages of congratulation to Rochambeau, as did the minister of war, who said that the count's performance of his duty had "completely fulfilled every expectation of His Majesty." The king ordered a Te Deum to be sung in the Metropolitan Church in Paris on November 27, and an ordinance directed "all the bourgeois and inhabitants" of the city to illuminate the front of their houses to celebrate the great victory. And on December 15, in Williamsburg, the Te Deum was also sung, the garrison moved out to parade and gave three salutes, followed by "Vive le Roi" and a volley from the artillery, and that evening Rochambeau invited the most prominent citizens to a ball. The ladies, one guest wrote, "show a partiality for the Minuet and dance it fairly well. . . . without exception

[they] are charmed with our French quadrilles and also find our French manners to their taste."

By the first week in November the area around Yorktown had begun to empty out of soldiers. The American militia had already departed by then and the Continentals split up, with most of them destined to join Washington on the Hudson, while Anthony Wayne with the Pennsylvania line and Arthur St. Clair with Maryland and Delaware recruits headed south to reinforce Greene. The British left in stages: the troops, including the Hessians and Anspach regiments, were bound for Winchester and Fort Frederick, where they were to spend their time in captivity; those officers who were not with the captives and had been granted parole headed for New York or England. The French, after razing the works around Yorktown and Portsmouth, went into winter quarters in Virginia—mainly Williamsburg, their headquarters, where the Deux-Ponts, Bourbonnais, and several artillery companies were stationed, with the Soissonnais at Yorktown and others at Gloucester and West Point, which Clermont-Crèvecoeur described as "a little hamlet of 7 or 8 houses at the confluence of the Mattaponi and Pamunkey rivers."

During the winter of 1781–1782 the French had little to do beyond resting and making acquaintances in the neighborhood, and with time on their hands officers enjoyed sitting around a fire in the evening ruminating on the qualities and effectiveness of the American troops. What seems to have impressed them most was their expertise with the carbine, or long rifle, which they used to great effect on the English. They rarely missed their mark, Jean-Baptiste-Antoine de Verger observed, and the tactic they employed was to face the enemy individually, not as a unit, slipping from bush to bush until they brought their quarry within range, then picking off a sentry and vanishing. An Anspach officer told him that riflemen killed eight sentries in this manner on the day they arrived. The English were so fearful of their abilities that they gave them no quarter if caught.

The Continental soldiers, the Frenchmen agreed, were "very

war-wise and quite well disciplined." They were thoroughly inured to hardship of all kinds, which they tolerated with little complaint as long as their officers set them an example, but it was imperative that those leaders equal their troops in firmness and resolution.

That was certainly true of the militia outfits, which were worse in the South than elsewhere, the French agreed. When these men had superior numbers or an advantageous position, from which they could ambush the enemy, they gave occasional examples of bravery. But they had to have room in their rear to enable them to retreat; if not, their high opinion of the British or their fear of capture might make them useless in defending a fort. And yet, "We have seen parties of militia in this country perform feats that veteran units would have gloried in accomplishing. They only do so, however, when the persuasive eloquence of their commander has aroused in them an enthusiastic ardor of which immediate advantage must be taken."

It was agreed by the French officers that of all the American corps the light infantry was the best. But whether they were light infantry, cavalry, Continentals, or militia made no difference in one respect: every one of them had "supreme confidence in General Washington."

Once he had settled into his Williamsburg quarters, Clermont-Crèvecoeur observed how hospitable everyone was, receiving the French in a most cordial manner, but went on to say that the residents were exceptionally lazy. "The gentlemen, as well as those who claim to be but are not, live like lords. Like all Americans they are generally cold, but the women are warmer. They have the advantage of being much gayer by nature than the northern women, though not so pretty. They love pleasure and are passionately fond of dancing, in which they indulge both summer and winter." As he had in Rhode Island, he kept a close eye on the women in Virginia, finding that they, like the men, had very poor teeth—the result, he declared, of eating too much salt meat. (Because of the heat, fresh-killed meat had to be eaten within twenty-four hours or it would spoil—hence, much salted poultry, beef, and lamb.) Even more than in the north, a Virginia girl lost her freshness after the age of twenty; she would pass for thirty-five in France, he said. The men, who were not very active, drank and chewed tobacco a lot and left the responsibility of the household to their wives.

Rochambeau and his aides made occasional forays into the countryside, one of which was the source of much regret—a night's lodging at the home of a former Virginia militia major named Johnston. Baron Closen, who was with his chief, claimed that he "had never seen a dirtier, more shocking, and more stinking barracks than that of this major, who, himself, was the greatest pig that the earth has produced. . . ." During the night the baron and his companions couldn't sleep; they bedded down on straw, he said, and had their ears "tickled by rats!" General Rochambeau, who at least had a bed, was "eaten by vermin" and declared the place "the worst lodging he had found in all America."

As the summer heat increased, Rochambeau and his friends suffered intensely, for the nights seemed even hotter than the days and they were tortured by invasions of gnats. The Americans told him it was dangerous to bathe—they maintained that it loosened the bowel and caused fevers, and the only times to do it were before dawn or after sundown. But he went bathing at all hours and never felt the slightest ill effects. What did bother him was the American habit of leaving their wells and springs uncovered, so that the water was warm or brackish and unpleasant to drink. He solved this problem by following the American custom of drinking grog (rum and water) "which fortifies and invigorates you without stopping perspiration."

★   ★   ★

GENERAL WASHINGTON HAD hoped to persuade de Grasse to ferry his army to Charleston and join him in besieging the British force there. But the French admiral replied that orders from Versailles, his commitments to the Spaniards, and other projects would not permit him to do so, and off he sailed to the West Indies. As the General wrote to Congress, his hopes of finishing the war in the

South and destroying any British foothold there had come to naught, so he was reinforcing Greene with some troops and marching with the remainder of the army to the Hudson River, "where they would be ready, at the ensuing Campaign, to commence such Operations against N. York as may be hereafter concerted." Meanwhile, he had a most important report to make—a mission to be entrusted to a man who richly deserved the honor of delivering it.

The morning of October 20, 1781, dawned behind a scrim of haze and smoke rising from hundreds of smoldering campfires in and around Yorktown when Tench Tilghman awoke, fighting fatigue and illness. For two nights he had had almost no sleep and he was suffering from a recurrent fever (probably malaria), but as weak as he was, he was determined to carry out the task given him by General Washington, which was to deliver the official news of Cornwallis's surrender to the Continental Congress in Philadelphia in the shortest possible time. This particular assignment was a glowing reward for the man who had been the General's loyal and most devoted aide for seven years of selfless service.

Tilghman was not quite thirty-seven years old, slender, five feet ten inches tall, and weighed about 150 pounds, with a ruddy complexion, gray eyes, and auburn hair tied in a queue. By all accounts he was charming, witty, and graceful, an excellent horseman. (On his black horse he was a conspicuous figure on the march or on a battlefield.) One of six brothers—two of them loyalists like their father—he was reserved, soft-spoken, and very tough. He grew up in a prominent family on the eastern shore of Maryland and at the age of fourteen began attending the College and Academy of Philadelphia, which was founded by Benjamin Franklin. Along with his many other assets, he brought to his present assignment a thorough knowledge of the terrain and water routes from Yorktown to Philadelphia.

As he rode off to the waterfront, Lafayette, the Duc de Lauzun, and several other men came along to wish him Godspeed. It was a dreary scene he was leaving behind: long piles of freshly dug dirt that covered the dead, the ruins of Yorktown, tents and the detritus of camps sprawled out across the fields, and at the water's edge the bloated bodies of slaughtered horses and, beyond, the charred hulks of sunken ships. Tilghman and Lauzun dismounted, handed their reins to an orderly, and stepped into the boats that were waiting for them. The American was heading north to Annapolis, where he would board the packet for Rock Hall. From there he expected to travel the 130 miles to Philadelphia with a relay of horses. The Frenchman was going downstream for a final conference with de Grasse before he boarded the *Surveillante*, bound for France.

Tilghman's boat set sail, picked up a six-knot breeze, and after clearing the mouth of the York River and old Point Comfort was soon out in the open waters of Chesapeake Bay. Day turned to night, and sometime in the darkness Tilghman was awakened with a huge jolt. Although he could see nothing, he recognized the problem immediately: the skipper had tacked too far in order to avoid the shoals off Tangier Island and had run aground on a sandbar. The only option was to wait for high tide, which cost Tilghman hours of frustrated waiting. By the morning of October 21, they were out in deep water again with a fresh wind, and it looked as though they would reach Annapolis in good time. But off Little Choptank River, about thirty miles from their destination, the wind died, and it was the morning of the 22nd before they arrived at Annapolis.

There, in the capital of Maryland, he met with the Committee of Safety, delivered his glorious news, and made arrangements for the continuation of his journey. He learned, to his annoyance, that a letter from de Grasse to Governor Lee had already been forwarded to Congress, conveying the news of Cornwallis's surrender to that body. The packet that ran between Annapolis and Rock Hall, carrying passengers as well as horses, some light freight, and wagons, normally took about two and a half hours, but Tilghman seemed to be jinxed by the weather. The packet, like his boat from Yorktown, was becalmed and took the entire day to reach Rock Hall on the evening of October 22.

Desperate to get moving, Tilghman was off the packet and on a fresh horse as quickly as possible, riding for Chestertown—where his father, two sisters, and a brother were then living—shouting his news to everyone he passed along the way. The *Maryland Journal* carried an account of his arrival in Chestertown and the celebration that followed—a great event attended by "a large number of worthy citizens," which featured "the roaring of Cannon, and the Exhibition of Bonfires, Illuminations, etc." before the gentlemen repaired to a suitable hall and drank thirteen toasts—first to General Washington and the allied armies, last to the state of Maryland, with an appropriate list of notables in between, including the French and Spanish kings and the officers who had rallied to the American cause. The next evening an "Elegant Ball was given by the Gentlemen of the Town" so the ladies might participate in "the general joy of their Country," but Tilghman was not among those present.

He was still sick and exhausted, and after delivering his message spent the night of the 22nd at his father's house. Next morning he was up at daybreak, riding again for Philadelphia. All that day and into the following night he rode hard, stopping only for a fresh horse when he could locate one. Just after 3 A.M. on October 24 he entered the outskirts of Philadelphia and cantered through the empty streets of the city to the house of his old friend Thomas McKean, president of the Continental Congress. Tilghman pounded on his door so violently that a night watchman appeared and threatened to arrest him for disturbing the peace. Fortunately, McKean arrived in his bed-clothes, heard the news, and immediately shared it with the night watchman, an elderly German, who continued his rounds, calling out, "Basht dree o'glock, und Gornwallis isht da-ken!"

Tilghman was right to worry about arriving late with his news. As he wrote to Washington, de Grasse's letter to Governor Lee had been delivered to Congress, but "I knew both Congress and the public would be uneasy at not receiving dispatches from you; I was not wrong in my conjecture, for some really began to doubt the matter." Regrettably, the fatigue of his journey brought back his fever, and he was in bed almost continuously after arriving in Philadelphia. He met with a committee of Congress that wanted more details on the capitulation—the motives that had led to several of the articles, in particular—and Tilghman was delighted to inform the commander in chief that the committee was "perfectly satisfied with the propriety and expediency of every step which was taken." In fact, the Congress as a whole concurred—all except the South Carolinians, "whose animosities carry them to that length, that they think no treatment could have been too severe for the garrison, the officers, and Lord Cornwallis in particular." One member of that delegation had even argued that the British officers should be held until the further order of Congress, but his proposal was unanimously rejected as an affront to Washington and the Congress. In closing, Tilghman informed the General that as soon as he was well enough he would ride to Chestertown and await further orders, adding that he would join him without delay when summoned. In the meantime, he had one more official duty to perform.

The Congress had presented him with "a horse properly caparisoned, and an elegant sword," testifying to their high opinion of his merit and ability. Presumably, that was the horse he rode to Chester, where he met his fellow aide, David Humphreys, who was bringing to Congress the colors surrendered by the British and German troops. The financier Robert Morris, who was a great friend of Tilghman, described the arrival of the captured colors. The city troop of light horse went out to meet them, he said, and became the standard-bearers—each of twenty-four privates carrying one of the flags, with the American and French colors preceding the trophies down Market Street and eventually to the State House, where "they were laid at the feet of Congress who were sitting." Several members spoke to Morris later and told him that instead of regarding the transaction as one more in a series of joyous ceremonies, "they instantly felt themselves impressed with ideas of the most solemn and awful nature."

The whole city went wild with joy. Lighted candles and lamps appeared in every window; people of all ages poured out of houses into the streets, jumping up and down, shouting, hugging their neighbors. In the morning members of Congress met to hear the reading of the dispatches and questioned Tilghman at length about the siege, the articles of capitulation, and what was being done about the prisoners the allies had taken. Cannons on the State House grounds were fired throughout the day, as were guns on ships in the harbor, all of which ran up their colors. At two o'clock that afternoon congressmen proceeded in a body to the Dutch Lutheran church to attend a service held by one of their chaplains, the Reverend Mr. Duffield, and, returning to the State House, passed a resolution of thanks to the army and voted to erect a commemorative monument in Yorktown. (Regrettably, no money was appropriated to build the monument, and years went by before it was erected.)

Tench Tilghman also discovered that the congressional till was empty when he requested reimbursement for his out-of-pocket expenditures. Congressman Elias Boudinot noted ruefully, "It was necessary to furnish him with hard money for his expenses. There was not a sufficiency in the treasury to do it, and the members of Congress, of which I was one, each paid a dollar to accomplish it."

As it happened, the city of Newport, Rhode Island, heard the news almost as early as Philadelphia did. On the afternoon of October 24 the schooner *Adventure*, with Captain Lovett in command, arrived in the harbor, having left Chesapeake Bay on the 20th with the "GLORIOUS NEWS of the SURRENDER of LORD CORNWALLIS and his ARMY Prisoners of War to the ALLIED ARMY, UNDER THE COMMAND OF OUR ILLUSTRIOUS General, and the French fleet, under the Command of his Excellency, the *Count de Grasse*," as an excited printer headlined the news, which was then sent on to Providence and Boston. As the joyous tidings spread from one community to another, the celebrations continued across the countryside. In the Highlands, Heath's army devoted an entire week to salutes and banquets. In New Haven, Connecticut, Yale students sang a triumphal hymn, and their president, Dr. Ezra Stiles, wrote a grandiose letter to Washington that began: "We rejoice that the Sovereign of the Universe hath hitherto supported you as the deliverer of your country, the Defender of the Liberty and Rights of Humanity, and the Mæcenas of Science and Literature." As the *New York Journal* reported, the remarkable capture of an entire British army, four years to the day after the surrender at Saratoga—"an event in which the hand of heaven has been visibly displayed—has been celebrated, in various expressions of thankfulness and joy, by almost every town and society in the thirteen United States."

I NOW TAKE LEAVE OF YOU

In the lazy summer days of 1780, before Lord Cornwallis's army descended on the little town of York, sixteen-year-old Mildred Smith wrote her friend Betsy Ambler, who was a year younger and had recently moved with her family to Richmond.

"When you left our dear little town," Mildred said, "I felt as if every ray of comfort had fled." Oh, the other local girls were charming and very fond of her, but they were all older and their "freedom and levity, almost amounting to indiscretion," was troubling and made her blush for them.

When a party of visiting French officers arrived on the scene, the older girls' "heads seemed turned" by the flattering attention of the elegant foreigners. Though not one in ten of the latter spoke a word of English, "their style of entertaining and their devotion to the ladies of York are so flattering that almost any girl of sixteen would be enchanted." It was a good thing that her well-loved Betsy was removed from these "scenes of amusement and dissipation" for *her* giddy, fifteen-year-old brain would have been turned.

On and on went the teenage chatter, to which Betsy responded in kind, telling of a party given for her and her sister when they had reached Williamsburg, consisting of "more Beauty and Elegance than I had ever witnessed before . . . a most charming entertainment, and so much attention did your giddy friend receive as almost turned her poor distracted brain."*

A year later the tenor of the girls' letters was transformed, with Betsy writing from Richmond to tell Mildred of an alarm that morning, with the British approaching by way of the James River. The next installment was from "the Cottage," noting that when the British landed her family fled "in a winkling" with "Governor, council, everybody scampering." (One reason for her apprehension was that her father was treasurer of Virginia.)

In each subsequent letter the news grew worse, and she was grateful that Mildred's residence was too remote for her to suffer "the outrages of these barbarians." The enemy had chased them out of Richmond along with Jefferson, "our illustrious Governor, who, they say, took neither rest nor food for manor or horse till he reached C-----r's Mountain."

Writing from Louisa Court House, she told how her father had taken to spending nights in his carriage in order to get out of harm's way quickly, while the rest of them crowded into the overseer's tiny building.

"When or where shall we find rest?" another letter begins. During that night they heard a terrible clatter of horses and the dreaded words "The British!" but upon opening the door discovered some "miserable militia"—local boys—who had come to tell them the enemy was marching through the country, but had no idea which route they had taken. Betsy's family decided to move at once and "traveled through byways and brambles" until they reached the plantation of a friend on the way to Charlottesville. No sooner had they

---

*One of the attentive young swains she identified only as "Marshall." His first name was John, and twenty-one years later he became chief justice of the United States Supreme Court.

arrived and spread pallets on the floor to get some rest than they were warned that "Butcher" Tarleton had just passed by and would catch the governor before he reached Charlottesville. Panicked by the thought that their father had taken the same route, they soon learned that he had been warned in time to escape and, sure enough, here he came to hurry them off to the same place they had spent the night. "Great cause have we for thankfulness," she added.

Another year later, in 1782, Mildred Smith wrote from Yorktown to her friend Betsy, beginning,

> Again are we quietly seated in our old mansion. But oh! How unlike it once was! Indeed, were you to be suddenly and unexpectedly set down in the very spot where you and I have so often played together—in that very garden where we gathered flowers or stole your father's choice fruit—you would not recognize a solitary vestige of what it once was. *Ours* is not so totally annihilated, being more remote from the shock and battery—but Heaven knows, it is shocking enough! Others that remain are so mutilated . . . as to grieve one's very soul. But it is over! . . . the great end is accomplished. Peace is again restored, and we may yet look forward to happy days.

But despite Mildred Smith's assurance, the war was not over.

★   ★   ★

IN FACT, THE whole of America was in a state of watchful waiting, dreading a continuation of the fighting, wondering where and when and how it would break out again. Most of the waiting had to do with outside forces, beyond the control or ken of Americans, notably which of the European nations would prevail at sea, and during the winter months the balance of naval power began shifting against the French. De Grasse and the French fleet had sailed for the West Indies, but the British were determined he would not seize Jamaica, and with reinforcements joining the fleet, by April the Royal Navy outnumbered the French fleet. Rodney, who was now in command of the British, had thirty-six ships of the line, while de Grasse's numbers had been reduced to thirty, and when the inevitable clash came off Guadeloupe de Grasse was taken prisoner, five of his vessels were seized, and two more struck their colors and surrendered to Hood a week later.

★　★　★

GEORGE WASHINGTON WAS painfully aware of the continuing presence of British troops in Halifax, in Wilmington, North Carolina, in Charleston, Savannah, St. Augustine, and, of course, Clinton's forces in New York—some thirty thousand enemy soldiers, altogether. For all he knew, the ministry would send reinforcements to America in time to launch a fresh campaign in the spring of 1782, and when the Comte de Grasse informed him that he could remain here no longer and sailed for the West Indies on November 4, it was obvious that the British were once again in command of American waters. After lingering at Mount Vernon for a badly needed rest and time dedicated to his plantation and family, Washington rode northward to rejoin his army. Writing to Nathanael Greene, he said he would stop in Philadelphia and try to stimulate Congress to prepare the way for a vigorous and decisive campaign. His greatest fear was that the delegates, persuaded by the victory at Yorktown that "our work [is] nearly closed, will fall into a state of Languor & Relaxation."

Greene himself was in desperate straits. As he informed Virginia's governor, Thomas Nelson, "I have the mortification to hear no troops are coming from Virginia & but few from the other States." If he received no reinforcements, the Carolinas and Georgia might well be lost to the enemy, which, with the reinforcements he heard were coming, would soon outnumber him three to one, not counting the Tories. The southern states had already been "ravaged and distressed so as to pain the humanity of every observer"; his own little army had no meat, not a drop of spirits, hardly a bushel of salt. If neither Virginia nor other states could send him Continentals or state troops, he continued, "I beg you will order out Two Thousand good militia immediately, well-appointed, well-armed, and properly officered to serve three months after their arrival at Camp."

As ever, Washington wanted to be "prepared in every point for war"—not because he wanted hostilities to continue, only that the Americans must be ready for any eventuality. He had ordered the Pennsylvania, Virginia, and Maryland troops to join Greene in South Carolina, while the rest of his army headed toward their old quarters in New Jersey and on the Hudson. Fortunately for Greene, the rumored British reinforcements proved false, and while he did get some Delaware and Maryland troops, no Virginians turned up; they refused to march unless they were paid for past duty.

Lafayette, who departed for France in late December, two months after Cornwallis surrendered, arrived at Versailles just in time to celebrate, with his wife and various members of the French court, the birth of the dauphin—a glorious event that had been awaited for eleven and a half years since Louis XVI and Marie Antoinette were married.

In the Carolinas, sporadic fighting broke out between Greene's troops and loyalists, between Greene's men and those of General Leslie, but talk of peace was in the air, American officers were resigning, the "sickly season" of summer took such a toll that funeral services were omitted, and eventually neither the British forces nor Greene's were strong enough to attack the other. Finally, more than a year after Cornwallis's surrender, some of the loyalists and the remaining British troops boarded transports and evacuated Charleston.

★ ★ ★

FROM THE TIME news of Yorktown reached England, what was to happen in the next session of Parliament was the question that riveted the attention of most Britons and Americans. One dark November day, from his house in Berkeley Square, Horace Walpole was writing a characteristically chatty letter to a close friend, Sir Horace Mann. On the previous Sunday, Walpole had learned that Washington and the French had captured Cornwallis and his army, and he was glad to hear it. At least the troops were not all cut to pieces, he wrote, though it could hardly have come at a worse moment; Parliament was to meet on the morrow, and this news put the king's speech and others "a little into disorder." Pleased though he was, Walpole could not find it in himself to "put on the face of the day and act grief," since whatever brought an end to the war in America would save thousands of lives—millions of money, too. It is not honorable, he concluded, to boast of having been in the right when your country's shame is what you predicted; nor would anyone want to join in celebrating France's triumph.

To the Earl of Strafford Walpole revealed his emotions. "I have no patience with my country! And shall leave it without regret! Can we be proud when all Europe scorns us? It was wont to envy us, sometimes to hate us, but never despised us before. James the First was contemptible, but he did not lose an America! His eldest grandson sold us, his younger lost us—but we kept ourselves. Now we have run to meet the ruin—and it is coming!"

Walpole was outraged at the way Cornwallis had abandoned the loyalists. The general surrendered to save his own hide and ensure his safe return to England, and for the sake of his garrison; "but lest the loyal Americans who had followed him should be included in that indemnity, he demands that they should not be *punished*—is refused— and leaves them to be hanged!"

The devastating news from America found Lord George Germain at the same time Walpole heard it. The secretary of state for the colonies was at home in Pall Mall, speaking with a visitor, Lord Walsingham, when a messenger arrived with official intelligence of the surrender. Without saying anything to another person, the two got into a hackney carriage, picked up several other ministers, and drove immediately to Downing Street, where they knocked on Lord North's door.

Someone asked Germain how the prime minister took the news

when they informed him. "As he would have taken a ball in the breast," Lord George replied, saying that North spread his arms and exclaimed wildly as he paced up and down the room, saying again and again, "Oh God! it is all over!"

Germain sent a message to the king, who was at Kew, and George III hesitated not an instant, returning his reply by the same messenger. After lamenting the misfortune in Virginia, the king—obdurate as ever—added, "I trust that neither Lord George Germain nor any Member of the Cabinet will suppose that it makes the smallest alteration in those principles of my conduct, which have directed me in past time, and which will always continue to animate me under every event, in the prosecution of the present contest."

The king and Germain were as one on the subject of the war: as the latter put it, "we can never continue to exist as a great or powerful nation after we have lost or renounced the sovereignty of America." For the next four months, while the opposition fumed, the king's supporters, the country gentlemen—those conservative stalwarts who had backed George III's policies loyally for so long—were beginning to turn against him, dropping off one by one. Meanwhile, the government was adrift, and no decision was forthcoming.

★   ★   ★

FROM LONDON, THE rumor mill suggested that the king was determined to continue the war, but the public mood was shifting—the American war had proved too costly by far, as the country gentlemen had finally recognized. On both sides of the Atlantic, the war had bled the participants dry for years. As Vergennes had observed, "This war has gone too slowly; it is a war of hard cash, and if we drag it out the last shilling may not be ours." (In fact, as early as the spring of 1781, with French finances nearing the breaking point and Vergennes fearing that the Spanish might give up and make a separate peace with England, Versailles had appeared willing if necessary to sacrifice the Americans for the sake of peace.)

When news of Yorktown reached the British public, the general reaction matched North's sentiments—"Oh God! it is all over!" It was, after all, the second time an entire British army had been surrendered to the American rebels, and the reaction was one of anguish and anger. London was a city in mourning, with "the wisest and most intelligent asking each other what was next to be done, to which the wisest and most intelligent could give no answer," as one Englishman put it. Adding salt to the wounds, French sea power had made possible the victory at Yorktown, and for all anyone knew, that sea power might cost the empire its other colonies, its fisheries, and its commerce to boot. But Vergennes was a realist: Yorktown was an extraordinary success, it was true, "but one would be wrong to believe that it means an immediate peace; it is not in the English character to give up so easily."

In a sense, he was right, for the war would drag on for another year, but it was no longer war on the same scale in America. There, neither side had the stomach for it, and nothing much was happening.

Then, on the penultimate day of February, 1782, the House of Commons repudiated Lord North's American policy by voting against further prosecution of the war, and a few days later passed a bill authorizing the crown to make peace with the former colonies. That was it for North, who announced his ministry's resignation on March 20. A week later the ministry of Charles Wentworth, Marquis of Rockingham, swept into office, bringing a new broom to the task.

Still, there was no peace, but in America, the first action in what might be called the campaign of 1782 was not made until late August, when Washington's army moved down the Hudson from Newburgh to Verplanck's Point. This was in no sense a military maneuver, merely a move to a fresh supply of food and forage. From mid-September to mid-October Rochambeau's troops were camped nearby, on their leisurely journey to Boston, whence they would sail to the West Indies. So for a month or more the comrades-in-arms enjoyed the reunion with real affection—a pleasure darkened for the American officers by their inability to repay the Frenchmen's hospitality. All they had to offer, Washington observed, was "stinking whiskey—and not always that—and a bit of beef without vegetables." Most of the Americans, the French were glad to see, were transformed—they were newly "uniformed and well-groomed"—but Congress's parsimony was visible to one and all, as was the army's status as "the most neglected and injured part of the community."

The impotence of Congress was frightening. As James Madison reported to Arthur Lee in late May of 1782, "Notwithstanding the importance of the present crisis the number of states in Congress does not exceed 8, sometimes 7 only, and most of those represented by two members. The president is directed to write to the unrepresented states on this subject and urge them to supply the deficiency."

★　★　★

EVEN AFTER THE victory in Virginia the army was largely ignored, its supplies as meager as ever, its demands for payment shunted aside, and despite new uniforms for some, many of its men were confined to quarters because they lacked clothing to cover their nakedness. It was disturbingly clear, however, that the troops were no longer willing to be put off by a do-nothing Congress, and a three-man committee was delegated to deliver a petition to the legislators in Philadelphia. The document was a list of the officers' minimum demands, including an advance of part of the pay due them, plus security for the remainder. In place of the half-pay for life that had been agreed upon earlier, they were willing to accept a lump sum or full pay for a reasonable number of years, but they insisted on the clothing, ration, and forage allowances due them, and the closing paragraph of the petition warned that "It would be criminal in the officers to conceal the general dissatisfaction which prevails, and is gaining ground in the army. . . ."

General Alexander McDougall (who had been paid only twice in eight years) led the three-man delegation that included John Brooks of Massachusetts and Matthias Ogden of New Jersey, and they had instructions to remain in Philadelphia until Congress acted, when they were to report back to the army. At first they had reason to hope they would be successful, since twelve of the thirteen states ratified the agreement that federal funds would be forthcoming. Only Rhode Island, the smallest, had not yet ratified. Then suddenly the picture changed entirely—word was received that Rhode Island had refused and Virginia changed its vote from yes to no, and the reason was not hard to find. Congress was bankrupt.

To General Henry Knox, who had prepared the petition to Congress, it was imperative that the new nation have a strong, responsible central government, and the current predicament of the army was a reflection of that lack. It was obviously absurd to have thirteen separate state armies; as he wrote to Gouverneur Morris, "America will have fought and bled to little purpose if the powers of government shall be insufficient to preserve the peace. . . . why do not you great men call the people together and . . . have a convention of the States to form a better Constitution? . . . Let something be done before a peace takes place, or we shall be in a worse situation than we were at the commencement of the war." Later, he wrote to Alexander McDougall, "Posterity will hardly believe that an army contended incessantly for eight years under a constant pressure of misery to establish the liberties of their country, without knowing who were to compensate them or whether they were ever to receive any reward for their services." There is a point beyond which there is "no sufferance," he added, and he prayed that he and his comrades had not passed it.

Knox was a moderate, mild-mannered man, but other highly placed officers saw the situation in a different light and saw, moreover, opportunity for personal gain.

On March 10, the first signs of what appeared to be a military conspiracy surfaced at Newburgh, New York, making it clear that unknown forces in the army were determined to capitalize on the increasingly dangerous situation. Copies of an anonymous address appeared on handbills in camp, calling on the officers to meet the next day to consider a way to deal with the army's grievances. Since this summons to action was not authorized by (or known to) Washington and was therefore contrary to regulations, it implied a mutinous movement. Upon investigation, the General made the disturbing discovery that his old antagonist and troublemaker Horatio Gates was behind the agitation, supported in Newburgh by Colonel Walter Stewart, Major John Armstrong, and Colonel Timothy Pickering, the quartermaster general, their moves masked by "the most perfect dissimulation and apparent cordiality."

On the heels of the call for a meeting, a document appeared that made eloquently clear what the meeting was to consider. The author,* who described himself as "A fellow soldier, whose interest and affections bind him strongly to you," related how he had loved private life and left it with regret to share with others the toils and hazards of the military, the "cold hand of poverty," and other hardships, and until lately believed in the justice of his country. Now, instead of justice, he could see "a country that tramples upon your rights, disdains your cries, and insults your distresses." And at the very moment when swords were to be removed from the soldiers' sides "and no remaining mark of military distinction left but your wants, infirmities, and scars . . . Can you consent to wade through the vile mire of despondency and owe the miserable remnant of that life to charity, which has hitherto been spent in honor? If you can—GO—and carry with you the jests of Tories and scorn of Whigs—the ridicule and, what is worse, the pity of the world. Go starve and be forgotten."

Although the precise nature of the plot is murky, the idea seems to have been that Washington would be asked to endorse armed intimidation of the state legislatures. If he refused, which was likely, then Gates, as next in line of seniority, would step in and lead the army to Philadelphia and force political action.

Determined to prevent the officers from "plunging themselves into a gulf of civil horror from which there might be no receding,"

---

*Gates's aide Major John Armstrong is generally believed to have written the "Newburgh Addresses."

Washington issued an order disapproving "such disorderly proceedings" as the assembly had been illegally summoned, and announced a meeting of his own for the following Saturday. The anonymous author of the Newburgh Addresses published another paper agreeing with the change while hinting that Washington's action indicated his sympathy for the Gates group's plans.

★   ★   ★

ON MARCH 15, 1783, the officers of the Continental Army crowded into a structure known as the Temple at noon. The building had been erected by the troops to serve as a church on Sundays and a dance hall at other times, and it was filled from wall to wall with officers. When Washington called the meeting, he had said that the senior officer present would "preside and report the results of the deliberations to the Commander in Chief." Since the General was not among those seated on a small platform in the large room, it was assumed that he would not attend and that Gates would take charge. Then, suddenly, a door opened onto the platform, and to everyone's astonishment His Excellency emerged, looking "sensibly agitated," and began reading from a speech he had prepared.

He first reminded the officers that he had never left their side for one moment except when called away on public duty; he had witnessed and experienced their distresses; he considered his own military reputation to be inseparable from the army's; and "it can *scarcely be supposed*, at this late stage of the war, that I am indifferent to its interests."

Moving on, he asked how those interests were to be promoted by those who had initiated this meeting. The "dreadful alternatives" proposed were "of either deserting our country in the extremest hour of her distress or turning our arms against it (which is the apparent object, unless Congress can be compelled into instant compliance). . . ."

He was confident that Congress held "exalted sentiments of the services of the army" and would act justly, while the soldiers could count on his own support in obtaining the rights that were theirs. "Let me conjure you," he went on, "to express your utmost horror and detestation of the man who wishes, under any specious pretenses, to overturn the liberties of our country, and who wickedly attempts to open the flood gates of civil discord and deluge our rising empire in blood." By the dignity of their conduct in this matter, he added, the officers would enable posterity to say, "had this day been wanting, the world had never seen the last stage of perfection to which human nature is capable of attaining."

That concluded the speech he had prepared, yet a hostile, chilly mood remained in the hall. From the look on most men's faces it was evident that he had failed to persuade them. He told them he had a letter he wanted to read, reached in his pocket, and drew out a paper, stating it was from a member of Congress and that it would show them what the problems of that body were and what the members were trying to do.

But something was wrong—very wrong. The General was obviously unable to read and seemed bewildered. Fumbling in another pocket, he drew out what only his close aides had seen him wear—a pair of glasses. Putting them on, he said quietly, "Gentlemen, you will permit me to put on my spectacles, for I have not only grown gray but almost blind in the service of my country."

As he read the congressman's letter, it was obvious that his simple statement had achieved what his speech had not. Many of the officers had tears in their eyes as the tall, gray-haired man they loved, with his innate sense of the dramatic, walked out of the room without another word, mounted his horse, and disappeared from view.

Behind was Gates, presiding now, and Pickering, who rose to his feet in a desperate effort to get the meeting back on the track the conspirators wanted. Fortunately, Henry Knox had other ideas and offered several resolutions thanking Washington for his wise counsel and expressing the officers' unshaken attachment to the commander in chief.

Another paper was drawn up and approved unanimously, informing Congress that the officers had served their country from the outbreak of hostilities "from the purest love and attachment to the rights and liberties of human nature," and that under no circumstances would they sully the reputation they had acquired during the years of war. They viewed the anonymous addresses with "abhorrence and reject with disdain the infamous propositions" they contained. They were confident, they added, that the army would not be disbanded until arrangements for back pay and pensions were made.

Congress was badly frightened by the episode at Newburgh, and rightly so. Washington's account of the near coup d'état and his pleas that the army's requests be granted persuaded the legislators to accept most of the officers' demands, including commutation of half-pay for life into five years at full pay, drawing 6 percent interest, for officers who chose that option. But as much as Washington wanted all men to receive some cash—three months' pay, at a minimum—Congress had no such resources and voted to send most of the troops home on furloughs that would become permanent when peace was declared. (As a farewell gift Congress voted to give them their arms, which many sold on their way home for travel money.)

For many of these men, parting from their companions was heartbreaking. As Joseph Plumb Martin wrote, they had lived together as brothers for years, sharing the hardships, dangers, and sufferings common to a soldier's life; had sympathized with each other in trouble and sickness; had done their best to lighten their friends' burdens; "had endeavored to conceal each other's faults or make them appear in as good a light as they would bear." As a result, they "were as strict a band of brotherhood as Masons and, I believe, as faithful to each other. And now we were to be . . . parted forever; as unconditionally separated as though the grave lay between us."

As devastating as Congress's solution was for the soldiers, it was thought to give the financial community time to raise funds. But even that proved a mirage.

When the hour approached for the army to disband, the superintendent of finances, Robert Morris, announced his inability to find enough cash to finance certificates for one month's pay, let alone three, since he did not have enough money even to buy paper for printing the certificates.

That was the final straw for George Washington's fellow veterans, and the General suddenly became the object of enormous resentment for placing them, as they saw it, in this position. Instead of attending a final farewell dinner at which he was to be the honored guest, most of the Continental officers headed for home, angry and disgusted. As heartbreaking as this was for the General, he understood, and confided to Congress, "a parting scene under such peculiar circumstances will not admit of description."

He was the leader they had followed for seven terrible years. They had given him their best, and when at last they relied on him to obtain compensation that was so richly deserved for what they had done, he failed them—or so it must have seemed. Many of them clearly felt that Gates was right, that they should have marched on Philadelphia if necessary and demanded their rights at the point of a gun.

Yet what could Washington have done? At Newburgh he had narrowly averted the disaster of a coup d'état that might well have put Gates and a military dictatorship in control of the new nation, with God only knew what consequences.

He took the only alternative left him and put his prestige behind a letter that was circulated to the states, indicating that since he planned to retire from public service forever, this was his final official communication. In it he urged that the Articles of Confederation form the basis of a central government—"an indissoluble union" that would establish a peacetime army and navy sufficient to the nation's needs, "a sacred regard for public justice," which would include paying the men of the Continental Army the money owed to them, and the elimination of "local prejudices" that divided the nation. Under the circumstances, it was all he could do.

Regrettably, the states refused to accept their obligations and come up with revenue to meet the veterans' needs or the multitude of other claims against the government. Finally, Robert Morris resigned in disgust as superintendent of finances, but when no one volunteered to take the thankless job he said he would stay on until the army was paid and demobilized. But not until the summer of 1784 did John Adams succeed in securing a desperately needed loan from Holland, which finally enabled Morris to fulfill his pledge to the army.

Soldiers who are in a hurry to return to home and family at the end of a war write few letters and record few thoughts in their diaries, and so it was with the officers and enlisted men of the Continental Army. In 1782 and 1783 the organization all but vanished as if it had been a phantom, and except for a few hundred three-year enlistees no one remained.

★　★　★

WASHINGTON COULD NOT know it when he was at Newburgh, but King George III had issued a proclamation on February 14, 1783, notifying the world that hostilities had ceased between Great Britain, France, Spain, Holland, and the United States of America. It amounted to an armistice, but it went deeper than that: the war was over.

Following that stunning announcement, the Earl of Shelburne—who became prime minister upon the sudden death of Rockingham—initiated talks with the other European belligerents and the Americans, represented by John Adams, Benjamin Franklin, and John Jay. Their negotiations dragged on, seemingly endlessly, until the third day of September, 1783, when the peacemakers gathered to sign the definitive treaty, in which the opening sentence of Article I proclaimed what the Declaration of Independence had resolved seven years earlier: "His Britannic Majesty acknowledges the said United States . . . to be free, sovereign and independent states."

The three American delegates, ignoring the instructions of Congress—which would have required them to abide by the wishes of the French foreign ministry—skillfully managed to obtain a settlement that gained the new nation virtually everything they wanted for it. (At the time, it turned out, Vergennes had been secretly informing the government in London that he opposed many of the American claims, including their "pretentious ambitions" concerning boundaries and fisheries.)

What suddenly emerged was a new nation that was unlike any other in the world. In helping to make it so, the delegates had achieved a triumph—made even more remarkable when the ever practical Benjamin Franklin cannily succeeded in persuading Vergennes to grant the newly minted United States of America a loan of yet another 6 million livres.

★　★　★

FOR A WAR that yielded such far-reaching consequences for the entire world, it was not easy to fathom how it had been achieved. No one could say with certainty that the rebels—with the inestimably valuable help of France—had won the war, or whether the conflict had been lost by the British.

To begin with, the physical handicaps confronting the British were simply staggering. The awesome logistics of the operation required that every article of clothing and weaponry needed by the army be transported three thousand miles across the unforgiving North Atlantic. Moreover, few Englishmen grasped the fact that the geography of America and the difficulties of communication within and without were at the root of many insurmountable problems. But as one perceptive officer observed, the English supply system was based not only on the Atlantic Ocean but on the rivers flowing into it, a fact of life that "had absolutely prevented us this whole war from going 15 miles from a navigable river." And of course the effect of those three thousand ocean miles had a paralyzing effect on communications between Whitehall and the front lines in America.

Beyond that, the blundering, slothful British high command deserved much blame for the loss. Take the condescending attitude of British officers toward the rebels, which took its toll on the eventual outcome. From the very beginning they disliked and underestimated Americans, of whom they were contemptuous, and disliked the conflict itself as infra dig. It would be an easy war, they knew, against men they denounced as cowards, scoundrels, rascals, vermin, who made war "like savages," and were "the poorest mean-spirited scoundrels that ever surely pretended to the dignity of rebellion."

As General James Murray saw it in July 1776, "we shall beat them this autumn if we know how to set about it," and in that hint of doubt lies another reason for their ultimate defeat. Senior officers were seen by their juniors, who bore the brunt of the fight, as negligent, inefficient, inactive, and inept, men who did *not* "know how to set about it." Lord Rawdon complained bitterly about those superiors: "It is not only the lives of many valuable members of society which are risked by the[ir] negligence, but the whole empire of Great Britain in America is hazarded." In December of 1775 Charles Stuart described the British generals in America as "a pack of the most ordinary men . . . who give themselves trouble about the merest trifles, whilst things of consequence go unregarded"; three years later he said, "hardly one General Officer . . . does not declare his intention of going home, the same with officers of all ranks who, could they procure leave, would be happy to leave the Army."

As the behavior of Clinton and Cornwallis revealed, not only did generals quarrel with one another, but each blamed the other for every reversal.

Behind many of the blunders made by Britain's civilian and military authorities was the king—a not very intelligent man who had no military experience whatever, was an obsessive meddler, and was to blame for much that went wrong. Rigid, moralistic, quick-tempered, he never forgot a grudge and insisted that on every major decision he had the final word and intended to keep it that way, no matter what. Thanks in large measure to His Royal Majesty, the deck was heavily stacked against the British.

⋆ ⋆ ⋆

A HAUNTING QUESTION is whether a true majority of Americans had wanted the Revolution in the first place. Chances are that they did not. If, in John Adams's colorful phrase, "We were about one third Tories, and [one] third timid, and one third true blue," this suggests that somewhere between a majority and two-thirds may have opposed the war. And if one assumes that Adams was speaking of public opinion as he remembered it at or near the time the Revolution began, what were the figures seven years later when the terrible war weariness had penetrated all levels of society and diminished what enthusiasm had once existed?

Among those uncommitted, many had opposed the war on religious grounds or because they yearned for unity and peace; others— merchants, tradesmen, shipowners, and small farmers—because of its effect on business; still others because they simply wanted nothing to do with a war and refused to take sides. So you might say the American Revolution was fought and won by a determined minority—a minority whose leadership, mercifully, consisted of conservatives who were men of considerable standing and influence.

Unfortunately, by 1783 most of the best minds had left Congress to return to their states, where their hearts lay. Nationhood was unfamiliar, unexplored territory, after all, yet if ever there was a need for leadership by a strong civil authority this was it, for Congress was hopelessly inadequate, a hollow shell of an organization, too often incapable even of mustering a quorum. The army was the only entity with a cadre of leaders—men accustomed to making decisions and acting upon them. And to only one of those men was leadership in the civil area an ingrained habit.

As early as 1777, with the army in winter quarters in Morristown, George Washington had begun operating as a leader of the confederated states, devoting much of his time to members of Congress and state officials, on top of his military duties. Throughout the war he acceded to the wishes of Congress, always seeking its approval of his plans and actions, providing direction when it was sought. But now, when the country needed them most, the majority of those civil authorities were nowhere to be seen, and matters were coming to a head, precipitated by the long-overdue payment of the army.

As the year wound down and the British army prepared to leave, it was increasingly evident that leadership of the American people would be the next great challenge the states would have to face.

★   ★   ★

FOR MORE THAN seven years, Manhattan had been occupied by a British army. So by the autumn of 1783, when the time came at last for the Americans to reclaim the city, little remained of the rebel presence that had once been so important.

The two generals—for the Americans, George Washington; for the British, Sir Guy Carleton, who had replaced Sir Henry Clinton—had agreed that the British would evacuate New York City on November 25, 1783.

The day dawned crisp and sparkling, with the wind out of the northwest, and as Washington and his troops approached Manhattan Island from their camp on the Hudson, they saw no autumn foliage as one might expect. Everything that could be used for fuel had been cut by the British—forests, orchards, fences, outbuildings—everything. In this wasteland, mansions belonging to patriot leaders, which had been used by British officers, were run-down, deserted, unpainted, and overrun by weeds.

One-third of New York's buildings—including Trinity Church—had been destroyed by fire in 1776 and never rebuilt, so what remained of a huge area of town was charred timbers and blackened, freestanding chimneys. This was a shabby, unloved city of filthy streets and deserted houses with shattered windows, derelict remains of what had once been a vibrant seaport town.

As Washington and his men entered Manhattan, clusters of citizens came out to cheer them, but they were few in number.

The small American army—each man with a union cockade on his left breast and a sprig of laurel in his hat—marched as far as the Battery and halted, broke ranks, and sat down on the grass to wait for the British to withdraw. At one o'clock the redcoats formed up and headed for the wharves on the East River, where they were rowed out to the waiting transports.

In their footsteps came the American military: General Washington, mounted on a magnificent gray horse, accompanied by Governor George Clinton, escorted by troops under General Henry Knox, a corps of dragoons, the light infantry, artillery, and a battalion of Massachusetts men. Years later a New York woman who had been an eyewitness of the scene wrote that she and her friends had been accustomed for a long time to the British military display of finery, troops in scarlet uniforms and burnished arms, whereas the American troops that marched into town that day were "ill-clad and weather beaten and made a forlorn appearance; but then they were *our* troops, and as I looked at them and thought upon all they had done and suffered for us, my heart and my eyes were full, and I admired and gloried in them the more, because they were weather beaten and forlorn."

Then came civilians, some mounted and riding eight abreast, many more of them on foot, also marching eight abreast, and as the marchers passed the people lining the streets, cheering and clapping, everyone's eyes were on George Washington, the hero of the Revolution, who had kept the cause alive even in the darkest days of suffering and defeat.

For the next few days, while British ships remained in the harbor, taking on the last soldiers and some loyalists, surrounded by American and French vessels—all of them flying their country's colors—a succession of dinners was given, all of them with speeches eulogizing Washington. Each speech called for a response from the General and fortunately his aide David Humphreys was on hand to compose a more or less standard reply, thanking the speaker for the tribute while acknowledging the aid of Providence in all that happened, and expressing his faith in the future of America.

At last it was time to say farewell before he and his aides were taken by barge from Whitehall in lower Manhattan to Paulus Hook in New Jersey, where horses would be waiting for them. It was Friday, December 4, and the General had arranged for his officers to convene with him at Fraunces' Tavern at noon. Shortly after the clock struck the hour, he entered the long room and saw those officers who had entered the city with him on the 25th, plus a few others who lived nearby and returned to the city. But it was a disappointing turnout, since many failed to appear because of their anger over his failure to obtain payment they had expected from Congress. Of twenty-nine major generals, only three were present: Knox, Steuben, and McDougall. Of forty-four brigadiers, only one: James Clinton. A handful of colonels and majors was there, along with more junior officers, some of them unknown to the commander in chief, but whether or not these officers thought of it in such terms, they represented to Washington the men who had stood at his side throughout the desperate years of poverty and suffering while their own families scraped by at home, pinching their pennies, seeing men who had refused to serve remain comfortable and prosper.

The proprietor had laid out a collation in the room, and Washington tried to eat something, thought better of it, and filled a glass with wine, passing the decanter on to the others. When bottles had gone around the room and everyone had a drink in his hands, the General raised his glass and, in a voice choked with emotion, said, "With a heart full of love and gratitude, I now take leave of you. I most devoutly wish that your later days may be as prosperous and happy as your former ones have been glorious and honorable."

The response was an awkward chorus of thanks and words of appreciation, as the men drank the wine in what was almost a communion gesture.

Washington looked out at them, his eyes filled with tears, and said in a halting voice, "I cannot come to each of you, but shall feel obliged if each of you will come and take me by the hand."

As it happened, the officer standing closest to the General was Henry Knox, the self-taught master artillerist who in eight years had been a pillar of strength for his leader. Now he stepped forward with his hand outstretched, and Washington held out his own, then realized, as he looked into his friend's eyes, all that Knox had meant to him, threw his arms around the big man, and kissed him. And so it went with everyone in the room, from Steuben down to the youngest officer, one after the other stepping up to embrace the General, their eyes streaming tears and no one trusting himself to say a word. As Benjamin Tallmadge, the daring dragoon, wrote years later, "The simple thought that we were then about to part from the man who had conducted us through a long and bloody war, and under whose conduct the glory and independence of our country had been achieved, and that we should see his face no more in this world seemed to me utterly insupportable."

The room was silent as the tall, uniformed figure raised his arm in a farewell gesture, walked over to the door and out of the tavern into the cobbled street where a guard of honor waited, then down the way toward the waterfront.

At the wharf a throng had assembled, eager for a glimpse of the great man, many of them holding their children in the air for a sight they would remember years afterward. Few of the spectators could have understood how difficult it must have been for Washington to keep his emotions in check as he strode out on the dock, walked past the crowd, and climbed down into the waiting barge. When it moved out into the river, he gave a single, all-embracing wave of farewell and settled down as the rhythmic motion of the oarsmen took him farther and farther away from the waving, cheering crowd and the tearful officers, who stood watching, in "silence, military grief," as long as the barge and the figures in it could still be seen.

★ ★ ★

CONSIDERING WHAT MIGHT have been, Washington's farewell to his fellow officers was a disappointing anticlimax. Even so, it was a solemn, unforgettable moment. Some of these men—Henry Knox and Alexander McDougall, among them—had been with him from the beginning in 1775. They and the others who had served so self-lessly, enduring such hardships as few armies had known, had achieved a miracle. They had made the impossible possible as they struggled to bring independence to a new nation at a time in the history of the world when it was simply inconceivable that such a transformation could occur.

The American Revolution was a war of liberation from foreign rule—the first of many such uprisings that would take place over time. Yet its significance was in going much further than a war for freedom. Winning the conflict they had begun was the first step. Beyond that was their determination to achieve independence with constitutional guarantees.

As Benjamin Rush put it in his Fourth of July address in Philadelphia in 1781, "There is nothing more common than to confound the terms American Revolution with those of the late American War. The American War is over, but this is far from being the case with the American Revolution. On the contrary, [only] the first act of the great drama is closed."

★　★　★

FOR GEORGE WASHINGTON one more duty remained to be performed.

Setting off to the south, he and his aides, David Humphreys, David Cobb, and Benjamin Walker, rode through New Brunswick, Trenton, and Philadelphia (where Cobb, who had serious financial problems, left him). All along the road he was greeted by joyful, cheering people begging him to stop and say a few words; in every village, church bells rang and cannon boomed in salutes. There was hand-shaking, speeches to deliver, local notables to accommodate, finally a night's rest and back in the saddle the next morning. In Wilmington an "elegant supper" was given him, followed by festivities, and he delivered the expected speech the next morning; in Baltimore another dinner awaited him, followed by a ball that lasted until two in the morning; then it was on to Annapolis, where the Congress of the United States was sitting.

Sitting, that is, after a fashion. General Washington's imminent arrival had thrown that body into a crisis. In the first place, until December 13 not enough states were represented to constitute a quorum, which meant that Congress had been completely impotent before that date. Even after December 13, only seven states were present, so it was voted unanimously that a Congress of seven states could act on Washington's resignation.

No protocol existed for such a formality as the resignation of a commander-in-chief, so a committee was appointed to create one, and on December 23, 1783, in a moving, emotionally charged ceremony, Washington submitted his commission to the president of Congress. After saying good-bye to each congressman, he left the building and mounted his horse.

He and his two aides galloped off at once. After spending the night at a tavern, they pushed on the next day, riding hard through the rolling countryside of Maryland, halting no longer than was absolutely essential to please the groups of happy people that waved to them to stop and visit. Then it was on to the ferry crossing of the Potomac. As the late afternoon light was fading from the sky, they trotted up the long drive to Mount Vernon. It was Christmas Eve, and George Washington was home at last.

PRINCIPAL CHARACTERS

John Adams (1735–1826). A Boston lawyer, diplomat in Europe, and second president of the United States. A delegate to the First and Second Continental Congresses and initially fearful of separation from England, he supported the Declaration of Independence in 1776. During the war he served on diplomatic missions and, with John Jay and Benjamin Franklin, negotiated the Treaty of Paris ending the war. He was Washington's vice president and, in 1796, president.

Major John André (1751–1780). An ambitious, capable young man who organized dramatic performances in Philadelphia, where he met Peggy Shippen (later Arnold). He became Sir Henry Clinton's aide, handled his correspondence with secret agents, and was involved with Benedict Arnold. Captured carrying incriminating documents, he was hanged in 1780.

Admiral Marriot Arbuthnot (1711–1794). A terrible choice for commander in chief on the American station, he was both incompetent and uncooperative, especially with General Sir Henry Clinton. He was succeeded by Admiral Thomas Graves in 1781.

Major General Benedict Arnold (1741–1801). As a youth in Connecticut, he worked as a bookseller and druggist and became a successful merchant. A captain of a militia company, he took part in the capture of Fort Ticonderoga and led the heroic march to Quebec that ended in defeat. He assembled a small fleet with which he fought the British at Valcour Island in 1776, losing the battle but forcing the enemy to delay for a year an invasion from Canada. He fought with distinction at Saratoga, where he was badly wounded. In 1775 he commanded in Philadelphia and later at West Point, the scene of his treason.

Margaret Shippen Arnold (1760–1804). Daughter of a wealthy, conservative Philadelphia jurist, she socialized with British officers, including John André, in the occupied city. When the British evacuated Philadelphia, she was courted by Benedict Arnold, twenty years her senior. They married in 1779, and Peggy helped her husband convey information to Sir Henry Clinton. After the war she remained a faithful partner to her husband, despite his increasing poverty.

Dr. Edward Bancroft (1744–1820). Massachusetts-born doctor, scientist, inventor, and double agent, he was largely self-educated. After adventures in Dutch Guiana he moved to England and began working as a spy for Benjamin Franklin. Then he started spying for the British. Through a cozy relationship with Silas Deane, he leaked information about American relations with the French.

Pierre-Augustin Caron de Beaumarchais (1732–1799). Writer, musician, inventor, and playwright, he arranged secret aid to the Americans before the alliance with France. At Versailles he was "Watchmaker to the King" and established the fictitious firm Hortalez et Cie as a conduit for 21 million livres' worth of munitions, gunpowder, and clothing to the rebel army. He barely escaped death in the French Revolution and fled to Germany, where he remarried twice—at seventy-six and eighty-six.

Louis-Alexandre Berthier (1753–1815). An aide to the French quartermaster general, Berthier was a diligent planner and route finder. During the French Revolution he was chief of staff to Comte d'Estaing, then Lafayette, and later an important friend and aide to Napoleon.

Claude Blanchard (1742–1803). Chief commissary to Rochambeau's corps, he was responsible for organizing hospitals, quarters, fuel, food, and supplies for the army—a formidable task in a foreign land.

Charles-Louis-Victor, Prince de Broglie (1756–1794). Colonel in the Saintonge regiment, he returned to France after Yorktown, was president of the national constituent assembly, and, though a proponent of liberty, was sent to the guillotine in 1794.

Lieutenant General Sir Guy Carleton (1724–1808). Irish-born, he served under General Jeffrey Amherst and General James Wolfe and was named governor of Quebec in 1767. He is said to have drafted the Quebec Act and was the commander of British forces in Canada after 1775. Largely because of his leadership, England was able to retain Canada. After Cornwallis's defeat he went to New York and oversaw the cessation of hostilities.

John Champe (c. 1756–c. 1798). A member of Henry Lee's cavalry command, Champe was sent in 1780 to New York on a mission to capture Benedict Arnold, after feigning desertion from the Americans. He was taken to Arnold, who made him a sergeant major in his loyalist legion. Champe's plans were foiled, and when he escaped from the British he was discharged to protect him from retaliation by the enemy.

François-Jean de Beauvoir, Chevalier de Chastellux (1734–1788). He entered the army at the age of thirteen and later won modest fame as a philosopher. After joining Rochambeau's army in 1780, he was third in command at Yorktown. His *Travels in North America* (1786) was a popular account. He died of an illness before the French Revolution.

Jean-François-Louis, Comte de Clermont-Crèvecoeur (1752–c. 1824). He fought under Rochambeau from 1780 to 1783, returned to France, and served in the army until he emigrated in 1792 with other loyalists.

General Sir Henry Clinton (1730–1795). As a general in America, Clinton sparred with his peers, Sir William Howe, John Burgoyne, and Lord Cornwallis, and when Burgoyne lost at Saratoga and Howe resigned, he succeeded the latter as commander. He requested a competent, cooperative admiral, only to get Arbuthnot; his communications with Cornwallis were abysmal; and though the capture of Charleston was a triumph, after Cornwallis took matters into his own hands the war turned against the British. Even so, Clinton was made the scapegoat for Yorktown.

Baron von Closen (c. 1754–1830). A nobleman from Bavaria, he served as an aide to Rochambeau, accompanying him on all his American campaigns. After the war he continued to serve in the French army, resigning during their revolution. He later served under Napoleon.

Colonel David Cobb (1748–1839). A Harvard-educated doctor, he served as delegate to the Massachusetts Provincial Congress in 1775. As a rebel soldier, he fought in New Jersey and Rhode Island before becoming a trusted aide to Washington. Cobb delivered important messages between the General and Rochambeau and negotiated the evacuation of New York with British general Sir Guy Carleton.

Charles, Earl Cornwallis (1738–1805). As a member of Parliament, he voted against the Stamp Act and was sympathetic to the interest of the colonies. He pursued but failed to trap Washington's army at Trenton—a major blunder—and in 1778 left for England, where his wife was dying. On his return he took charge of the war in the South and had some major successes until Greene arrived. Moving to Virginia, he took a questionable position in Yorktown, where he was bottled up.

Silas Deane (1737–1789). A member of the Continental Congress, he was sent to France in 1776, where he arranged for ammunition, weapons, and clothing to supply the Continental Army. In Paris he met his friend Edward Bancroft, not knowing he was a double agent, and they hoped to make a killing by purchasing supplies and profiteering. He helped Benjamin Franklin and Arthur Lee negotiate commercial and military treaties with France in 1778. Congress ordered his return from Paris after Lee accused him of corruption. He died a poor man in exile.

Henry Dearborn (1751–1829). A New Hampshireman, he fought at Bunker Hill and marched with Benedict Arnold to Quebec, where he was imprisoned. Exchanged, he was with Alexander Scammell's regiment at Ticonderoga and Saratoga before joining John Sullivan's expedition against the Iroquois. He assisted Timothy Pickering, quartermaster general, at Yorktown.

Oliver DeLancey, Sr. (1718–1785). Prominent New York loyalist, politician, and merchant. At the outbreak of war DeLancey was the senior loyalist officer in the British army and raised a brigade for the defense of Long Island. Of his three battalions, two served in the South, the third in Queen's County, New York. With British defeat DeLancey lost all his property and went into exile, dying in England two years later.

Vice Admiral Charles Hector Theodat, Comte d'Estaing (1729–1794). His fleet provided the first formal assistance to rebel forces in 1778. He also caused tension between the allies by leaving the waters around Rhode Island against the wishes of American forces. He commanded the national guard at Versailles in 1789 and was guillotined.

Guillaume, Comte de Deux-Ponts (1754–1807). He led a crucial attack at Yorktown on Oct. 14, 1781, where he lost one-fifth of his troops in seven minutes. He was chosen by Rochambeau to bring the news of victory to Louis XVI. Deux-Ponts was from Bavaria, and during and after the French Revolution he went by his German name: Wilhelm Graf von Forbach und Freiherr von Zweibruecken. He helped the royal family flee from Varennes in 1791 but survived the revolution to return to his home.

Rear Admiral Robert Digby (1732–1814). Named in 1781 as a commander of the North American station, he allowed Admiral Thomas Graves, who had been passed over for Digby, to stay in command until the Yorktown siege ended. He remained in America to evacuate the British army.

Comte Mathieu Dumas (1753–1837). Aide to Rochambeau and assistant quartermaster general. In 1791 he was directed to conduct Louis XVI back to Paris after he tried to flee. A moderate, he fell from favor and fled to Switzerland. His brother was guillotined in 1794.

Major Patrick Ferguson (1744–1780). Inventor of the first breech-loading rifle used in the British army—a very accurate weapon with a rapid rate of fire. He was wounded at Brandywine, was at the Charleston siege, and was killed at Kings Mountain, where almost all his command was lost. He had been a soldier for twenty-one years when he died at thirty-six.

Comte Axel von Fersen (1755–1810). A Swede who sought service in America and, through his connections, became an aide to Rochambeau. A personal favorite of Marie Antoinette, he drove the coach in which the royal family tried to flee Paris. He escaped to Sweden.

Benjamin Franklin (1706–1790). Born in Boston, he established himself early in life as a printer and author in Philadelphia, winning fame and financial success with the publication of *Poor Richard's Almanack*. Dividing his time between politics, business, and science, he was easily America's best-known colonist. He was deputy postmaster of the colonies (1753–1774), proposed the plan of union at the Albany Congress of 1754, helped draft the Declaration of Independence, was a peace negotiator with Britain after the war, and took part in the 1787 Constitutional Convention. His natural son William was the last royal governor of New Jersey.

Major David Franks. An aide to Benedict Arnold in Philadelphia and at West Point, he escorted Peggy Arnold to Philadelphia after discovery of her husband's treachery.

Major General Horatio Gates (1728–1806). Son of a duke's housekeeper in England, he joined the British army, was present at General Braddock's defeat in 1755, and retired on half-pay in 1765. With Washington's help he settled on a Virginia plantation, supported the revolutionary cause, and was commissioned in the Continental Army. Gates commanded rebel forces at Saratoga and in 1778 was the willing choice of the Conway Cabal to replace Washington as commander. His reliance on militiamen cost him a major defeat at Camden. He was replaced by Nathanael Greene.

George III (1738–1820). King of Ireland and Great Britain from 1760 until his death sixty years later, he became the symbol of oppression after the Revolution began. He was increasingly hardened against independence and even considered abdication rather than give in to a Parliament committed to making peace.

Lord George Germain (1716–1785). After being denounced as "unfit to serve . . . in any military capacity whatever" (he had been convicted of disobeying orders as commander of British forces at Minden in 1759), he became secretary of state for the American colonies, where his misguided efforts to manage the war from London were disastrous.

François Joseph Paul, Comte de Grasse (1722–1788). The French admiral whose fleet was instrumental in trapping Cornwallis's army at Yorktown was a big, strapping man. His naval career began at the age of eleven. He was defeated and captured by the British in 1782.

Admiral Thomas Graves (1725?–1802). His career marked by setbacks and accusations, Graves was made second in command to Marriot Arbuthnot and was in charge during the Battle of the Virginia Capes that set up the defeat of Cornwallis at Yorktown.

Major General Nathanael Greene (1742–1786). Son of Rhode Island Quakers, Greene became an ironworker, then defied his pacifist origins to become a soldier. In 1775 he organized a militia company whose men rejected him as an officer because of his stiff knee—an affliction since childhood. Nevertheless, he became a general (regarded by Washington as his best), was appointed quartermaster general in 1778, and returned to field command to succeed Horatio Gates as commander of the southern troops. He retired to a plantation given him by Georgia.

Alexander Hamilton (1757–1804). As secretary and aide to Washington, Hamilton had a very responsible job and was a trusted adviser until the two had a falling out. Hamilton sought and received a field command and performed ably at Yorktown. After the war he wrote more than half of the *Federalist Papers* and was Washington's treasury secretary.

Brigadier General William Heath (1737–1814). A Massachusetts farmer, Heath won a commission as brigadier after service in the siege of Boston. When he seriously mishandled an attack on Fort Independence in 1777, he was removed from command. He helped Washington prepare for the coming of Rochambeau's army in 1780.

Admiral Sir Samuel Hood (1724–1816). A quarrelsome man, he was one of the best British naval officers of his day. In 1780 he became second in command to Sir George Rodney, and when the latter left for England, he joined Thomas Graves but failed to defeat the French off Chesapeake Bay.

Colonel John Eager Howard (1752–1827). A Maryland officer, Howard not only fought but distinguished himself again and again—at White Plains, Germantown, Monmouth, Camden, and Cowpens. Nathanael Greene called him "as good an officer as the world affords." After the war he was elected governor and senator from his state.

Brigadier General Isaac Huger (1743–1797). Son of a wealthy South Carolina planter, Huger began soldiering in the Cherokee War of 1760. He served in the state militia and in 1779 became a brigadier in the Continental Army. He tried unsuccessfully to defend Georgia and later commanded a detachment of Virginians at Guilford and Hobkirk's Hill.

Lieutenant Colonel David Humphreys (1752–1818). A sentimental and sometimes dramatic figure, this Connecticut poet and statesman gave up a tutoring position at Yale to join the state militia. He developed a sharp military mind and in 1780 became a valued aide to Washington.

John Jay (1745–1829). As a delegate to the First Continental Congress, Jay represented the interests of conservative merchants, but he became a supporter of revolution after the Declaration of Independence. He was elected president of the Congress in 1778, and later served as commissioner to Spain. In 1782 he joined Franklin and Adams in Paris to negotiate peace with Great Britain. After the war he was secretary of foreign affairs, chief justice of the Supreme Court, and governor of New York, and he wrote the *Federalist Papers* with James Madison and Alexander Hamilton.

Thomas Jefferson (1743–1826). A many-talented man, Jefferson embodied the Enlightenment ideas of his time. Trained in the law, he entered politics at the onset of the Revolution. Recognized as a fine writer, he was chief author of the Declaration of Independence. During the war he was governor of Virginia (1779–1781) and narrowly escaped capture by the enemy. He succeeded Benjamin Franklin as commissioner to France in 1784 and after returning to the United States began arguing against the ideas of Alexander Hamilton and the Federalists. He was elected president in 1800 and served two terms.

Major General Henry Knox (1750–1806). A Boston bookseller, Knox married Lucy Flucker, daughter of the royal secretary of Massachusetts, who remained loyal to the crown. Knox's career as the army's chief artillerist spanned almost all of the important campaigns. His first achievement was moving heavy cannon from Fort Ticonderoga three hundred miles to Boston in winter, where they ended the British siege. His last was making critical cannon emplacements at Yorktown. During Washington's presidency he served as secretary of war and was responsible for the creation of the military academy at West Point.

Colonel Thaddeus Kosciuszko (1746–1817). Polish army officer who volunteered to serve in the Continental Army and was commissioned as colonel of engineers. He fortified the battleground at Saratoga and was in charge of transportation in the race for the Dan.

Marie Joseph Paul Yves Roch Gilbert du Motier, Marquis de Lafayette (1757–1834). In the summer of 1775 the idealistic young nobleman decided to join the American cause, knowing that Louis XVI would disapprove. Leaving France surreptitiously, he received a cold reception from Congress, but was commissioned a major general without command when he offered to serve as a volunteer. He joined Washington and, given increased responsibility, served with considerable distinction and was helpful in obtaining French troops to support Washington.

Colonel John Lamb (1735–1800). Son of a reputed burglar who came to the colonies and became a successful mathematical instrument maker, Lamb was fluent in several languages, was a good speaker, and became a leader of New York's Sons of Liberty. Commissioned in the Continental Army, he was captured at Quebec in 1777. After release he commanded the artillery for Benedict Arnold at West Point.

Henry Laurens (1724–1792). A South Carolinian of Huguenot descent, he made a fortune trading rice, hides, indigo, and slaves. He was elected to the Continental Congress in 1777 and became president, succeeding John Hancock the same year. In 1780, on a mission to seek a large loan from Holland, he was captured at sea and imprisoned in the Tower of London under conditions so severe that his health was impaired. After his release he was exchanged for Cornwallis and briefly joined Benjamin Franklin, John Jay, and John Adams as peace negotiator. His son John was one of the Revolution's last casualties.

John Laurens (c. 1754–1782). Educated and married in England, he returned to America in 1777 and joined Washington as an aide. The General used him to help calm tensions between Americans and French officers and sent him on secret missions. Captured at Charleston, he was released and sent by Congress to Europe to raise money. In 1781 he was back with the army at Yorktown and helped Vicomte de Noailles negotiate surrender terms. He was killed in a minor skirmish in 1782.

Armand-Louis de Gontaut-Biron, Duc de Lauzun (1747–1793). He brought to America a regiment of volunteers from at least fifteen foreign countries. Rochambeau picked him to carry the news of Yorktown to Versailles. A moderate who initially supported the French Revolution, he was condemned to die. Sharing a last meal with his executioner, he observed, "You need courage in prosecuting a trade like yours."

Arthur Lee (1740–1792). Educated in Edinburgh and London as a doctor and lawyer, he became a follower of John Wilkes, at whose house he met Beaumarchais and hatched a plan for French aid that resulted in the formation of Hortalez et Cie. A morbidly suspicious man, he joined Benjamin Franklin and Silas Deane in France and proceeded to accuse the latter of using his position for financial gain, ruining him.

Lieutenant Colonel Henry ("Light-Horse Harry") Lee (1756–1818). A member of the influential Lee family of Virginia, he became a brilliant cavalryman at an early age and was given his own legion by congressional resolution. A trusted friend of Washington, he was a lieutenant colonel at twenty-four. In 1781 he joined Greene in the Carolinas, where he and his troops distinguished themselves. After the war he served in Congress and as governor of Virginia, before unlucky land speculation landed him in debt and prison. He was the father of Robert E. Lee.

Richard Henry Lee (1732–1794). After study in England he became a member of the House of Burgesses and an ally of Patrick Henry. In the Continental Congress he was close to John and Samuel Adams and was an advocate of attacks on the king rather than the ministry. Lee played a key role in persuading Virginia to send Congress resolutions for independence, and he signed the Declaration of Independence. He opposed adoption of the Constitution, arguing that it must have a bill of rights, and his proposals found their way into the first ten amendments.

Major General Alexander Leslie (1731–1794). In a career marked more by personal courage than by performance, he served from 1775 to 1782, when he succeeded Cornwallis and oversaw the British evacuations of Charleston and Savannah.

Major General Benjamin Lincoln (1733–1810). This Massachusetts farmer became a lieutenant colonel in the militia and commanded troops around Boston in the siege, where he impressed Washington. Congress appointed him a major general. He was badly wounded in the Saratoga campaign. As commander of the southern department, he had the bad luck to have his army abandoned by d'Estaing in Savannah, and he lost most of his forces at Charleston in 1779.

Louis XVI (1754–1793). King of France at the age of twenty, he was finally persuaded by Vergennes to give secret aid to the colonies through Hortalez et Cie, and then approved the French alliance. He and his wife, Marie Antoinette, were sent to the guillotine in 1793.

Chevalier Anne-Cesar de La Luzerne (1741–1791). He became France's minister to the United States in 1779 and, though he spoke little English, exerted a great influence. He oversaw the purchase of supplies for the French army and acted as go-between for Washington and Rochambeau.

James Madison (1751–1836). A Princeton graduate whose keen interest in the controversy between the colonies and England fueled his desire to enter politics. As a delegate to the Virginia convention, he helped frame its constitution and bill of rights and was elected to the Continental Congress in 1780. After the war he wrote twenty-nine of the *Federalist Papers* and the Bill of Rights. He was Jefferson's secretary of state and his chosen successor as president from 1809 to 1817.

Colonel Francis Marion (1732–1795). The "Swamp Fox" attained the rank of brigadier general of militia, but Congress never awarded him more than a colonelcy. His enormous skill in guerrilla tactics made him one of the most feared fighters in the South after all organized resistance there was destroyed, and he and his brigade (which included as many as 2,500 men) became the bane of British and loyalist forces.

George Mason (1725–1792). A tidewater aristocrat, he served in the House of Burgesses before becoming an influential revolutionary figure through his political writings. With Madison he framed Virginia's constitution and bill of rights, which influenced the Declaration of Independence and French revolutionary thought. As a delegate to the Constitutional Convention, he refused to sign the final draft because of his opposition to slavery and his belief that it must have a bill of rights.

Brigadier General Alexander McDougall (1732–1786). A Scot who emigrated to New York, as a boy he delivered milk from his father's cows, went to sea at an early age, and became a successful privateer and merchant. An active Son of Liberty, he was jailed for writing a controversial pamphlet and became known as the "Wilkes of America." During the war he commanded at West Point after Benedict Arnold's treason; afterward he became a congressman and later president of the Bank of New York.

Captain Allen McLane (1746–1829). A Pennsylvanian, he fought with Virginia militia on Long Island and was promoted to captain on the field at Princeton by Washington. After the British evacuated Philadelphia McLane tried unsuccessfully to reveal Benedict Arnold's profiteering to Washington. In June 1781 he bore a message urging de Grasse to sail north to the Chesapeake, and during the Yorktown campaign he was posted on Long Island to inform Washington if the British were reinforcing Cornwallis.

Brigadier General Daniel Morgan (1736–1802). Leaving home at seventeen, he became a farm laborer and wagoner. Two years later he joined General Edward Braddock's expedition as a teamster and got to know Washington. He fought in the French and Indian wars, led Benedict Arnold's march to Quebec, was captured and exchanged. His riflemen played a decisive role at Saratoga. Resigning in 1779 after being passed over, he later took charge of an elite corps after the disaster at Camden, went on to win the pivotal victory at Cowpens, and finally left the army because of ill health. In 1797, by which time he owned 250,000 acres of land, he was elected to Congress.

Robert Morris (1734–1806). English-born merchant who was known as the financier of the Revolution. A partner in a Philadelphia import-export firm, he became a leader in the patriot cause and signed the nonimportation agreement in 1765. He was in the Congress while continuing his commercial activities, and brokered deals to supply rebel troops. He personally financed the Yorktown campaign. Like many others, his postwar downfall resulted from land speculation.

Governor Thomas Nelson (1739–1789). Educated in England, he returned to serve in the House of Burgesses, as brigadier general in the state militia, in Congress, and as governor of Virginia, succeeding Jefferson. War debts turned him into a poor man.

Louis-Marie, Vicomte de Noailles (1756–1804). Lafayette's brother-in-law, he fought at Yorktown and helped negotiate surrender terms with the British. Back in France, he was elected to the Estates-General but during the Reign of Terror fled to England and then to the United States.

Lord North, courtesy title of Frederick, second Earl of Guilford (1732–1792). Appointed first minister in 1770 by George III, for whom he was a pliant agent. North's administration bears much blame for the loss of the colonies. After Yorktown he finally lost faith in the cause and resigned.

Brigadier General Charles O'Hara (1740?–1802). After service in Africa he came to America in 1778 and later joined Cornwallis in the South, where he spearheaded the pursuit of Nathanael Greene to the Dan and represented the earl at the Yorktown surrender.

Major General William Phillips (1731?–1781). A brilliant artillerist, he was captured at Saratoga and, when exchanged, led two thousand troops to join Benedict Arnold in Virginia. There he died of typhoid fever in May 1781.

Andrew Pickens (1739–1817). An austere South Carolina farmer and justice of the peace, he became a brigadier general of militia and fought in numerous engagements, including Cowpens, with his irregulars, whom he paid in goods and slaves taken from loyalists.

Colonel Timothy Pickering (1745–1829). Author of a training manual for militia, he served in the Lexington alert and the New York and New Jersey campaigns. In 1780 he replaced Nathanael Greene as quartermaster general. Earlier he wrote, "If we should fail at last, the Americans can blame only their own negligence, avarice, and want of almost every public virtue." He was not an admirer of George Washington.

Francis, Lord Rawdon (1754–1826). Distinguished at Bunker Hill, he became an aide to General Sir Henry Clinton, then recruited a provincial regiment called "Volunteers of Ireland" and led them to the South. He fought at Camden and was left behind by Cornwallis to take charge of South Carolina and Georgia. Ill, he was captured by the French en route to England.

Beverley Robinson (1721–1792). A New York loyalist who became a hugely wealthy landowner. He raised a regiment of loyalists and served as an intelligence agent for Clinton. His property on the Hudson was confiscated, and he was exiled to England.

Jean-Baptiste-Donatien de Vimeur, Comte de Rochambeau (1725–1807). After several decades of fighting in Europe, he was chosen to lead French expeditionary forces in America. Fortunately, he accepted a subordinate role to Washington and maintained good relations with the American, which, with the help of the French fleet, led to the triumph at Yorktown. Jailed during the Reign of Terror in France, only the death of Robespierre saved him from the guillotine.

Donatien-Marie-Joseph de Vimeur, Vicomte de Rochambeau (1755–1813). During the Revolution, he was an aide to his father, the Comte de Rochambeau. After the war he served in the West Indies and was captured by the British.

Admiral Sir George Rodney (1718–1792). He played almost no part in the Revolution beyond capturing Admiral de Grasse in 1782, but by then the war was all but over.

Benjamin Rush (1745–1813). Trained in medicine at Edinburgh, he became the colony's best-known physician as well as a member of Congress and signer of the Declaration of Independence. Appointed surgeon general of the army, he complained about Washington's handling of military matters and started what became the Conway Cabal. He resigned when confronted with evidence of his disloyalty.

Claude Henri, Marquis de Saint-Simon (1760–1825). He entered the army in 1775 and took part in the Yorktown campaign with three thousand men.

John Montagu, fourth Earl of Sandwich (1718–1792). As first lord of the Admiralty, he and his corrupt department were responsible for the wretched condition of ships and naval personnel during the Revolution. He liked to eat meat held between two slices of bread; hence the name.

Colonel Alexander Scammell (1747–1781). A surveyor and brigade major in John Sullivan's militia, he served at the siege of Boston, in Canada, and distinguished himself at Saratoga. As Washington's adjutant general, he arrested Charles Lee and had John André executed. One of the most admired field officers, he was mortally wounded at Yorktown.

Major General Philip Schuyler (1733–1804). One of four major generals commissioned under Washington, he was a huge landowner in the Hudson Valley and an ardent patriot. His leadership was plagued by tensions between New Yorkers and New Englanders and by friction with General Horatio Gates. He resigned but continued to advise Washington.

Colonel Isaac Shelby (1750–1826). A frontier surveyor, he became a militia colonel and led troops to important victories in the Carolinas, notably at Kings Mountain. He became Kentucky's first governor after the war.

Lieutenant Colonel John Graves Simcoe (1752–1806). Commander of the Queen's Rangers, a Tory corps, he fought around Boston, at Brandywine, and in Virginia, where he was posted at Gloucester during the Yorktown siege.

Joshua Hett Smith (1736–1818). Brother of William and an active Whig, perhaps quite innocently he helped John André meet with Benedict Arnold by taking him ashore from the British ship *Vulture*. He accompanied André on part of his journey, leaving him before they reached British lines.

William Smith, Jr. (1728–1793). A distinguished jurist and historian of New York, Smith was a fence-sitter when war broke out. He refused to take the oath supporting the rebel cause and remained in New York City until war's end, when he moved to England and was appointed chief justice in Canada.

Baron Friedrich Wilhelm von Steuben (1730–1794). The bogus "baron" had served under Frederick the Great and was sent to America by Benjamin Franklin. Here he had great success in training rebel soldiers and teaching them discipline. His "blue book" was the official drill manual until 1812.

David Murray, Viscount Stormont (1727–1796). As British ambassador to France, he tried to block the French alliance, employing a network of spies to help. As secretary of state for the northern department, he persuaded the king to declare war on Holland in 1780.

Major General John Sullivan (1740–1795). A Maine lawyer, he was in the Continental Congress and served at the siege of Boston and the invasion of Canada. He was captured at Long Island, fought at Trenton, Princeton, and Brandywine, and led an expedition against the Iroquois. As a military diplomatist with the French at Newport, he was a failure.

Major Benjamin Tallmadge (1754–1835). A Yale graduate, he saw action from Long Island to Monmouth before taking over Washington's secret service from 1778 to 1783. His initiative after the capture of John André led to the revelation of Benedict Arnold's treachery.

Lieutenant Colonel Banastre Tarleton (1754–1833). An accomplished cavalryman, he was a favorite of Cornwallis and anathema to rebels, who called him "Butcher" and "Bloody Tarleton" for his tactics. Badly beaten at Cowpens, he fought Lauzun at Yorktown and asked to be surrendered to Rochambeau rather than to the Americans, for fear of what they would do to him.

Charles-Louis d'Arsac, Admiral the Chevalier de Ternay (1722–1780). He was commissioned to transport Rochambeau's army from Brest to Rhode Island. He died not long after arriving.

James Thacher (1754–1844). After apprenticeship to a Massachusetts doctor he became an army surgeon and witnessed many important events, which he described in his journal. It provides a unique glimpse into the cold, hungry lives of the troops.

Lieutenant Colonel Tench Tilghman (1744–1786). He sold his Philadelphia business on the eve of the Revolution and in 1776 began work as volunteer military sec-

retary to Washington. A favorite of the General, after assisting him for five years he was made a lieutenant colonel. He had the honor of taking news of Yorktown to the Congress. He died young of hardships suffered in the war.

Carl Gustaf Tornquist (1757–1808). A Swedish officer in the French navy, he served under de Grasse in 1781 and wrote a valuable memoir.

Lieutenant Colonel Jonathan Trumbull (1740–1809). Son of the Connecticut governor, he was paymaster general in the northern department and later first comptroller of the currency. In 1781 Washington chose him to replace Alexander Hamilton as an aide, and he served in the Yorktown campaign. After the war he was a congressman and governor of Connecticut.

Lieutenant Colonel Richard Varick (1753–1831). At first he was an aide to Philip Schuyler, then to Benedict Arnold at West Point. After Arnold's treason was revealed, Varick was investigated and found innocent. Between 1781 and 1783 he was Washington's official recording secretary.

Charles Gravier, Comte de Vergennes (1717–1787). He became a diplomat as a young man and as a favorite of Louis XVI became secretary of foreign affairs in 1774. In that role he helped Benjamin Franklin and Silas Deane secure secret military and financial aid and persuaded the king to sign a treaty of alliance.

Jean-Baptist-Antoine de Verger (1762–1851). As a teenager, he joined the Deux-Ponts regiment and fought under Rochambeau. With the fall of the French monarchy in 1792, he emigrated to Germany.

Antoine Charles du Houx, Baron de Vioménil (1728–1792). He entered the army at twelve and was Rochambeau's second in command in America. At Yorktown he led a charge that was decisive. He died of injuries sustained while defending the French royal family in 1792.

Charles-Joseph-Hyacinthe, Comte de Vioménil (1734–1827). Younger brother of the baron, he commanded the French artillery at Yorktown. In 1792 he joined other émigrés fighting to restore the monarchy, became leader of the Portuguese army, and moved to England in 1808.

Horace Walpole, fourth Earl of Orford (1717–1797). Third son of Sir Robert Walpole, known as the first prime minister of England, he was a prolific writer of letters and memoirs, providing a vivid picture of Georgian England. He opposed North's ministry and the colonial war.

General George Washington (1732–1799). A Virginia planter, surveyor, and militia colonel, he became prominent during the French and Indian War. As a member of his province's House of Burgesses, he opposed British legislation affecting the colonies. He was a delegate to the First and Second Continental Congresses, which chose him as commander in chief of the Continental Army. After the war he advocated a strong national union and was president of the Constitutional Convention in 1787. Two years later he was elected the nation's first president and served two terms before retiring to his estate, Mount Vernon.

Colonel William Washington (1752–1810). A distant relative of George Washington, he studied for the ministry before the war, when he became a captain in the Virginia infantry. Wounded at Long Island and Trenton, he moved to the South to join Benjamin Lincoln and organized a cavalry brigade, which skirmished often with Banastre Tarleton (notably at Cowpens).

Brigadier General Anthony Wayne (1745–1796). A Pennsylvania tanner, Wayne was active in the revolutionary movement from its earliest days. His fiery leadership won him the nickname "Mad Anthony." He served in Canada, at Brandywine, Paoli, Germantown, Monmouth, Stony Point, and was with Steuben in the Yorktown campaign, then with Nathanael Greene.

Brigadier General George Weedon (c. 1730–1793). Known to his tavern customers as "Joe Gourd," he fought at Brandywine and Germantown and commanded the Virginia militia at the siege of Yorktown.

Paul Wentworth (?–1793). Though George III never trusted him, calling him a "stock jobber," he was chief of the loyalist secret agents in London, and after he tried to persuade Benjamin Franklin to seek peace, Louis XVI agreed to a Franco-American treaty. Edward Bancroft reported to him.

Colonel Otho Williams (1749–1794). An outstanding commander under Nathanael Greene, Williams fought at Fort Washington and Camden, where he performed ably. He covered Greene's race to the Dan and then led the army into North Carolina, where he distinguished himself at Hobkirk's Hill and Eutaw Springs.

SOURCE NOTES

The notes that follow indicate the chief sources of quotations or assertions for readers interested in pursuing a subject further or knowing what publications I found most useful. Wherever possible I have based the text on contemporary evidence as recorded by eyewitnesses, and I have indicated where such material may be found.

Citations of documents in the Gilder Lehrman collection include the abbreviation GLC or MA followed by the appropriate item number.

Prologue

The quotations from and about Washington and Congress are from Flexner 2:9, 13–14.

Jefferson's comment is quoted in Van Doren *Benjamin Franklin* 529, and Abigail Adams's remark is from the same source, 541.

The footnote about Napoleon's statement is taken from Flexner 2:543fn.

Descriptions of Washington's face by Houdon and Stuart appear in Flexner's *Gilbert Stuart* 127.

Prince de Broglie's observation is in Ferrière 468.

1. So Much Is at Stake

A splendid account of the battles of Lexington and Concord may be found in David Hackett Fischer's *Paul Revere's Ride*.

Estimates of the Continental Army's strength are in Scheer and Rankin 376.

Thacher 185 describes the horrendous winter at Morristown.

Flexner 2:354–55 and Martin have more details on the soldiers' suffering, and the former quotes Webb's angry outburst on p. 355.

Stokes 5:161–62 has William Smith's opinion of France.

Freeman 5:161–67 is the source of information on the orders to French troops and Lafayette's reaction to the Continental Army's distress.

Freeman 5:177–78 has the General's warning of how the French might react to his soldiers' condition. The number of new recruits coming into camp appears in the same source.

Washington's appeal to the states is from Freeman 5:178.

Ebenezer Huntington's outburst appears in Freeman 5:174–75.

Washington's comment on the history of war as one of false hopes and temporary expedients is from his letter to James Duane of Oct. 4, 1780, Hamilton Papers 2:454. The footnote about Samuel Tate is from GLC 1422, dated May 1780.

The description of the states as a potential many-headed monster comes from Flexner 2:355–56, as does the concern about "seditious combinations."

Washington's fear that the army might vanish may be found in Flexner 2:357. From the same source, p. 359, comes the General's cynical jibe about his borrowed horse and the figure on expiring enlistments.

Whitridge records Vergennes's perceptive comment on the loss of Canada.

Bemis 18 has Vergennes's remark concerning the Turks. Einstein's first two chapters are entertaining and illuminating on the topic of British spies and their efforts to uncover what the American commissioners were up to at Versailles.

Whitridge 65fn6 contains Vergennes's statement about England's importance to the balance of power in Europe.

France's arrangements for getting money and arms to America are described in Bemis 19–21 and Van Doren *Benjamin Franklin* 568.

Franklin in Paris is ably described in Van Doren *Benjamin Franklin* 570–75.

Van Doren *Benjamin Franklin* 572 and 579 has information on Lafayette and Steuben.

How the news of Saratoga was delivered to Franklin is in Van Doren *Benjamin Franklin* 587–88 and Ketchum *Saratoga* 441–45.

Bemis 28–30 contains details of the treaty with France.

Commager and Morris 743–45 is the source of information on the double agent Bancroft.

Einstein 16–25 *passim* discusses Silas Deane; Van Doren's chapter 20 *Benjamin Franklin* is informative on spies. The footnote concerning the Carlisle commission is drawn from Boatner 844–45.

Bemis 30–31 deals with congressional ratification of the treaties.

Heath 225 and Scheer and Rankin 377 describe the French arrival in Newport.

Information on the French chevalier appears in Chastellux 2–13 *passim*.

Closen 107 continues his description of the Atlantic passage and discusses himself, xxii–xxvi.

Chadwick 13 and Freeman 5:179–80 treat British naval superiority and its effect on Washington's plans.

Rice and Brown 1:18fn9 includes Clinton's belief that British failure to deal with the French in Rhode Island was a turning point of the war. This book is an invaluable source.

2. *France Will Turn the Tide*

Washington's despair that the army must disband is in Freeman 5:181–82fn.

The same volume also has Arnold's early attempt to beg off active command (182–83) and Washington's reluctant decision to scavenge the countryside (184–85).

Flexner 2:365 is the source of Washington's decision to use Lafayette as a conduit to the French, and 414fn gives the reason French officers did not care to serve with Lafayette's command.

Boatner 939 has a good summary of Rochambeau's career.

Rochambeau's comments on Washington's plans are in Flexner 2:366–67, and Freeman 5:187fn has his plea to the General to deal directly with him.

Gottschalk 2–3 is the source for Lafayette's decision to come to America.

Boatner 591–92 and Flexner 2:213–15 have useful information on Lafayette and his relationship with Washington.

Flexner 2:367 quotes Washington's reluctance to leave his army.

Arbuthnot's failure to act against Newport is in Whitridge 90.

Willcox 328 contains Clinton's acid comment about the admiral.

The story of Clinton's efforts to get Arbuthnot to act, Rodney's arrival and attitude are detailed in Willcox 324–44 *passim.*

Washington informed Congress in a letter to the Committee of Congress for Co-operation, dated Aug. 17, 1780, which is in GLC 6488.

Freeman 5:188 cites Washington's letter to his brother Samuel.

Alexander Hamilton to James Duane, Sept. 6, 1780, is from GLC 6671.

Hamilton Papers 2:422 contains his letter to Elizabeth Schuyler.

American proposals to the French are in Freeman 5:193 and fn.

The draft proposal for the Hartford meeting is in Hamilton Papers 2:3391–96.

A discussion of Joshua Hett Smith is in Boatner 1015 and Smith *Historical Memoirs* 1–7.

Freeman 5:192 and Flexner 2:371–72 describe conversations between Washington and Arnold and the General's ride to Hartford.

Mackesy's *The War for America* is very informative on naval matters.

Flexner 2:366 and 371–73; also Rice and Brown 1:241 (Berthier journal); Johnston; Chinard 62–65 are good sources of French comments.

Hamilton Papers 2:391–93 contains an excellent account of the Hartford meeting and the American proposals. More may be found in Flexner 2:371–72.

Whitridge is an excellent study of Rochambeau. See especially chapter 6 of that volume for details on the selection of the count and the staff that accompanied him to America.

3. *So Hellish a Plot*

The story—perhaps apocryphal—about Wayne and Washington appears in *New York*, WPA Guide series, 605.

Boatner 1066 has the story of Wayne at Stony Point.

Flexner 2:382 relates the meeting between Washington and Arnold.

Shreve 133 quotes the diary of Tobias Lear, Washington's private secretary, to whom he dictated the story while on his deathbed of giving Arnold the command at West Point.

Washington's instructions to Arnold appear in Flexner 2:383.

Van Doren *Secret History* 294–95 and 345–47 is very informative on the Arnold story.

Brandt 205 also has a fine account of what occurred.

I turned to Flexner 2:385; Chastellux 1:89–90; and Thacher 216 for a description of West Point at this time.

An article in *Life*, Feb. 23, 1968, contains the report from Jameson.

Commager and Morris 760–61 and Freeman 5:200 have André's story. The footnote explaining Colonel Sheldon's absence is based on Freeman 5:208fn.

Lafayette to La Luzerne described Arnold's flight, in Commager and Morris 754–55. The same source, 751–52 and 758, describes Arnold's escape.

Flexner 2:383 mentions the delay of Arnold's letter.

Van Doren *Secret History* 289 notes Smith's invitation to Mrs. Arnold.

Hamilton to Laurens, in Commager and Morris 759–60, describes the plotters' meeting.

Scheer and Rankin 380–81 has the account of Smith and André trying to elude capture.

Jones 1:732 states that the captors of André were not militiamen but "farmer's boys" who were on a mission to steal cattle. Two of them could neither read nor write, he said; the third, John Paulding, stated at the trial of Joshua Hett Smith that he had held on to André "because he said he was a British officer. Had he pulled out General Arnold's pass first, I would have let him go."

Scheer and Rankin 375–88 has the full account of Arnold's treason and André's fate.

Freeman 5:208 is good on the capture of André.

Commager and Morris 758–59 and Boatner 475 describe André and his execution.

Hamilton's letter to his fiancée is in his Papers 2:441–42.

Lamb's letter to a fellow officer is in Leake 250–52.

Van Doren *Secret History* 165–66, 185–86 describes Arnold's activities in Philadelphia. The same source, 187–88, has the fullest account of Arnold's treachery, based on the then recently acquired British headquarters papers.

John André to Joseph Chew, June 18, 1780, is in GLC 05533.

Brandt 154–95 *passim* is an excellent source on Arnold's treason.

Scheer and Rankin reprints Greene's general orders (384) as well as Scammell's condemnation of Arnold (388).

Van Doren *Secret History* 352–53 describes the march of Wayne's Pennsylvanians, and this is supplemented in Commager and Morris 753–54.

Scheer and Rankin 385–86 contains Tallmadge's account of André's death.

Flexner 2:392–94 notes the attempt to persuade Clinton to surrender Arnold to the Americans.

Commager and Morris 762–63 reports Arnold's threat to Washington.

Maguire 237–40, 243fn, and 244fn provides a graphic picture of André's final moments.

Scheer and Rankin 387 prints the artificer's description of the hanging.

Freeman 5:221fn, Thacher 226–31, and Commager and Morris have anecdotes from the scene of André's execution.

Brandt 155 and elsewhere discusses Arnold's motivations.

Washington's comment on Arnold is in Freeman 5:223.

Brandt discusses the public outrage against Arnold.

Lloyds's Evening Post (London), Dec. 11–13, 1780, quoted in Scheer and Rankin 388, has the observation regarding Arnold's unpopularity with British officers.

Brandt 230–31, 233–37 describes Arnold's activities after his treason was discovered, including efforts to recruit volunteers.

Thayer 280 has Greene's letter to his wife.

The fullest account of John Champe's remarkable story is the article in *American Heritage* by George Scheer. Additional material is in Boatner 193–94.

4. *Beware the Back Water Men*

The hurricane is described in Rice and Brown 1:20 and fn13.

Loughrey 33 quotes Fersen on Rochambeau.

Numerous accounts of the French stay in Rhode Island exist, notably those in Rice and Brown (see especially Berthier journal). In addition to the journals of French officers, Stevens's "The French in Rhode Island" is useful. Simpson has an amusing account on whether the French paid for their lodging.

Rice and Brown 1:21 (Clermont-Crèvecoeur journal) describes American table manners.

Blanchard 78–79 contains his comments on the American diet.

Closen's observations are on pp. 49–51.

Bundling is discussed in detail by Clermont-Crèvecoeur in Rice and Brown 1:39.

The Verger journal in Rice and Brown describes the Indian visit (123); and Clermont-Crèvecoeur's journal in the same source has commentary on the Quakers (21–22).

News of Leslie's assignment is in Closen 45–46, and his mission is noted in Clinton 467 (Clinton to Leslie, Oct. 12, 1780).

Flexner 2:405 has details on the correspondence captured from American generals.

Clinton 461–62 has a copy of the purloined Hamilton letter.

Clinton 466 discusses the capture of Henry Laurens.

Closen 43–47 and 47fn describes the death of Ternay, the Christmas storm, and the aborted mission to capture Clinton.

Accounts of the mutiny of the Pennsylvania line appear in Freeman 5:235, 236–41.

Clinton 240–41 discusses his efforts to capitalize on the mutiny. The footnote explaining why veterans got a discharge and reenlisted is from Flexner 2:406.

Freeman 5:510, appendix 3, contains material on Clinton's moves.

Several sources offer valuable material on the mutiny of the Pennsylvania line: Freeman 5:236–48, Flexner 2:407–8, and Clinton 240–41.

Freeman 5:243 prints the letter from Sullivan to Washington.

Flexner 2:406–7 describes the General's doubts about the army's continued existence.

Robert Howe's settlement of the New Jersey mutiny is described in Freeman 5:247–49.

Lumpkin 1–4 has a good account of initial plans for war in the South.

Clinton notes being out of fashion in Clinton xxxii.

Flood 110; Boatner 285–89; and Clinton xxxviii–xl all shed light on Sir Henry's personality.

The rare agreement between Clinton and Arbuthnot is noted in Clinton xxxii ff.

Washington reported his anxiety about the South to James Duane, Oct. 4, 1780, in Freeman 5:226.

Johnston 23 notes that Clinton could "ill spare" Arnold's command.

The Thomas Jefferson broadside of Jan. 19, 1781, is in GLC 0448; William North to Lewis Morris, Jan. 25, 1781, is in GLC 04829.

Closen 56 has his diary note.

Ward *The War of the Revolution* 2:740 describes Ferguson.

Scheer and Rankin 413–16 has accounts of the battle preliminaries.

Boatner 1174–75 discusses the massacre of Buford's men.

Ward *The War of the Revolution* 2:741 has an apt description of the over-mountain men.

Scheer and Rankin 416–21 and Commager and Morris 1140–41 have details on the Kings Mountain battle.

Freeman 5:227 has Washington's reaction to news of the battle.

Clinton 476 contains Cornwallis's letter to General Clinton.

5. *A Little Persevering and Determined Army*

Greene 280, 285–91 relates his move to the South.

Commager and Morris 1151–52 has the remark about the state treasuries, Greene's anger at slackers, and his letter to Joseph Reed.

Greene 64–67 has details about his experience in the siege of Boston.

Scheer and Rankin 427–28 includes Greene's message to Morgan, Tarleton's plan, and comments about Greene by his men.

Boatner 1087–88 has an entry on Tarleton.

Commager and Morris 1158 has Morgan's decision to stand and fight.

Greene's battle plans and the action are discussed in Scheer and Rankin 430–32 and Commager and Morris 1153–55.

Commager and Morris 1157 and Flood 375 have material on Colonel Howard and the British captain.

Casualty figures are from Flood 376 and Scheer and Rankin 432, and the latter source, 433, has Walpole's comment.

Cornwallis's reaction and plans are in Flood 381–82.

Ward *The War of the Revolution* 2:765–76 discusses the race to the Dan, as does Thayer 315–18.

My description of the Yadkin comes in a letter from Ethan K. Murrow.

Ward *The War of the Revolution* 2:769 relates the story about Greene and Mrs. Steele. That same excellent source describes the race to the Dan and the skirmishing between Greene's and Cornwallis's men.

For Arnold's activities in Virginia, I have drawn on Brandt 146 and 240–41; and Lee 298–300, 394, and 408–10. Ward *The War of the Revolution* 2:868–70 also covers Arnold's movements.

Arnold's arguments to Germain appear in Brandt 235–36, and his request to return to New York is in the same source, 245.

Commager and Morris 1201 cites Cornwallis's letter to Phillips.

Greene's moves and his army's exhaustion are detailed in Commager and Morris 1164, and the same source includes Sergeant Lamb's rescue of Cornwallis at Guilford (1160), Greene's plans (1167–68), and Cornwallis's April 23 letter to Clinton (1161).

Richard Henry Lee's letter to Arthur Lee, June 4, 1781, is in Commager and Morris 1205.

Billias's *Opponents* 213 has casualty figures for Cornwallis's army, and the earl's comments on North Carolina are in the same source, 1168.

Scheer and Rankin 441 quotes Cornwallis's chagrin over the lack of Tory strength. The same source, 1169–70, has the Andrew Jackson story.

Boatner's entry on Marion, 675–79, is helpful. Greene's thanks are from the same source, 1173.

Freeman 5:304 and fn has Washington's praise for Greene.

6. *Our Deliverance Must Come*

Commager and Morris 1210–11 has the letter from Lafayette to Vergennes from New Windsor on the Hudson, Jan. 20, 1781.

Washington to Laurens, Apr. 9, 1781, is in Bonsal 251, appendix C.

Shreve 136 gives the figure of 5,835 for Washington's force on July 15, 1781.

Washington's journal observations are in Freeman 5:256.

Johnston 72 notes Washington's pessimism over his prospects.

Bonsal 79–80 cites Franklin's letter.

Young Rochambeau's news is in Rice and Brown 1:26.

Freeman 5:292 has Washington's call for a conference.

Flexner 2:429 indicates the General's hope for a blow at New York.

The difficulty of an attack on New York is examined in Shreve 143.

Closen 79 fn44 notes the French army's plans.

Flexner 2:430 discusses Rochambeau's letter to de Grasse and the difficulties of dealing with the former.

For Clinton's exchange with de Grasse, see Clinton 299, 306.

Flexner 2:365 mentions Washington's request that Rochambeau deal through Lafayette.

Tilghman's education is described in Shreve 35–36.

Blanchard 122 discloses how hard it was dealing with Rochambeau.

Chastellux's portrayal of Washington is in Flexner 2:399–401.

Chastellux 1:87 compares medicine in the rebel army with that in Agamemnon's.

The quotation about Americans from Lafayette appeared in Stacy Shiff's "Vive l'Histoire" in *New York Times*, op-ed, Feb. 6, 2003.

The Verger journal is in Rice and Brown 1:124.

Acomb, in Closen 82–83, has the details of the trip.

Rice and Brown 135 fn39 mentions the beautiful Polly Lawton.

The Tory threat is in Clermont-Crèvecoeur's journal, Rice and Brown, 1:28–29. His appraisal of the dragoons is on pp. 30–31.

Scheer *Yankee Doodle* 214 and Rice and Brown 1:32 fn30 describe the line of march. The site of the first brigade's camp, or bivouac, was on the outskirts of present-day Bedford Village, near the intersection of Seminary and Court roads.

Closen's remark is on p. 91.

Rhode Island's black regiment is noted in Rice and Brown 1:32–34. The same source, 33 fn34, quotes Rochambeau's letters to France.

Berthier's observations are from Rice and Brown 1:251, July 6, 1780.

Balch 162 relates the episode when Washington and Rochambeau were nearly stranded.

Closen 102 quotes his admiration for the rebel army.

Berthier's adventure is from Rice and Brown 1:251–52 and also notes his encounter with the Tories.

Closen's close call is on pp. 99–100.

Shreve 147 describes de Grasse's plans.

Washington's need for water transport is noted in Flexner 2:436, and the same source, 441, quotes Lafayette's description of York.

Johnston 59 quotes the young Frenchman's estimate of what Cornwallis's Virginia campaign cost.

The Internet "Maps" mileage from Newport to Williamsburg is 565.9, but this is over modern roads. The Vicomte de Noailles calculated the distance he walked from Newport to Yorktown at more than 750 miles.

Washington's allotments of his resources are in Freeman 5:310 fn68d and 313.

Scheer and Rankin 473 quotes the French officer on Clinton's lethargy.

Cumming and Rankin 318–19 mentions Prince William's arrival.

"A Gentleman from Philadelphia" to Capt. Beckwith, July 24, 1781, is in GLC 05223.

The hazards faced by the French navy are recited by Flexner 2:439–40; see also Freeman 5:312 and Ward *The War of the Revolution* 2:882.

"War Diary"; Anthony Wayne to Robert Morris, July 12, 1781, GLC 02620 describes how Wayne dealt with mutineers.

The source of George Mason's letter to his son George, June 3, 1781, is GLC 03256.

The captured letter is discussed in Flexner 2:431, as is the importance of the boats in persuading Clinton that the plan was to attack Staten Island. See also Clinton 307–9 and 531, which includes his belief that loyalists were of little use.

Freeman 5:314 fn97 has Thacher's comment comparing the situation to a theatrical exhibition. The same source, 315–17, relates the relative strength of the British and French fleets.

Rice and Brown 1:44 describes Washington's meeting with the French officers.

7. *A Partial Engagement*

George Washington to Governor Thomas Nelson, Aug. 27, 1781, and the Nelson broadside Sept. 1, 1781, are in GLC 04828, MA 488/1, 31.

Freeman 5:317 and 319 fn121 discusses Washington's visit to Philadelphia.

Closen 116–17 characterizes the French officers' reception at Morris's home.

Washington's letter to Lafayette is in Commager and Morris 1217.

Johnston 92 describes the troops' march through Philadelphia.

Martin's comment on marching is in Scheer *Yankee Doodle* 289.

Francis Barber to his wife, July 18, 1781, is in MA 0488/1, 114.

Flood 403 has Clinton's letter to Cornwallis about Washington's march south.

Bonsal 127, Johnston 92–93, Flood 403–4, Ward *The War of the Revolution* 2:884, and Thacher 271–72 all describe the triumphant French march through Philadelphia.

Clermont-Crèvecoeur's observations are in Rice and Brown 1:47–49.

Shreve 149 describes the unusually enthusiastic Washington.

Closen 123, Bonsal 129–31, and Flexner 2:443 discuss the episode.

Material on the Battle of Rhode Island is in Boatner 788–94; the quote is in Scheer and Rankin 341–42.

Freeman 5:68, 74 has more on the Battle of Rhode Island.

The unhappy saga of d'Estaing's career comes from Boatner and Scheer and Rankin.

Tornquist 35–42 describes the battle between the two fleets. The same source, 14 and 43–44, has material on Tornquist and his journal.

Mackesy 184 has the quotation from Germain and much information on British trade with the West Indies.

Tornquist 48 has the remarks quoted here.

Boatner 444–45, Balch 2:137–40, and Tornquist 53 have details on the French fleet and the search for money. Tornquist gives a figure of 700,000 piastres; Balch, chap. 13, states that the French government placed 6 million livres at Washington's disposal. Balch, chap. 15, says de Grasse was carrying 1.2 million livres for the American commander.

Tornquist 55 notes the arrival of de Grasse in the Chesapeake.

Flexner 2:445 lists the fleet's strength.

George Weedon to Nathanael Greene about the new Virginia governor, dated Sept. 5, 1781, is from MA 488/1, 96.

Blanchard 172 describes the drought in Head of Elk.

Freeman 5:323–24 fn11 quotes one of Clinton's informers.

The source for the footnote on Mordecai Gist is his letter to Smith and Wooton, Sept. 18, 1781, in MA 488/1, 147.

The fireships are described in Rice and Brown 1:52–53 fn91, and the same source, 55 fn98 and 56, lists the trials of other French soldiers.

Tornquist 57 has the author's experience near Hampton.

Freeman 5:324–28 and Flexner 2:445–47 tell of Washington at Mount Vernon and the message concerning de Grasse.

Scheer and Rankin 470 quotes the Marquis de Lafayette to George Washington; another message of July 8, 1781, between the two is in GLC 05467.

Johnston 96–99 tells of the plan to bottle up Cornwallis.

Freeman 5:328–30, Flexner 2:448, and Scheer and Rankin 476 describe Washington's arrival in Williamsburg and the festivities.

Tuchman discusses the Dutch salute to *Andrea Doria* in the first chapter.

Johnston notes how Graves missed Rodney's dispatch (99) and Graves's arrival off the Chesapeake (100–101).

The source for the footnote about the Doyles and Lord Rawdon is Closen 137 and fn.

Tornquist 58–61, Flood 406, Flexner 2:448 and fn, and Commager and Morris 1220–21 all provide valuable details on the sea battle. The last-named source includes a journal of an anonymous French officer with the French fleet—a good eyewitness account.

8. *Prepare to Hear the Worst*

The fascinating correspondence between and about Clinton and Cornwallis is in Clinton's *The American Rebellion*, and I have quoted from Sir Henry's letters of Apr. 10 and Apr. 23 to the earl; Apr. 23 to Germain; Apr. 24 to Phillips; Apr. 30, July 11, and July 14 to Cornwallis.

Gordon, in Peckham, *Narratives of Colonial America* 252 depicts Yorktown before the Revolution, and Lossing 2:301–3 has a description of the place in 1848.

Clinton has several letters recording the naval situation (559–63) as well as letters from Cornwallis and Clinton relating the arrival of the French fleet (563–64).

The journal of Johann Conrad Doehla has the description of unsanitary conditions inside British lines.

Willcox 429 cites the warning by General Robertson.

For the period Sept. 8 to Sept. 23, 1781, covering the conversations in New York about Cornwallis's plight, and the earl's increasingly desperate letters, I have relied on Clinton 565–72.

Flexner 2:449 describes Washington's meeting with de Grasse.

The arrival of the English brig alongside the *Ville de Paris* is mentioned in Rice and Brown 1:136–37.

Both Freeman 5:334–35 and Flexner 2:449 note de Grasse's decision to depart on Oct. 31. The latter source describes the spectacular *feu de joie* (450) and quotes the general's optimistic message (451).

Closen 138 records Washington's operational plans.

Freeman 5:335–43 and Closen 133–37 describe the visits of Washington and Closen.

Closen 138–39 has an account of the allies setting up camp.

9. *I Propose a Cessation of Hostilities*

Lee 496–98 has a long and comprehensive account of this affair. Other material is in Rice and Brown 1:57–58, 139 fn69, and Boatner 1179–80.

The firsthand account by Armand-Louis de Gontaut-Biron, Duc de Lauzun, is in Commager and Morris 1216–17.

Rice and Brown 1:57–58, 138–39 has the story of Lauzun's heroism.

Cornwallis's statement that only the promise of relief led him to defend Yorktown appears in Clinton 583.

Tucker 381 describes the terrain.

Cornwallis's optimistic assessment is in Billias's *Opponents* 218.

Johnston 111 has a complete list of regiments with a full breakdown of both armies on the next eight pages. For numbers of troops, see Doehla (a total of 7,414 British and German), Ward *The War of the Revolution* 2:889 (about 6,000), and Johnston 164–65 (7,157 surrendered; he also gives the round number of 7,500 besieged plus 800 marines).

Johnston has Wayne's criticism of the British movement (127) and Clinton's reassurance of Cornwallis (121).

Lee 496 has his comment on Scammell.

More on Scammell is in Johnston 123 and appendix 174–75; Lee 406; a letter from Colonel Smith in *Magazine of American History*, Jan. 1881, 21; and my *Saratoga* 148, 156–57, 395–97. With Scammell's death I felt that I had lost an old friend. I had been with him from Bunker Hill through the rest of the war and had nothing but admiration for him.

Dearborn 219 has his lament.

The Gregory diary 3 lists the size of the first parallel.

Scheer *Yankee Doodle* 218–19 includes Martin's observations on fascines and gabions; more appears on 230fn and in Closen, 143fn.

The frequency of artillery fire comes from Tucker 382 (Oct. 2).

Duncan's account is in Scheer and Rankin 480.

The quotation from Wayne appears in Johnston 127.

Tucker reports on the wounded (394) and on the dead horses (382–83).

Commager and Morris 1231 has the account of Washington's visit to the trenches.

Flexner 2:454 records the Reverend Evans's high dudgeon.

Commager and Morris 1229 discusses Hamilton's maneuver.

Scheer and Rankin includes Popp's statement (484), notes Martin's pride in seeing the flag raised (233), and describes the arcing shells (484). The damage to people and the town is in several accounts in this book, especially 386–87 and 484–85, and in Doehla 41–42.

Comments on Knox are from my *Decisive Day* 214–21.

Chastellux's appraisal of Knox is in Chinard 54.

Doehla 43–44 describes the British wounded.

Thacher's remark is in Commager and Morris 1232.

The actions of the French regiments appear in Rice and Brown 1:141–42, fn76 and 77.

Some events of Oct. 16 are reported by Cornwallis to Clinton, Oct. 20, in Clinton, Carrington 640, and Doehla 48.

Scheer and Rankin 488 has the Richard Butler account.

In Rice and Brown 1:60 and 143 the Clermont-Crèvecoeur and Verger accounts differ, especially as to the number of troops involved and other details, so I have tried to merge them without focusing on numbers.

Martin's exploits appear in Scheer *Yankee Doodle* 234–36.

Scheer and Rankin 488 quotes Captain William Stevens on Knox. The footnote describing the demise of Cochrane is from Cummings and Rankin 325.

Clinton 580–82 prints the Cornwallis letter ending with Oct. 12. The earl's letter of Oct. 15 appears in Scheer and Rankin 488–89, and the same source, 489, reports the activities of Hamilton and Knox.

Tarleton's *History of Campaigns in the Southern Provinces*, quoted in Commager and Morris 396–400, is the source of his advice to retreat. Cornwallis's comment on the storm is in the same source, 1238.

Freeman 5:374 quotes the American soldier. Tarleton's statement that all hope is gone appears in Commager and Morris 1235–36.

Doehla 49–50 mentions the flag of truce, and Cornwallis's letter to Clinton is printed in Commager and Morris 1238.

Denny's comment on the drummer boy is in Scheer and Rankin 490.

Freeman 5:376 quotes the American officer, and Cornwallis's letter to Washington is in MA 488/1, 2.

10. *The Hand of Heaven Displayed*

Dearborn's 1777 diary 111 has his comment on "Mr. Burguoyn."

Rice and Brown 1:143–44 and fn81 contains details on the surrender negotiations.

Tucker's description of the scene is in Scheer and Rankin 491.

Commager and Morris 1240 cites the honors to be granted.

The honors in the context of the Charleston surrender are discussed in Scheer and Rankin 1108–9 and 491–92. The same source, 492–93, states that Steuben planted the American flag on a British fort.

Governor Nelson's comment on his house appears in Rice and Brown 1:65, and Closen 180 cites his ownership of plundered farms and loss of hundreds of slaves. The footnote mentioning Governor Nelson's slaves is from Closen 180.

Balch 2:210–11 is a source of information on Governor Nelson.

Closen 154 and Balch 1:209 and 2:64 have information on the captured stores.

Closen 154–55 quotes the fear of pillaging.

The pitiable condition of Negroes is from Rice and Brown 1:64.

Doehla 60–64 mentions Popp's promotion.

My figures on casualties are from several sources, including Closen 154. Johnston 158 gives an entirely different count, totaling 10,069. Note the statement in Closen 154 and fn34 that Closen's figures are too high. Clinton 587 gives 6,630 surrendered, 552 killed, wounded, or missing, for a total of 7,182. To this must be added the number of Germans. Germain's letter of July 7, 1781, to Clinton states that 2,800 Germans will soon arrive. That would make the total 9,982. In his journal 393 St. George Tucker has a figure of 5,818, not counting the garrison at Gloucester.

Commager and Morris 1240–41 and Flexner 2:460–61 have information on the *Bonetta*.

Greene's letter to Knox is in Scheer and Rankin 493.

Thacher 288–90 describes the surrender.

Freeman made a thorough study of what tune was played by the British band and concluded that it was almost certainly "The World Turned Upside Down." See his 5:388 fn47.

Thacher 288–90 mentions the timbrel.

Information about the Blarenberghe paintings may be found in Rice and Brown 2:161–65, with views on 92–97.

Closen's quote is on pp. 153–54.

Commager and Morris 1239 quotes the New Jersey officer.

Doehla 57–58 gives his impressions of the size of the allied armies.

Shreve 157–58 describes the British and German reactions.

The American colonel's views of the antics of Americans appear in Scheer and Rankin 494–95.

The favors done by Rochambeau for Cornwallis are cited in Rice and Brown 1:64.

Clinton 583–87 has Cornwallis's letter to Sir Henry.

The treatment of Negroes is noted in Scheer and Rankin 241–43 and fn11.

Flood 412–13 has the Tarleton stories.

Bonsal 175–77 relates how the news reached Versailles.

Thayer 385 mentions Wayne's and St. Clair's reinforcement of Greene.

Rice and Brown 1:66 characterizes the French quarters, and the same source, 152, contains the Verger journal with its comments on American riflemen and the rebels' veneration of Washington. Clermont-Crèvecoeur's comments on American habits appear in the same source, 71–72.

Tilghman and his mission are reviewed in detail in Shreve 215, appendix 1, no. 15—Tilghman to Washington, Oct. 27, 1781, 158–66 and 168. Further details on the celebrations are in Scheer and Rankin 496 (quoted from Boudinot's journal) and Johnston 158–59.

11. I Now Take Leave of You

The letters between Mildred Smith and Betsy Ambler were published as "An Old Virginia Correspondence," *Atlantic Monthly* 34 (1899):535–39.

Mackesy 433–59 has an excellent section on the navies and their war.

George Washington to Nathanael Greene, Nov. 16, 1781, is in MA 488/1, 37.

The letter from Nathanael Greene to Thomas Nelson, Dec. 27, 1781, is in GLC 07884.09.

Van Doren *Benjamin Franklin* 627–30 mentions the dauphin's birth.

Closen 181–82 reports on events in the Carolinas, as does Greene 408–9.

The quotations from Walpole are in his *Letters* 8:115 and 118.

Johnston 179–81 quotes from Wraxall's memoirs, describing how the cabinet received the news of Yorktown.

Mackesy 386, 435–36, 462–70 quotes Vergennes and reports on London's state of mind and the Rockingham ministry.

Flexner 2:482–84 discusses Washington's movements and the reunion with the French.

James Madison reported the critical situation in Congress to Arthur Lee, May 28, 1782, GLC 3930.

Champagne 186 describes the army's growing discontent.

Rhode Island's refusal to ratify and Virginia's about-face appear in Flexner 2:486.

Brooks 170–71 appraises Knox's role.

Flexner 2:502–4, Champagne 196, and Brooks 172–74 relate events in Newburgh, and Freeman 5:433–36 follows Washington's actions there.

Flexner 2:507–8, 512, and 514–15 discusses Washington's difficult position and the failure of Congress to honor its commitments.

Boatner 744 provides information about Morris; McCullough 300 reports the loan from Holland.

The king's proclamation of Feb. 14, 1783, is in GLC 1731.

McCullough 281, 284–85 assesses the contribution of the American delegates to the peace conference and the treaty itself.

Robson xxiii–xxvi has the British officers' observations on the mediocre caliber of their superiors.

As for the merchants and shipowners who refused to reveal their loyalties, when I was doing research for the book *Divided Loyalties: How the American Revolution Came to New York*, my initial idea was to build the story around a small town, and one I had in mind was Salem, Massachusetts. I found to my astonishment that the splendid local historical society had few of the contemporary documents I required—that is, diaries, letters, journals of the period—and I was reminded by Will LaMoy that Salem was a seafaring town, full of businessmen and traders who almost certainly concealed their loyalties as best they could so as not to upset relations with clients or trading partners.

The quotation from the New York woman who was a spectator is in Freeman 5:462–63. Tallmadge's comment is in the same source, 468.

Both Freeman 5:466–68 and Flexner 2:523–26 provide fine summaries of Washington's last day with his officers. Much of this comes from the memoir of Benjamin Tallmadge, who was an eyewitness.

The material on Washington's appearance before the Congress and his return to Mount Vernon is based on Freeman 5:472–87 and Flexner 2:526–27.

BIBLIOGRAPHY

Primary Sources

BEAUMARCHAIS, PIERRE AUGUSTIN CARON. *Correspondence de Beaumarchais*. Brian N. Morton and Donald C. Spinelli, eds. Paris: A.-G. Nizet, 1969.

BLANCHARD, CLAUDE. *The Journal of Claude Blanchard, 1780–1783*. William Duane, trans. Thomas Balch, ed. Albany, N.Y.: J. Munsell, 1876. Reprint, New York: Arno Press, 1969.

BURNABY, ANDREW. *Travels Through the Middle Settlements of North America in the Years 1759 and 1760 with Observations upon the State of the Colonies*. London, 1775.

CHASTELLUX, MARQUIS DE. *Travels in North America in the Years 1780, 1781, and 1782*. 2 vols. Howard C. Rice, Jr., trans. and ed. Chapel Hill, N.C.: University of North Carolina Press for Institute of Early American History and Culture, 1963.

CLINTON, SIR HENRY. *The American Rebellion: Sir Henry Clinton's Narrative of His Campaign, 1775–1782*. William B. Willcox, ed. New Haven, Conn.: Yale University Press, 1954.

CLOSEN, BARON LUDWIG VON. *The Revolutionary Journal of Baron Ludwig von Closen, 1780–1783*. Evelyn M. Acomb, trans. and ed. Chapel Hill, N.C.: University of North Carolina Press for Institute of Early American History and Culture, 1958.

DEARBORN, HENRY. *Revolutionary War Journals of Henry Dearborn, 1775–1783*. Lloyd A. Brown and Howard H. Peckham, eds. Freeport, N.Y.: Books for Libraries Press, 1939.

DENNY, EBENEZER. *The Diary of Ebenezer Denny, 1781*. "Common Sense Americanism," www.csamerican.com/Doc.asp?doc=yorktown.

GIROUD, VINCENT. *The Road to Yorktown*. New Haven, Conn.: Yale University Library, 1992.

GOTTSCHALK, LOUIS, ed. *Lafayette: A Guide to the Letters, Documents, and Manuscripts in the United States.* Ithaca: Cornell University Press, 1975.

GRAVES, ADMIRAL SAMUEL. *The Graves Papers and Other Documents Relating to the Naval Operations of the Yorktown Campaign, July to October, 1781.* French Ensor Chadwick, ed. New York: DeVinne Press for the Naval History Society, 1916.

GREENE, NATHANAEL. *The Papers of General Nathanael Greene.* 9 vols. Richard K. Show-man, ed. Chapel Hill, N.C.: University of North Carolina Press for Rhode Island Historical Society, 1976–1997. (With vol. 9, Dennis M. Conrad became editor.)

HAMILTON, ALEXANDER. *The Papers of Alexander Hamilton.* Vols. 1 and 2. Harold C. Syrett, ed. New York: Columbia University Press, 1961.

HEATH, WILLIAM. *Memoirs of Major-General William Heath by Himself.* William Ab-batt, ed. New York: William Abbatt, 1901.

HOFFMAN, RONALD, AND PETER J. ALBERT, eds. *Diplomacy and Revolution: The Franco-American Alliance of 1778.* Charlottesville, Va.: University Press of Virginia for United States Capitol Historical Society, 1981.

HOOD, ADMIRAL SAMUEL. *Letters Written by Samuel Hood in 1781–82–83.* Vol. 3. David Hannay, ed. Publications of the Navy Records Society, 1895.

JONES, THOMAS. *History of New York during the Revolutionary War.* 2 vols. Edward Floyd DeLancey, ed. New York: New-York Historical Society, 1879.

LAFAYETTE, MARQUIS DE. *Correspondence.* Vol. 4, Apr.–Dec. 1781.

——. *Lafayette in the Age of the American Revolution: Selected Letters and Papers, 1776–1790.* Idzerda, Stanley, ed. Ithaca: Cornell University Press, 1977.

LEE, HENRY. *Memoirs of the War in the Southern Department of the United States.* Robert E. Lee, ed. New York: New York University, 1869. Reprint, New York: Arno Press, 1969.

MACKENZIE, FREDERICK. *Diary of Frederick Mackenzie . . . during the Years 1775–1781.* 2 vols. Cambridge, Mass.: Harvard University Press, 1930.

MACKENZIE, RODERICK. *Strictures on Lieutenant-colonel Tarleton's History.* London, 1781. Reprint, New York: Arno Press.

MARTIN, JOSEPH PLUMB. *Private Yankee Doodle: Being a Narrative of Some of the Adventures, Dangers & Sufferings of a Revolutionary Soldier.* George F. Scheer, ed. Boston: Little, Brown, 1962.

MURPHY, ORVILLE T. *Charles Gravier, Comte de Vergennes: French Diplomacy in the Age of Revolution, 1719–1787.* Albany: State University of New York Press, 1982.

MURRAY, SIR JAMES. *Letters from America, 1773–1780.* Eric Robson, ed. New York: Barnes and Noble, 1950.

"An Old Virginia Correspondence." *Atlantic Monthly* 34 (1899):535–39.

RICE, HOWARD C., JR., AND ANNE S. K. BROWN. *The American Campaigns of Rocham-beau's Army, 1780, 1781, 1782, 1783.* 2 vols. Princeton, N.J.: Princeton University Press, 1972.

RILEY, EDWARD M. "St. George Tucker's Journal of the Siege of Yorktown." *William and Mary Quarterly,* 3rd ser., vol. 5, no. 3 (July 1948).

ROCHAMBEAU, JEAN BAPTISTE DONATIEN DE VIMEUR, COMTE DE. *Memoirs of the Marshall Count de Rochambeau, Relative to the War of Independence of the United States.* New York: Arno Press, 1971.

RODNEY, GEORGE. *Letter-Books and Order-Book of George, Lord Rodney, Admiral of the White Squadron, 1780–1782.* 2 vols. New York: New-York Historical Society for the Naval History Society, 1932. (Vol. 1, July 6, 1780–Feb. 4, 1781; vol. 2, Dec. 1781–Sept. 1782.)

SMITH, WILLIAM. *Historical Memoirs of William Smith.* William H. Sabine, ed. New York: Colburn and Tegg, 1956.

STEVENS, BENJAMIN F. *The Campaign in Virginia, 1781: An Exact Reprint of Six Rare Pamphlets on the Clinton-Cornwallis Controversy.* 2 vols. London, 1888.

TARLETON, BANASTRE. *A History of the Campaigns of 1780 and 1781 in the Southern Provinces of North America.* London, 1787. Reprint, New York: Arno Press, c. 1970s.

THACHER, JAMES. *A Military Journal of the American Revolution.* Hartford, Conn., 1854.

TORNQUIST, CARL GUSTAF. *The Naval Campaigns of Count de Grasse during the American Revolution, 1781–1783.* Amandus Johnson, trans. Philadelphia: Swedish Colonial Society, 1942

WALPOLE, HORACE. *The Letters of Horace Walpole.* 9 vols. Peter Cunningham, ed. Edinburgh: John Grant, 1906.

WAR DIARY. The diary of an unknown soldier in what was probably the 3rd Regiment of the Pennsylvania line, from May 26, 1781, to July 4, 1782. Connecticut Society of the Sons of the American Revolution.

WILLIAMS, OTHO. *Calendar of the Papers of General Otho Williams.* Maryland Historical Society, 1940.

New-York Historical Society, New York, N.Y.
Gilder Lehrman Collection

The following works are from the Gilder Lehrman Collection on deposit in the New-York Historical Society, New York, N.Y.

KING GEORGE III TO EDWARD THURLOW, Nov. 25, 1779. GLC 7003

CHARLES PETTIT. Estimate of debts of Quartermaster Department under Nathanael Greene, c. 1780. GLC 03150.01

JOHN ANDRÉ TO JOSEPH CHEW, June 18, 1780. GLC 05533

GEORGE WASHINGTON TO CAESAR RODNEY, Aug. 17, 1780. GLC 06488

RICHARD VARICK TO REVEREND ROMEYN, Sept. 24, 1780. GLC 03265

Troop strength under EARL CORNWALLIS, c. Nov. 15, 1780. GLC 05220

ANTHONY WAYNE TO GEORGE WASHINGTON, Dec. 25, 1780. GLC 04863

GEORGE WASHINGTON TO NATHANAEL GREENE, Jan. 2, 1781. GLC 07675

HENRY LEE TO NATHANAEL GREENE, Jan. 21, 1781. GLC 02487

WILLIAM NORTH TO LEWIS MORRIS, Jan. 25, 1781. GLC 04829

GEORGE WASHINGTON TO PRESIDENT OF CONGRESS, Mar. 11, 1781. GLC 07471

EDMUND PENDLETON TO JAMES MADISON, Mar. 19, 1781. GLC 00099.061

MARQUIS DE LAFAYETTE TO NATHANAEL GREENE, June 3, 1781. GLC 06323

GEORGE MASON TO GEORGE MASON, JR., June 3, 1781. GLC 03256

MARQUIS DE LAFAYETTE TO GEORGE WASHINGTON, July 8, 1781. GLC 05467

NATHANAEL GREENE TO HENRY LEE, Aug. 22, 1781. GLC 07884.06

NATHANAEL GREENE TO HENRY LEE, Aug. 25, 1781. GLC 07884.07

SMITH AND WOOTON, Sept. 18, 1781. MA 488/1, 147

GEORGE WEEDON TO NATHANAEL GREENE, Sept. 5, 1787. MA 488/1, 96

Pierpont Morgan Library, New York, N.Y.

GEORGE WEEDON TO GEORGE WASHINGTON, Sept. 5, 1781. MA 488/1, 96
CORNWALLIS amnesty offer, Mar. 8, 1781. MA 3162

Colonial National Historical Park, Yorktown, Va.

JOURNAL OF JOHANN CONRAD DOEHLA, 1777–1785, Robert J. Tilden, trans.
DIARY OF MATHEW GREGORY at Yorktown, 1781
LETTERS TO AND FROM ST. GEORGE TUCKER, Oct. 1–Oct. 15, 1781, Michael
   Hubbell, ed.

Secondary Sources Containing Primary Materials

COMMAGER, HENRY STEELE, AND RICHARD B. MORRIS. *The Spirit of '76: The Story of
   the American Revolution as Told by Participants.* 2 vols. New York: Bobbs-Merrill,
   1958.
MAGUIRE, J. ROBERT. "A Self-Portrait by Major John André." *Bulletin of the Fort
   Ticonderoga Museum* 16, no. 3 (2000).
MOORE, FRANK. *Diary of the American Revolution from Newspapers and Original Docu-
   ments.* New York: Scribner, 1858.
PECKHAM, HOWARD H., ed. *Narratives of Colonial America, 1704–1765.* Chicago:
   Donnelley, 1971.
SCHEER, GEORGE F. *Private Yankee Doodle, Being a Narrative of Some of the Adventures,
   Dangers and Sufferings of a Revolutionary Soldier.* Boston: Little, Brown, 1962.
SCHEER, GEORGE F., AND HUGH F. RANKIN. *Rebels and Redcoats.* New York: World,
   1956.
STOKES, I. N. PHELPS. *The Iconography of Manhattan Island, 1498–1909.* 6 vols. New
   York: The Lawbook Exchange, Ltd., 1998.

General Works

BALCH, THOMAS. *The French in America during the War of Independence of the United
   States, 1777–1783.* 2 vols. T. W. Balch, trans. Introduction and preface by
   George Athan Billias. Boston: Gregg Press, 1972.
BASS, ROBERT D. *The Green Dragoon: The Lives of Banastre Tarleton and Mary Robin-
   son.* New York: Holt, 1957.
BEMIS, SAMUEL FLAGG. *A Diplomatic History of the United States.* New York: Holt,
   1936.
BILLIAS, GEORGE. *George Washington's Opponents.* New York: Morrow, 1969.
BONSAL, STEPHEN. *When the French Were Here.* Garden City, N.Y.: Doubleday, 1945.
BRANDT, CLARE. *The Man in the Mirror: A Life of Benedict Arnold.* New York: Ran-
   dom House, 1994.
BROOKS, NOAH. *Henry Knox: A Soldier of the Revolution.* New York: Da Capo Press,
   c. 1900.

BUCHANAN, JOHN. *The Road to Guilford Courthouse: The American Revolution in the Carolinas.* New York: Wiley, 1997.

BURNETT, EDMUND CODY. *The Continental Congress.* New York: Norton, 1941.

CARRINGTON, HENRY B. *Battles of the American Revolution, 1775–1781.* New York: Barnes, 1876.

CHAMPAGNE, ROGER. *Alexander McDougall and the American Revolution.* Schenectaday, N.Y.: Union College Press, 1975.

CHINARD, GILBERT, ed. *George Washington as the French Knew Him.* Princeton, N.J.: Princeton University Press, 1940.

CHRISTIE, IAN R. *The End of North's Ministry, 1780–1782.* London: Macmillan, 1958.

CUMMING, WILLIAM P., AND HUGH RANKIN. *The Fate of a Nation: The American Revolution through Contemporary Eyes.* London: Phaidon, 1975.

DULL, JONATHAN. *The French Navy and American Independence: A Study of Arms and Diplomacy, 1774–1787.* Princeton, N.J.: Princeton University Press, 1975.

EINSTEIN, LEWIS. *Divided Loyalties: Americans in England during the War of Independence.* London: Cobden-Sanderson, 1933.

ETTER, SUSAN ATKINS. "Colonel Richard Clough Anderson (1750–1826)." *Cincinnati Fourteen* 39, no. 2 (spring 2003).

FERRIÈRE, JAMES L. "The Prince de Broglie in America." *Lippincott's Magazine* (November 1881).

FLEXNER, JAMES THOMAS. *George Washington in the American Revolution (1775–1783).* Vol. 2. Boston: Little, Brown, 1967.

FLOOD, CHARLES BRACELEN. *Rise, and Fight Again: Perilous Times along the Road to Independence.* New York: Dodd, Mead, 1976.

FONER, PHILIP S. *Blacks in the American Revolution.* Contributions in American History, No. 55. Westport, Conn.: Greenwood Press, 1976.

FREEMAN, DOUGLAS SOUTHALL. *George Washington.* Vol. 5, *Victory with the Help of France.* New York: Scribner's, 1952.

GOTTSCHALK, LOUIS. *Lafayette and the Close of the American Revolution.* Chicago: University of Chicago Press, 1942.

———. *Lafayette in America, 1777–1783.* L'Esprit de Lafayette Society of Arvoyres, France: 1975. (Copyright University of Chicago.)

GRUBER, IRA D., ed. *John Peebles' American War.* Mechanicsburg, Pa.: Stackpole, 1998.

JOHNSTON, HENRY P. *The Yorktown Campaign and Surrender of Cornwallis, 1781.* New York: Harper, 1881.

KENNEDY, PAUL. *The Rise and Fall of the Great Powers: Economic Change and Military Conflict from 1500 to 2000.* New York: Random House, 1987.

KENNETT, LEE. *The French Forces in America, 1780–1783.* Westport, Conn.: Greenwood Press, 1977.

KETCHUM, RICHARD M. *Decisive Day: The Battle for Bunker Hill.* New York: Owl Books, 1999.

———. *Saratoga: Turning Point of America's Revolutionary War.* New York: Holt, 1997.

KIERNER, CYNTHIA. *Traders and Gentlefolk: The Livingstons of New York, 1675–1790.* Ithaca, N.Y.: Cornell University Press, 1992.

LANDERS, COLONEL H. L. *The Virginia Campaign and the Blockade and Siege of York-town, 1781*. Washington, D.C.: U.S. Government Printing Office, 1931.

LARRABEE, HAROLD. *Decision at the Chesapeake*. New York: Clarkson Potter, 1964.

LEAKE, ISAAC Q. *Memoir of the Life and Times of General John Lamb*. Albany: Joel Munsell, 1850.

LEWIS, CHARLES LEE. *Admiral de Grasse and American Independence*. Annapolis: United States Naval Institute, 1945.

LOSSING, B.J. *Pictorial Field Book of the Revolution*. 2 vols. New York: Harper and Brothers, 1860.

LOUGHREY, MARY ELLEN. *France and Rhode Island, 1686–1800*. New York: King's Crown Press, 1944.

LUMPKIN, HENRY. *From Savannah to Yorktown: The American Revolution in the South*. New York: Paragon House, 1987.

MACKESY, PIERS. *The War for America, 1775–1783*. Cambridge, Mass.: Harvard University Press, 1964.

MAHAN, ALFRED THAYER. *The Major Operations of the Navies in the War of American Independence*. Boston: Little Brown, 1913.

MCCULLOUGH, DAVID. *John Adams*. New York: Simon and Schuster, 2001.

MORRIS, RICHARD B. *The American Revolution Reconsidered*. New York: Harper and Row, 1967.

PANCAKE, JOHN S. *This Destructive War: The British Campaign in the Carolinas, 1780–1782*. University, Ala.: University of Alabama Press, 1985.

RANDALL, WILLARD STERNE. *Benedict Arnold: Patriot and Traitor*. New York: Morrow, 1990.

SCHEER, GEORGE F. "The Sergeant Major's Strange Mission." *American Heritage* 8, no. 6 (Oct. 1957).

SHREVE, L. G. *Tench Tilghman: The Life and Times of Washington's Aide-de-Camp*. Centreville, Md.: Tidewater, 1982.

SIMPSON, ALAN. "The French in Newport: Paying Guests or Free-Loaders?" *Newport History* 56 (summer 1983).

STEVENS, JOHN A. "The French in Rhode Island." *Magazine of American History* 3 no. 7 (July 1879).

THAYER, THEODORE. *Nathanael Greene: Strategist of the American Revolution*. New York: Twayne, 1960.

THOMAS, PETER D. G. *Lord North*. New York: St. Martin's, 1976.

TUCHMAN, BARBARA W. *The First Salute*. New York: Knopf, 1988.

VAN DOREN, CARL. *Benjamin Franklin*. New York: Viking, 1938.

———. *Secret History of the American Revolution*. New York: Viking, 1941.

WALKER, ANTHONY. *So Few the Brave: Rhode Island Continentals, 1775–1783*. Newport, R.I.: Seafield Press, 1981.

WARD, CHRISTOPHER. *The Delaware Continentals, 1776–1783*. Wilmington, Del.: Historical Society of Delaware, 1941.

———. *The War of the Revolution*. 2 vols. New York: Macmillan, 1952.

WHITRIDGE, ARNOLD. *Rochambeau*. New York: Macmillan, 1965.

WILLCOX, WILLIAM B. *Portrait of a General: Sir Henry Clinton in the War of Independence*. New York: Knopf, 1964.

WRIGHT, ESMOND. *Franklin of Philadelphia*. Cambridge, Mass.: Harvard University Press, 1997.

Reference Sources

BOATNER, MARK MAYO, III. *Encyclopedia of the American Revolution*. New York: David McKay, 1966.
GARRATY, JOHN, AND MARK CARNES, eds. *American National Biography*. New York: Oxford University Press, 1999
Webster's Biographical Dictionary. Springfield, Mass.: Merriam, 1965.

ACKNOWLEDGMENTS

Some years ago my friend Stephen Ward Sears, historian of the Civil War, urged me to write about the Yorktown campaign. That it has taken me so long to act on his suggestion does not diminish my gratitude to him.

As with my other books, I have enjoyed welcome offers of handholding and assistance from members of my family—particularly from my wife, Barbara Bray Ketchum, who has been unflagging in her support; as well as our daughter, Liza Ketchum, and her husband, John Straus; our son, Thomas Bray Ketchum, and his wife, Pauline; our two oldest grandsons, Derek and Ethan Murrow (the latter investigated some important terrain in the South for me and provided photographs and descriptions); and my sister, Janet Whitehouse, who has a boundless enthusiasm for history.

It is immensely gratifying to have what amounts to a cheering section of people who wish you well, offer to help, or have a friendly interest in the project. Among them are Frederick Buechner, Harvey Carter, John O. Chesley, Jr., Austin Chinn (who informed me that the word *bullet* was used as early as the fifteenth century), Art Cohn,

Rudyard Colter, Jan Crowley, Osborne Day, Castle Freeman, Robert Frothingham, John Hand, Jonathan Harwell, Robert Harwell III, Francis W. Hatch, Hervie Haufler, Gina Johnson, David S. Ketchum, J. Robert Maguire, David McCullough, Lex Nason, Rhoda Nason, Thomas O'Brien, Louise Ransom, Frank Smallwood, Richard Snow, Nicholas Westbrook, Corinna Wildman, Wallace Zellmer, as well as Michael Oltedal and Nancy Oltedal, who helped to unravel what are to me profound computer mysteries.

A special word of thanks goes to four friends without whose assistance this work would have taken even longer: Pauline Dunbar, Robert Matteson, Daniel O'Leary, and Virginia Pearson.

I benefited immensely from the staff at the Gilder Lehrman Institute of American History—first, when that remarkable collection of documents was housed at the Morgan Library, where Leslie Fields gave me invaluable assistance; and second, when the collection was moved to the New-York Historical Society, and I was so ably aided by Sandy Trenholm and Lauren Eisenberg. At the institute, Lesley Herrmann was a staunch supporter.

Much assistance was forthcoming from the Colonial National Historical Park in Yorktown, Virginia, chiefly from Karen Rehm, Diane Depew, and Chris Bryce. Thanks to my old friend Margot Waite, I got in touch with a number of very helpful people in Providence, Rhode Island, notably Karen Eberhart and Robin Flynn at the Rhode Island Historical Society. In Newport I was assisted as well by Bert Lippincott at the Newport Historical Society; and by Sally Small, Daphne Dirlam, and Carol Cummins. And Connell Gallagher, at the University of Vermont, Special Collections, did a great favor.

Quite unexpectedly, I heard from Allen Breed, who is with the Associated Press in North Carolina. He is a descendant of the family that owned Breed's Hill in Charlestown, Massachusetts, where the battle of June 17, 1775, was fought, and has a lively interest in history. Through him, I obtained a number of useful papers dealing with the Yorktown campaign.

Michael Blow, a friend and former colleague, whose family once owned a substantial property in Yorktown, generously loaned me several hard-to-find books dealing with the town and the campaign.

Once again, Peter Drummey, the librarian at the Massachusetts Historical Society, was exceedingly helpful in guiding me to sources of information. I am also indebted to Margaret Heilbrun, formerly of the New-York Historical Society, for assistance at that splendid institution.

As usual, my agent, Carl Brandt, was a source of support and cheerful encouragement. My editor, John Macrae, who always astonishes me with his acute knowledge of American history, has my gratitude for his incisive comments and suggestions.

As ever, members of the staff at the excellent Northshire Book Store in Manchester Center, Vermont—especially Barbara Morrow and Bill Lewis—were very supportive.

Alison Macalady was extremely helpful in the preparation of a dramatis personae.

It goes without saying that responsibility for any flaws or errors in the book rests entirely with me, not with these unfailingly generous people.

INDEX

ABOUT THE AUTHOR

RICHARD M. KETCHUM has written a number of books about American history, including five others on the Revolutionary War: *Decisive Day, The Winter Soldiers, Saratoga, Divided Loyalties,* and *The World of George Washington.*

As editorial director of book publishing at American Heritage Publishing Company, he edited many of that firm's volumes, including *The American Heritage Picture History of the Civil War,* which received a Pulitzer Prize Special Citation.

He was the cofounder and editor of *Blair & Ketchum's Country Journal,* a monthly magazine about country living.

Born in Pittsburgh, Pennsylvania, he graduated from Yale University and commanded a subchaser in the South Atlantic during World War II.

He and his wife have a sheep farm in Vermont and are active conservationists.